LECTIO DIVINA WITH THE SUNDAY GOSPELS

Contents

Introduction

Lectio Divina: A method of biblical reflection

The reflections proposed in this book are the fruit of lectio divina, a method of meditative Bible reading which goes back to the early centuries of our church, and continues to be a source of deep spiritual growth for many people throughout the world.

Lectio divina (a Latin expression which means sacred reading) is done in three stages:

- Reading: you read the passage slowly and reverentially, allowing the words to sink into your consciousness;
- Meditation: you allow the passage to stir up memories within you, so that you recognise in it your own experience or that of people who have touched your life;
- Prayer: you allow the meditation to lead you to prayer – thanksgiving, humility and petition.

The prayers given here, week by week, are intended to serve as models. You can use them as they are, but they will also suggest ways in which you can pray from your own meditations.

Now and then, prayers will be preceded by quotations from well known thinkers or spiritual writers. The quotations are there to remind us that through Bible reading we enter into the wisdom of the entire human family.

The basic principle of lectio divina is that Bible reading is a personal encounter with God, a communion which resembles (though different from) the communion of the Eucharist. This goes against what has prevailed in our church for some centuries: the text was seen as containing a message – doctrinal or moral – and once we got the message, the text had achieved its purpose. In lectio divina, we love the text, linger over it, read it over and over, let it remain with us.

When we approach the text in this way, we come face to face with the fact that it speaks to the imagination. A Bible text is not like a textbook or a newspaper, providing us with objective information. It was not written like that. Instead, it stirs up feelings; we find ourselves identifying with the characters – we feel for them, admire them or dislike them. We are caught up in the movement of the text, its suspense, its dramatic reversals of fortune, its unanswered questions.

Gradually, we 'recognise' the text; we find that we have lived the sequence of events ourselves, or have seen them lived in others who have touched our lives, for good or for ill. Reading the text becomes a homecoming – and a lifting up. We find ourselves caught up in the story of God's people, 'fellow citizens with the saints' (Eph 2:19); we are the lowly ones whom God 'lifts up from the dust and sets in the company of princes, yes the princes of his people' (Ps 113:7-8).

Lectio divina, like all imaginative communication – especially storytelling – teaches not directly but by changing the consciousness of those who practise it. By identifying ourselves with God's people – Jesus, the prophets and the great men and women of the Old and New Testaments – we find ourselves adopting their attitudes. We also recognise ourselves in the bad characters of the text – the Pharisees, Pharaoh, the apostles when they were jealous of each other – and find that we want to give up these attitudes.

The Bible, recognised as coinciding with our experience, reveals to us the truth about life – not abstract truth, but an ideal we hunger and thirst for and, from another perspective, an evil we recoil from. In the Bible text, therefore, we discover the double reality of every human person – a story of sin and a story of grace. They are not equally true, however – the story of grace is the deep truth of the person, their 'true name', the wheat which God will gather into his barn; sin is the chaff that will be burnt in a fire that never goes out (cf Mt 3:12).

Lectio blossoms spontaneously into prayer in three dimensions:
• Thanksgiving that Jesus is alive in the story of grace;
• Humility that the story of sin is alive;
• Petition that the story of grace may prevail – 'Come, Lord Jesus!'

In lectio divina we experience the true meaning of theology – entering through Bible reading into the wisdom of God or, more accurately, allowing God-alive-in-the-Bible to lead us into wisdom, humbly, gratefully and with awe, like St Paul on the road to Damascus. The wisdom of God gives us his perspective on every aspect of life: one-to-one relationships, but also economics, politics, agriculture, etc.

Lectio divina is best taught and practised with the church's Sunday lectionary as it was reformed after the Second Vatican Council. It has its shortcomings, but overall it is a wonderfully constructed three-year programme in Bible reading. By being faithful to the lectionary in this way, we experience ourselves in communion with the church and, through the church, with all humanity, sharing in the grace and the sin of our contemporaries. We can say of Bible reading what St Paul says of the Eucharist: 'We, though many, form one body because we partake of the one bread' (1 Cor 10:17).

I would like to thank all who have helped me with the preparation of this collection of reflections on the Sunday readings for Year A, and especially Elena Lombardi-French in Dublin and Brendan Clifford OP in Limerick.

Advent: The Mystery of Waiting

Advent is the liturgical season when we pay special attention to the mystery of waiting. We have a real problem here because most of us don't like waiting, we don't see it as something to celebrate. In fact this may well be one of the reasons why people don't understand Advent correctly – although it may also be true that not celebrating it as we should has led us to misunderstand the value of waiting.

Whereas waiting bores and often irritates us, the Bible teaches us that if we approach it in the right spirit, waiting is a creative moment when we grow spiritually. When we wait we are in touch with an essential aspect of our humanity which is that we are dependent on God and on one another. It is also an act of love since, by waiting for others, we pay them the respect of letting them be free.

Waiting is a mystery – God waits and nature waits – so that when we as individuals wait we go beyond ourselves and enter into a sacred life-giving process, experiencing that we are made in the image and likeness of God. This is why Advent is a time of celebration. It is the season when we remember with gratitude creative experiences of waiting in our lives or the lives of people we have known, the people who have waited for us at one time or another. We also remember the great waiting experiences in human history, in the Bible, and especially in the life of Jesus.

But we must also make Advent a time of teaching. During this season all those involved in the work of Christian education, whether as catechists or preachers or guides, should explore the mystery of waiting: true and false ways of waiting, the danger of not knowing how to wait, ascetical practices that will help us wait more creatively.

Finally, waiting can be, as we know from our own experience, a time of suffering and sometimes of despair. In Advent, we make a special effort to feel for those who are crying out in their agony, 'How long, O Lord?' – those we can name and the countless others 'whose faith is known to God alone'. Through our meditation we can let the special grace of the season flow through us to these brothers and sisters of ours, turning their mourning into dancing and their time of barrenness into one of abundance and fertility.

The liturgy of the word is a teaching moment. It is not abstract teaching, where truths are presented to be learnt, but teaching by celebration. We celebrate biblical stories which exemplify the spirit of the particular season, identifying with the persons in them. In the process we learn more about biblical values, experience repentance as we become more aware of how we (and the whole church) have failed to practise those values, and pray that we will enter more fully into God's plan for us – that his kingdom will come. The main person we identify with is Jesus himself. At each liturgical season we celebrate one particular stage of his life on earth, not as a past event but as a way in which he continues to live among us.

The grace of Advent is hope, the virtue by which we human beings can recognise and welcome God present in the world but not experienced with our senses. The corresponding stage in Jesus' life which we celebrate in this season is when he was in the womb of Mary. It was a time in the history of salvation when the Word was made flesh, but was not visible, his presence was real but an object of hope, like the tiny mustard seed which we trust will eventually become a great tree in whose branches the birds of the air will shelter.

The fruit of Advent then is that we grow in the virtue of hope that God is present even when he is hidden. We are undaunted by evil, do not give up on our dreams, face with confidence the present historical moment (ours, that of our society and of the modern world), welcome the people he sends us, and help them get in touch with the best in themselves – where God is present.

In celebrating Jesus in the womb of Mary we celebrate all the times, in the Bible and in history, when human beings have been invited by God to recognise his hidden presence in the world. The liturgical readings for the season then present us with biblical persons who are models of hope.

The Bible teaches this through stories, not abstract definitions. It does not attempt to define what hope is, but invites us to meditate on people of hope. We celebrate them and enter into their attitudes, how they interpreted the events of their time and how they related to their contemporaries.

By doing this we celebrate our own experiences of hope, in ourselves and others. In the process we experience conversion, renew our hope which had grown cold. We also pray that those in despair will turn to hope and we commit ourselves to bringing hope into the world.

First Sunday of Advent

Gospel Reading: Matthew 24:37-44

37Jesus said to his disciples: 'As it was in Noah's day, so will it be when the Son of Man comes. 38For in those days before the Flood people were eating, drinking, taking wives, taking husbands, right up to the day Noah went into the ark, 39and they suspected nothing till the Flood came and swept all away. It will be like this when the Son of Man comes. 40Then of two men in the fields one is taken, one left; 41of two women at the millstone grinding, one is taken, one left. 42So stay awake, because you do not know the day when your master is coming. 43You may be quite sure of this that if the householder had known at what time of the night the burglar would come, he would have stayed awake and would not have allowed anyone to break through the wall of his house. 44Therefore, you too must stand ready because the Son of Man is coming at an hour you do not expect.'

The passage comprises several teachings of Jesus, all on the general theme of waiting. However, each teaching forms a unit on its own, so begin by identifying which section you want to meditate on.

Verses 37 to 39 describe what happens 'when the Son of Man comes', the story of the Flood being the model. Make sure you get the precise point of the teaching. It is not that the people were bad or immoral – that is not the point Jesus is making. He is stressing only the suddenness and unexpectedness of the coming.

Verses 40 and 41 are another description of the coming but the point here is quite different: it is the indiscriminate way in which some are taken and some left. Be creative in interpreting the meaning of 'taken' and 'left', starting of course from your experience.

Verses 42 and 44 are two exhortations of Jesus; they are nearly identical although the metaphor in each is slightly different – 'stay awake' in verse 42 and 'stand ready' in verse 44. The stress is slightly different in each too – 'you do not know' in verse 42 and 'an hour you do not expect' in verse 44. In your meditation be faithful to the exact text.

Verse 43 is a parable which you should take on its own. Enter into the parable as it stands, in particular the metaphor of the burglar who breaks through the wall of the house. Your meditation will help you feel for this image of God's unexpected coming.

* * *

Lord, we remember a time in our lives when disaster struck:
    - we lost what seemed a secure job;
    - we were betrayed by a spouse or a friend;
    - we fell again into an evil habit we thought we had finished with;
    - there was a sudden death in the family.
We were like people in the days before the Flood
– eating, drinking, taking wives, taking husbands,
right up to the day when Noah went into the ark.
We too suspected nothing
till this terrible flood came and swept all away.
We recognise now that it was a coming of the Son of Man,
a moment when you showed us how vulnerable we are,
but also when we felt your presence with us.

Lord, it is strange how life turns out.
We remember when we were starting on our careers,
with members of our family, our friends at school.
Today, years after, some of us have done well
and others have not
– in marriage, at work, in health, in spiritual growth.
Much of it was chance.
How true it is that in life two men are working the fields,
one is taken and one left;
of two women at the millstone grinding,
one is taken and the other is left.
Lord, into your hands we commend ourselves.

'There must be no passing of premature judgement. Leave that until the Lord comes. He will light up all that is hidden in the dark and reveal the secret intentions of our hearts.' 1 Cor 4:5
Lord, forgive us, church people, that we usurp your authority,
presuming to pass judgement
on who is fit to enter your kingdom,

as if we could look at two men working in the fields
and decide which will be taken and which one left,
or two women at the millstone grinding
and decide which will be taken and which one left.

Lord, things were going well in our church community.
We thought that we had everything under control.
Then one day trouble appeared again
and the community was torn apart.
You had sent us Jesus to teach us that we must stay awake,
like a householder who knows
that there are burglars always hovering around
and they can break through the wall of his house
at any moment.

'Nobody said that the search for a lasting peace, a peace that is based on
justice, would be easy, but that does not mean that we should not go on
trying.' Bishop Fortich of the Philippines
Lord, we pray today for those who are striving for peace
in countries that are torn by war.
Let them work with hope,
like people who know that at some hour they do not expect
the Son of Man will come.

'The quest for truth is an everlasting process from which civilised people never graduate.' President Hassanali, Divali, 1989
Lord, help us, in our search for truth, to stay awake,
never thinking that we are secure
because at any time we might find
that our house has been broken into,
never despairing because you will show yourself
at an hour we do not expect.

Lord, we thank you that when we were foolish, irresponsible or
stubborn,
some people did not give up on us but stayed awake,
confident that we would return at an hour they did not expect.

Second Sunday of Advent

Gospel Reading: Matthew 3:1-12

¹In due course John the Baptist appeared; he preached in the wilderness of Judaea and this was his message: ²'Repent, for the kingdom of heaven is close at hand.' ³This was the man the prophet Isaiah spoke of when he said: 'A voice cries in the wilderness: "Prepare a way for the Lord, make his paths straight".' ⁴This man John wore a garment made of camel-hair with a leather belt around his waist, and his food was locusts and wild honey. ⁵Then Jerusalem and all Judaea and the whole Jordan district made their way to him, ⁶and as they were baptised by him in the river Jordan they confessed their sins. ⁷But when he saw a number of Pharisees and Sadducees coming for baptism he said to them, ⁸'Brood of vipers, who warned you to fly from the retribution that is coming? But if you are repentant, produce the appropriate fruit, ⁹and do not presume to tell yourselves, "We have Abraham for our father", because, I tell you, God can raise children for Abraham from these stones. ¹⁰Even now the axe is laid to the roots of the trees, so that any tree which fails to produce good fruit will be cut down and thrown on the fire. ¹¹I baptise you in water for repentance, but the one who follows me is more powerful than I am, and I am not fit to carry his sandals; he will baptise you with the Holy Spirit and fire. ¹²His winnowing-fan is in his hand; he will clear the threshing-floor and gather his wheat into the barn; but the chaff he will burn in a fire that will never go out.'

This is a long passage with many themes worked into it. Identifying the different themes before starting your meditation will help you to enter into the passage.

Verses 1 to 5 summarise the story of John the Baptist, but even in this section there are various points being made: the fact that John preached in the wilderness; that he appeared 'in due course', meaning at the time fixed by God; that he was fulfilling the prophecy of Isaiah.

The text of Isaiah in verse 3 is often misunderstood. What it is saying is that prophets always announce to people who are experiencing lostness and abandonment that they can relax because God is going to show himself to them.

In verse 4 the Baptist's garments are symbolic: they are the traditional garments of the prophets. His diet is simple and taken from the environment.

The rest of the passage gives us individual teachings of John the Baptist, each of them symbolic and a typical teaching of a prophet.

In verse 7 to 9 the mentality of all who are complacent is exposed, one that we will certainly recognise as typical of us who are religious people.

Verse 10 expresses dramatically an experience of a 'coming of the Son of Man'.

Verse 11 gives us an insight into the spirituality of John the Baptist, and of all who are involved in a work of God. There is deep humility combined with trust in our particular vocation.

Verse 12 is another dramatic image of God's coming and its effects. In your meditation you can enter into it as a message of comfort in a time of fear.

* * *

Lord, we thank you for conversion experiences:
- a parish retreat;
- a serious illness;
- one of our friends telling us off;
- meeting a great person.
At the time we were drifting, wrapped up in our own concerns.
Then this John the Baptist appeared;
he spoke to us in our wilderness
and his message was simply this:
we must re-think our values totally.
We recognise that this was the experience the prophets spoke of
when they said that no matter how desolate the wilderness
we find ourselves in,
you will speak to us there.
In fact, we can prepare for your coming. Thank you, Lord.

Lord, we thank you
for what is happening in South Africa today.
We thank you for the great leaders
who in due course appeared in that wilderness,
Nelson Mandela, Walter Sisulu, Desmond Tutu, Allan Boesak.

Like John the Baptist
they wore the garments of the ancient prophets,
nourishing themselves from the resources of their culture,
and proclaiming that a decisive moment has come
and the country must take a new path.
We thank you that the people responded.
As in the time of John the Baptist, when Jerusalem and all Judaea
and the whole Jordan district made their way out to him,
so today the people are abandoning their passivity,
confessing that they have played their part in the system,
and committing themselves to the new South Africa.
Naturally some are coming forward
like the Pharisees and Sadducees
only because they wish to escape
from the violence that is coming,
but your leaders are challenging them
and calling on them to produce the appropriate fruit.

'We wish to remind all how crucial is the present moment,
how urgent the work to be done.
The hour for action has now sounded.
At stake are the peace of the world and the future of civilisation.'
Paul VI, *Populorum Progressio*, 1967
Lord, we thank you
that recent popes have been John the Baptist,
preaching to the wilderness of the modern world
that a moment of decision is at hand,
that even now the axe is laid to the roots of our civilisation
and if it does not produce good fruit
it will be cut down and thrown on the fire.
Lord, don't let us Christians
presume that we can escape this retribution
because we are the children of Abraham;
remind us that you can raise children for Abraham from stones.

'The great problem for the church today is not survival but prophecy.'
Thomas Merton

Lord, as a church, we often wonder
why more people don't make their way to us,
ask for baptism and confess their sins.
Perhaps it is that we do not wear the garments of the prophets,
and we do not nourish ourselves
from the simple wisdom of our culture.

Lord, we thank you for those who bring the gospel message
in areas of society which are looked down upon
    - the worker priests;
    - those who work with gay people or with prostitutes;
    - Alcoholics Anonymous.
They proclaim in the wilderness that you are there
and all people need is to open themselves to your presence.

Lord, we thank you for the deep joy of knowing,
like John the Baptist,
that we are the humble servants of your great work,
that others will follow us
who will be more powerful than we are,
and so we can be content to baptise with water for repentance
because others will baptise with the Holy Spirit and with fire.

Lord, evil discourages us
– the evil within ourselves, in our church community, in society.
We thank you that every once in a while
you send us people like John the Baptist
who remind us that you are there
with your winnowing fan in your hand
and you will clear your threshing floor.
All that evil which frightens us,
you will burn in a fire that will never go out,
whereas goodness which seems so frail to us
is your precious wheat which you will gather into your barn.

Third Sunday of Advent

Gospel Reading: Matthew 11:2-11

²*John in his prison had heard what Christ was doing and he sent his disciples to ask him,* ³*'Are you the one who is to come, or have we got to wait for someone else?'* ⁴*Jesus answered, 'Go back and tell John what you hear and see;* ⁵*the blind see again, and the lame walk, lepers are cleansed, and the deaf hear, and the dead are raised to life and the Good News is proclaimed to the poor;* ⁶*and happy is the man who does not lose faith in me.'* ⁷*As the messengers were leaving, Jesus began to talk to the people about John: 'What did you go out into the wilderness to see? A reed swaying in the breeze? No?* ⁸*Then what did you go out to see? A man wearing fine clothes? Oh no, those who wear fine clothes are to be found in palaces.* ⁹*Then what did you go out for? To see a prophet? Yes, I tell you, and much more than a prophet;* ¹⁰*he is the one of whom scripture says: 'Look I am going to send my messenger before you; he will prepare your way before you.'* ¹¹*I tell you solemnly, of all the children born of women, a greater than John the Baptist has never been seen; yet the least in the kingdom of heaven is greater than he is.'*

The passage is clearly in two sections:
– verses 2 to 6: The meeting between John's disciples and Jesus.
– verses 7 to 11: Jesus speaks of John.

You can read verses 2 to 5 as a journey into a deeper faith which John the Baptist made, letting your meditation guide you to interpret this journey from your own experience. What was John's prison? Why did he send disciples? What was the purpose of his question?

You can, on the other hand, concentrate on Jesus, looking at his ministry for example, or, if you prefer, looking at how he responded to the question of John's disciples. You might like to enter deeply into the final saying in verse 6, identifying with the 'blessedness' spoken of by Jesus.

If you are meditating on verses 7 to 10, enter into the movement of the passage, identifying with the two options that Jesus puts forward – the 'reed swaying in the breeze' and the 'man in fine clothes' – before identifying with who John the Baptist really

was. The passage invites us to make that journey before arriving
there.

Verse 11 is a paradox and you must identify with both aspects of it, until you experience that things which seemed at first
contradictory can, in fact, come together in harmony. As always,
personal experience must be your guide.

* * *

*'Our philosophy of history constitutes a sort of intellectual prison. We
carry on as if we have been reduced to impotence and are completely incapable of any initiative on our own behalf.'* Lloyd Best
Lord, we are in a prison.
We are all the time looking for the one
who is to come and save us,
and if this one does not satisfy us,
we say that we must look for someone else.
Send us leaders like Jesus who will make us hear and see
the great things you are doing among us:
people who were lame now standing up
and doing things for themselves;
others finding new energy to live creatively;
the poor discovering the good news that they are not poor at all.
Leaders like this will teach us
the blessedness of not losing faith in ourselves.

Lord, we often read in the Bible of your great power,
how you have laid your axe to the roots of the trees
and any tree which fails to produce good fruit
will be cut down and thrown on the fire;
and how the winnowing fan is in your hand
and you will soon clear your threshing floor of chaff.
Yet, like John the Baptist, we find ourselves
still imprisoned by the injustice of the world.
You are teaching us the blessed way of Jesus
which is to conquer evil by doing good.

Lord, we thank you that in many parts of the world
the church is not concerned with answering abstract questions
such as 'Are you the one who is to come?'
but, like Jesus, is inviting people to hear and see
how the blind are seeing again,
the lame walk, lepers are cleansed, the deaf hear,
the dead are raised to life and
Good News is proclaimed to the poor.

'It is no business whatever of the Christian churches to be keeping peo-
ple passive and morally well-behaved while all the major questions of
their lives are settled by others.' Dr John Vincent, President of the
Methodist Conference of the United Kingdom
Lord, we pray that when people come to the church,
they may not find us following meekly
the dictates of the powerful,
like reeds swaying in the breeze,
nor concerned with fine garments,
like people who live in palaces.
May they find a prophet and more than a prophet,
an institution that will show up the false values of our society
and so prepare the way for your chosen ones
to carry out your work in the world.

'One day our grandchildren will visit each other and wonder what all
the pain and bloodshed were for. And perhaps they will be proud of us,
that we foresaw the happy future which they will take for granted.'
An Israeli woman writing to an Arab friend
Lord, help us, like John the Baptist, to play our part in history,
content in knowing that what we have worked hard
and suffered to achieve,
the least significant of the next generation
will enjoy as a matter of course.

'Looking to the past has much to offer; living in it nothing at all.'
John Harriot

Lord, the church today is very different from how it was some years ago:
- the various forms of lay ministry;
- collaboration with other churches and with people of other faiths;
- the contribution of every culture;
- the Bible opened to all.

Like Jesus remembering John the Baptist,
we remember with gratitude great people of the past
who could not accept these things.
None of us was as great as them,
but we must rejoice in all that even the least of us knows today.

Fourth Sunday of Advent

Gospel Reading: Matthew 1:18-24

[18]*This is how Jesus Christ came to be born. His mother Mary was betrothed to Joseph; but before they came to live together she was found to be with child through the Holy Spirit.* [19]*Her husband Joseph, being a man of honour and wanting to spare her publicity, decided to divorce her informally.* [20]*He had made up his mind to do this when the angel of the Lord appeared to him in a dream and said, 'Joseph son of David, do not be afraid to take Mary home as your wife, because she has conceived what is in her by the Holy Spirit.* [21]*She will give birth to a son and you must name him Jesus, because he is the one who is to save his people from their sins.'* [22]*Now all this took place to fulfil the words spoken by the Lord through the prophet:* [23]*'The virgin will conceive and give birth to a son and they will call him Immanuel,' a name which means 'God-is-with-us'.* [24]*When Joseph woke up he did what the angel of the Lord had told him to do: he took his wife to his home.*

The story of the virginal conception of Jesus is historical but is also deeply symbolic, and your meditation will reveal to you that this is how Jesus Christ always comes to be born into the world, in all the various ways in which this happens.

You can read it as a story of Joseph, symbolic of those whose vocation it is to welcome the one who bears God within her. You might like to stay with the long and painful journey which this vocation involves, identifying with Joseph's fears, his hesitations and eventually his total commitment. You might prefer to concentrate on his vocation to name the child.

It is also the story of Mary; although she does not say a word right through. She is the symbol of those who bear God within them and must wait until their collaborators welcome them and so allow God's work to be born. Do not, however, invent your own story of how Mary felt or what went through her mind; take the text exactly as you find it and you will find ample material to help you understand the work of God.

The fulfilling of prophecy is an important part of the passage and you might like to meditate on it as expressed in verses 22 and 23. It would help if you read the original passage in Isaiah;

as you will see there, the prophecy is a response to the king of
Judah who looked for security in alliances with the powerful
nations around him. Like all of us, he did not recognise 'how
Jesus Christ came to be born'.

* * *

Lord, any commitment involves a long journey.
We remember when we first committed ourselves:
   - we fought against racism or sexism or injustice at the work-
     place;
   - we decided to give up drink and work among addicts;
   - we accepted public office;
   - we began giving spiritual direction.
At first we felt very happy,
then one day we recognised that this was your work,
in which success could not be measured in earthly terms.
It was like when Joseph discovered that Mary, his betrothed,
was with child through the Holy Spirit,
and we too decided to extricate ourselves
as discreetly as we could.
But first, as we had made up our minds to do this,
you sent an angel to us, someone who told us not to be afraid
just because we now knew
that we were involved in a work of the Holy Spirit.
We thank you that when we thought about it
we found the courage to do what your angel told us to do.
Yes, this is always how Jesus comes to be born.

*'There is some spouse within us that we must meet and, failing that, we
fail wholeness. There is in the heart of us all some image of the Beloved
which we must not merely acknowledge but know, love and embrace.
Without this marriage there can be no real human life.'*
Matthew Kelty, Cistercian monk
Lord, Mary is that noble part of ourselves,
bearing your Son Jesus
who was conceived by the power of the Holy Spirit
– our generosity, the ability to sacrifice ourselves,
to give all to a cause.
That part of ourselves frightens us;

we would prefer to deny it is there at all,
to remain with our mediocrity and our compromises.
Send us your angel to reassure us
that we must not be afraid to take that Mary to ourselves,
so that through us your Son Jesus may be born into the world.

'We do not have to put God into the world. He is there. But we must
preserve his presence and aid our brothers and sisters to find him.'
A worker priest
Lord, as Christians we act
as if we are doing the world a favour by our service.
But the world is like Mary bearing divinity in her womb,
and you want us, like Joseph, to welcome her with reverence
because of this presence within her.
We must proclaim to all that
within the world we can find Emmanuel,
a name which means God-is-with-us.

Lord, people always think that the way to renew a society
is by enlisting the support of the powerful.
Today we can see clearly that once again
you are creating a new kind of civilisation
through small communities,
composed mainly of poor people,
fulfilling the word that you have often spoken
through the prophets,
that no great power but a humble maiden will conceive
and give birth to a new beginning for society
and the world will know that you are with us.

Lord, we think today of women who are pregnant
and are not being accepted.
Send your angel to those families,
telling them that they must not be afraid
to welcome this pregnancy
because it is your gift to them.

Lord, it sometimes happens that we have a project within us,
one that you conceived through your Holy Spirit.
Others, even those who love us deeply,
cannot understand what is happening to us.
They fuss and worry, give us up and then come back to us.
Teach us to wait like Mary, knowing that when the time comes,
they will take us to their hearts
and this project will come to birth.

Lord, there was a time
when we were afraid to come near to Jesus,
thinking that we were not good enough.
But you sent us Joseph, who named Jesus for us,
as one who saves us from our sins.

The Nativity of Our Lord

Gospel Reading: Luke 2:1-20

[1]*Now at this time Caesar Augustus issued a decree for a census of the whole world to be taken.* [2]*This census – the first – took place while Quirinius was governor of Syria,* [3]*and everyone went to his own town to be registered.* [4]*So Joseph set out from the town of Nazareth in Galilee and travelled up to Judaea, to the town of David called Bethlehem, since he was of David's House and line,* [5]*in order to be registered together with Mary, his betrothed, who was with child.* [6]*While they were there the time came for her to have her child,* [7]*and she gave birth to a son, her first-born. She wrapped him in swaddling clothes and laid him in a manger because there was no room for them at the inn.* [8]*In the countryside close by there were shepherds who lived in the fields and took it in turns to watch their flocks during the night.* [9]*The angel of the Lord appeared to them and the glory of the Lord shone round them. They were terrified,* [10]*but the angel said, 'Do not be afraid. Listen, I bring you news of great joy, a joy to be shared by the whole people.* [11]*Today in the town of David a saviour has been born to you; he is Christ the Lord.* [12]*And here is a sign for you: you will find a baby wrapped in swaddling clothes and lying in a manger.'* [13]*And suddenly with the angel there was a great throng of the heavenly host, praising God and singing:* [14]*'Glory to God in the highest heaven, and peace to men who enjoy his favour.'* [15]*Now when the angels had gone from them into heaven, the shepherds said to one another, 'Let us go to Bethlehem and see this thing that has happened which the Lord has made known to us.'* [16]*So they hurried away and found Mary and Joseph, and the baby lying in the manger.* [17]*When they saw the child they repeated what they had been told about him,* [18]*and everyone who heard it was astonished at what the shepherds had to say.* [19]*As for Mary, she treasured all these things and pondered them in her heart.* [20]*And the shepherds went back glorifying and praising God for all they had heard and seen; it was exactly as they had been told.*

This well-known story is very rich so we will focus on some aspects only, staying with Mary's perspective, especially in verses 6 to 7, and 16 to 20.

In verses 6 and 7 Luke tells us that Mary gave birth 'when the time came for her to have her child'. Contrary to the popular interpretation, he indicates no regret that there was no room in the inn. All happened as was foretold.

To understand the significance of verse 19, it is important to note that the Greek word which we translate as 'things' is *rhema*, which means both 'word' and 'event'. Mary, through her interior attitude of respectful listening, turns the event into a sacred word.

* * *

'Nothing happens before its time.' Trinidadian saying
Lord, we pray for those who are involved in lofty projects
and are becoming impatient:
  - parish youth leaders who are not getting co-operation;
  - a new party that has won no seats in the elections;
  - parents who are trying in vain to dialogue with their
    teenagers.
Help them to remember Mary and how when the time came
for her to have her child she gave birth to a son.
She was at peace, felt no great concern
that there was no room for them in the inn,
merely wrapped her child in swaddling cloths
and laid him in a manger.

Lord, these days we are all very busy.
At work or in school
we have to expend much effort to achieve success.
At home we are bombarded with information
from television and radio.
We have time only for the sensational
and we allow the ordinary events of life to come and go:
  - the signs of maturity in our children;
  - the life crises of those close to us;
  - new stirrings of resentment or of hope among ordinary people in our country.

Even in our relationship with you
we concentrate on the miraculous
and the extraordinary, glorify and praise you
because things turn out exactly as we were told they would.
Mary teaches us on the contrary
to see in every event a call to grow,
a sacred word you speak to us,
to be welcomed as a treasure and pondered in our hearts,
reflected on and integrated into our consciousness.
Lord, help us to be more like Mary.

'My cell will not be one of stone or wood, but of self-knowledge.'
St Catherine of Siena
Lord, we thank you for all the contemplatives in the world,
those in enclosed convents, and those called, like Mary,
to live in their families and in secular surroundings.
While others chatter and repeat endlessly
what they have been told,
these, like Mary, know how to be silent,
treasuring things and pondering them in their hearts.

The Holy Family

Gospel reading: Matthew 2:13-15;19-23

[13]*After the wise men had left, the angel of the Lord appeared to Joseph in a dream and said, 'Get up, take the child and his mother with you, and escape into Egypt, and stay there until I tell you, because Herod intends to search for the child and do away with him.'* [14]*So Joseph got up and, taking the child and his mother with him, left that night for Egypt,* [15]*where he stayed until Herod was dead. This was to fulfil what the Lord had spoken through the prophet: 'I called my son out of Egypt.'* [19]*After Herod's death, the angel of the Lord appeared in a dream to Joseph in Egypt* [20]*and said, 'Get up, take the child and his mother with you and go back to the land of Israel, for those who wanted to kill the child are dead.'* [21]*So Joseph got up and, taking the child and his mother with him, went back to the land of Israel.* [22]*But when he learnt that Archelaus had succeeded his father Herod as ruler of Judaea he was afraid to go there, and being warned in a dream he left for the region of Galilee.* [23]*There he settled in a town called Nazareth. In this way the words spoken through the prophets were to be fulfilled: 'He will be called a Nazarene.'*

This passage is in three sections; they are all important for us, and we therefore need to look at each one separately.

In the first section Joseph is inspired by 'an angel of the Lord'. He is told in a dream that he must 'get up' at once, and take 'the child and his mother with him'. They 'escaped into Egypt' and stayed there until he was told, once again in a dream, that he could move back home to Israel. This was to save Jesus from being put to death by order of Herod who was then king of Israel. Herod's purpose was to 'search for the child', and put him to death. We read about this search for Jesus later in the text, in verses 16 to 18, and we see Herod's anger taken out on all who were born at that time.

The text brings out very well Matthew's testimony to St Joseph. He was obedient to the word of the Lord – it did not really matter how it came to him.

Joseph stayed in Egypt for a long time. He waited 'until

Herod was dead'. This occurred around the year 4 AD, some years after the sad incident at Bethlehem.

The evangelist then illustrates his narrative with a text found in the Bible. The prophet Hosea spoke of Israel as a child who was dearly loved by his heavenly Father. It was said of him, 'When Israel was a child, I loved him and I called my son out of Egypt.' This is what happened to Jesus. He was God's beloved Son and the Father called him 'out of Egypt'.

We remember now situations in our own families. We too must allow ourselves, like Joseph, to be guided by God in all he wants us to do – for ourselves, and to help others we meet. Sometimes God will appear to us in a dream. Usually however it will be by some other intervention. It could be through friends who talk to us, or others we meet in our daily living.

In the second part of the passage, Matthew tells us that after Herod died, the angel appeared to Joseph once more. As usual it was 'in a dream'. He told Joseph to go back to the land of Israel, because 'those who wanted him killed are now dead'.

Joseph responded immediately. He 'got up' (notice the same words used as before) and he took the child and his mother and they headed back to Israel.

Joseph then learnt that Herod had bequeathed part of his country to his son, King Archelaus, who was now the ruler of the territory. Joseph was naturally afraid of the new king and so 'was afraid to go there'. Once more, he was 'warned in a dream' and he took the decision to go to Galilee, which was ruled by Herod's son, Herod Antipas. There Joseph decided to settle in a little town called Nazareth.

* * *

'All this doctrinal wealth is focused in only one direction, serving one another in our every condition, in our every ailment, in every way. In a certain way, the church has proclaimed herself as the handmaid of humanity.' Pope Paul VI quoted by Pope John Paul II in Sicily
Lord, we thank you for St Joseph.
We pray that we too may be guided by what you have told us.
The manner will be unique to us,
but we must be ready to recognise you.

Lord, we come to you in our various situations.
Some of us are single, some are celibates;
for others our original partner has gone from us
or has divorced us.
Help us always to be guided by your intervention
as St Joseph was,
to know that once we are led by you, all will be well for us.

*'The Word was made flesh in the incarnation, and ever since we have
tried to make that flesh into Word again.'* Cardinal Martini
Lord, we often find ourselves in a lost situation.
We find ourselves in some Egypt
or some other area we hadn't bargained for.
Help us to be like Joseph and follow your way
wherever you want to lead us.

Lord, when we know that our Herod is dead,
it is time to make our way home.
Help us to follow the right way,
to know when we must move to another town
where we will be known to be yours.
Jesus was called a Nazarene.
Help us to be whoever you want us to be.

Second Sunday after Christmas

Gospel reading: John 1:1-18

1In the beginning was the Word: the Word was with God and the Word was God. 2He was with God in the beginning. 3Through him all things came to be, not one thing had its being but through him. 4All that came to be had life in him and that life was the light of men, 5a light that shines in the dark, a light that darkness could not overpower. 6A man came, sent by God. His name was John. 7He came as a witness, as a witness to speak for the light, so that everyone might believe through him. 8He was not the light, only a witness to speak for the light. 9The Word was the true light that enlightens all men; and he was coming into the world. 10He was in the world that had its being through him, and the world did not know him. 11He came to his own domain and his own people did not accept him. 12But to all who did accept him he gave power to become children of God, to all who believe in the name of him 13who was born not out of human stock or urge of the flesh or will of man but of God himself. 14The Word was made flesh, he lived among us, and we saw his glory, the glory that is his as the only Son of the Father, full of grace and truth. 15John appears as his witness. He proclaims: 'This is the one of whom I said: He who comes after me ranks before me because he existed before me.' 16Indeed, from his fulness we have, all of us, received – yes, grace in return for grace, 17since, though the Law was given through Moses, grace and truth have come through Jesus Christ. 18No one has ever seen God; it is the only Son, who is nearest to the Father's heart, who has made him known.

This passage is the prologue to St John's gopel, a very deep teaching on the mystery of the incarnation. But do not let yourself be intimidated by the depth; remember that it was written for you; like the whole Bible, it was 'for you and for your salvation that it came down from heaven.'

It may be helpful to divide the passage as follows:

– verse 1: The Word of God which was made flesh had his beginnings with God before creation. Identify what in your experience was an incarnation of the Word and then remember when you knew that this word was with God from all eternity.

– verses 2 to 5: The story of creation, understood as an ongoing process.

– verses 6 to 8: The vocation of John the Baptist; recognise in him the vocation of all great people.

– verses 9 to 14: St John's presentation of the incarnation. Recognise the mystery from your own experience, in particular the strange mystery of the one who made and sustains humanity being rejected by this same humanity.

– verses 16 to 18: A further meditation on the mystery of the Incarnation. Note especially the process of growth 'from grace to grace', and the difference between Jesus and all others.

* * *

'To the end of our lives the Bible remains an unexplored and unsubdued land full of concealed wonders and choice treasures.'
Cardinal Newman
Lord, we thank you for the deep moments of Bible reading
when we know that we are in the presence of a Word
which existed from the beginning before time began,
which was with you before you created the world,
which was truly divine, with you from the beginning,
and which was made flesh and lived among us.

'In meditation I pass through my body which exists in time and space, and beyond my thoughts which reflect my body-consciousness. I discover my ground in the Word, my real Self which exists eternally in God and with God.' Bede Griffiths
Lord, we thank you for the moments of deep prayer
when we know that we have life in your Word,
that Word which was in the beginning,
which was with you and was you.

Lord, humanity today wants to live independently of you,
and even Christians speak as if you created the world
and then left it to its own devices.
We thank you for the teaching of St John
reminding us that all things come to be
only because you speak a Word,
and that every single thing that exists today

has its being because that Word continues to be spoken in it,
and the only way that anything which has come to be
has life today is because your Word lives within it.

'Perestroika shows that there are some live cells still left in our society,
battling against the disintegration of the Spirit.' A Russian writer
Lord, we thank you that the human spirit is unconquerable,
it is a light that comes from you,
a light that continues to shine even when there is great darkness,
a light that no darkness can overcome.

'Far from being the ultimate measure of all things, human beings can
only realise themselves by reaching beyond themselves.'
Paul VI, *Populorum Progressio*
Lord, how true it is that we can only find our dignity
as your sons and daughters
if we believe that there is more to us than a human birth,
the urges of the flesh and the human will
and that within us your love is at work.

'Of all the crimes of colonialism there is none worse that the attempt to
make us believe that we had no indigenous culture of our own.'
Julius Nyerere
Lord, we pray that as Christians
we may live the message of the Incarnation,
that your eternal Word was made flesh,
so that in every culture you are at work,
and if we look at our past in the light of faith
we will see your glory, Jesus at work in our history,
full of grace and truth.

Lord, a conversion experience is always a home-coming:
      - turning away from an addiction,
      - being reconciled with our family,
      - forgiving an old hurt,
      - going to confession after a long absence.
Once we are there we look back and wonder at our resistance.
Here was something that we needed in order to live,
and yet we did not recognise it;

the truth of ourselves demanded it,
and yet we did not accept to do it.
Now, Lord, by your grace,
we know that your Word has been made flesh
and found a home in us. Thank you, Lord.

*'One of the deepest joys of life is to be used for a purpose recognised by
yourself as a mighty one.'* George Bernard Shaw
Lord, we thank you for times
when we have the deep satisfaction of knowing
that we are working for a noble cause,
one that we know is far greater than ourselves,
even though we are making a contribution to it,
so that we can say like John the Baptist that what comes after us
ranks before us because it existed before us.

*'There is nothing in my former ministry that I would repudiate except
my many sins and shortcomings. My becoming a priest in the Roman
Catholic Church will be the completion and right ordering of what was
begun thirty years ago.'* Richard Neuhaus, Lutheran pastor, on entering
the Catholic Church and asking for ordination as a priest; October 1990
Lord, we pray for all those
who are becoming members of our church,
that they may experience their life up to now as being fulfilled,
as having received from your fullness,
the grace of the present fulfilling the grace of the past.

The Epiphany of the Lord

Gospel reading: Matthew 2:1-12

¹*After Jesus had been born at Bethlehem in Judaea during the reign of King Herod, some wise men came to Jerusalem from the east.* ²*'Where is the infant king of the Jews?' they asked. 'We saw his star as it rose and have come to do him homage.'* ³*When King Herod heard this he was perturbed, and so was the whole of Jerusalem.* ⁴*He called together all the chief priests and the scribes of the people, and enquired of them where the Christ was to be born.* ⁵*'At Bethlehem in Judaea,' they told him, 'for this is what the prophet wrote:* ⁶*And you, Bethlehem, in the land of Judaea, you are by no means least among the leaders of Judah, for out of you will come a leader who will shepherd my people Israel.'* ⁷*Then Herod summoned the wise men to see him privately. He asked them the exact date on which the star had appeared,* ⁸*and sent them on to Bethlehem. 'Go and find out all about the child,' he said 'and when you have found him, let me know, so that I too may go and do him homage.'* ⁹*Having listened to what the king had to say, they set out. And there in front of them was the star they had seen rising; it went forward and halted over the place where the child was.* ¹⁰*The sight of the star filled them with delight,* ¹¹*and going into the house they saw the child with his mother Mary, and falling to their knees they did him homage. Then, opening their treasures, they offered him gifts of gold and frankincense and myrrh.* ¹²*But they were warned in a dream not to go back to Herod, and returned to their own country by a different way.*

The feast of the Epiphany (from the Greek word for manifestation) celebrates the manifestation of God at the incarnation, and all his other manifestations to us and to people who have touched our lives, in every age. Every moment of grace can be called 'an epiphany': a conversion, a new insight, a new stage of spiritual growth.

As with all liturgical feasts, the Epiphany is 'wisdom teaching' on how to recognise epiphanies in our own lives and in the lives of those we are called to help, as parents, teachers, community leaders, spiritual guides, preachers, etc.

St Matthew's story of the 'manifestation' to the Wise Men

must be read as a parallel to St Luke's account of the one to the shepherds. The two 'manifestation stories' are alike and different:

- alike since there is only one God and he has one way of manifesting himself;
- different since as individuals and as groups we are all in unique situations.

The following are points of likeness that we will recognise from our experience:

1. Both groups are 'outsiders':
- shepherds in those days were looked upon as a marginal group;
- the Wise Men came 'from afar'.

A clear sign that we have experienced a true epiphany is the feeling that we have been brought in to a holy space from which we had felt excluded because of our sex, class, race, economic circumstances, status in the community.

2. They were invited to their epiphany by a sign from heaven:
- an angel in glory appeared to the shepherds;
- the Wise Men saw a star.

In every epiphany we have the sense that this is not of our doing. It comes not from 'flesh and blood' but from 'the Father in heaven'.

3. They rejoiced that the heavenly sign was fulfilled:
- the shepherds 'glorified and praised God' because what they had 'heard and seen' was 'exactly as they had been told';
- the Wise Men were 'filled with delight' at 'the sight of the star'.

Moments of grace are always experiences of homecoming.

What is special about the Wise Men is the long journey they made to their epiphany. Their story invites us to celebrate our own (or other people's) journey of grace. The text identifies its different stages, and we are free to remain with one stage or to re-live the entire journey.

Verses 1 and 2 tell us of the journey from 'the east' to Jerusalem. We remember a first searching which takes us some of the way, after which we get lost and have to resort to a religious centre, spiritual guide, religious community or place of pilgrimage.

Verses 3 to 9 tell of the meeting between the Wise Men and Herod – very dramatic and true to experience. We can read these verses from two points of view:

- the Wise Men are humble and open to learning from religious leaders even though these have bad motives;
- Herod is typical of those in positions of authority and privilege who become insecure at the possibility of new ideas (including religious insights).

Verses 10 and 11 are the touching story of the final moment of grace. We can identify three aspects of the moment:

- the joy of discovery – they 'fall on their knees';
- the sense of homecoming – they feel capable of 'opening their treasures';
- the extraordinary simplicity of the epiphany – 'a child with his mother'.

Popular devotion has given various interpretations to the 'treasures', but we might like to reflect on what they tell us about the givers: the Wise Men brought the gifts of their cultures. The important lesson for our time is that in the presence of Jesus all cultures 'open their treasures' to the universal church – surely the special 'epiphany' for the church today.

Verse 12 is very significant. Like all people who have had a deep experience of God, the Wise Men return to their ordinary lives but with a freedom they had not experienced before. Here is a further 'wisdom teaching' therefore: the fruit of a true epiphany is that we are able to 'return to our country by a different way'.

* * *

Lord, there comes a point in our lives when we finally discover what we want to give our whole lives to:

- a cause like racial equality, community development, women's rights;
- a spirituality which combines union with God and social involvement;
- the religious life or the priesthood;
- contemplative prayer.

We look back on the long journey that brought us to this point,

from the time we knew in some vague way
that we wanted to change our ways
– like the wise men seeing a star as it rose
and deciding to follow it.
Then, as it always seems to happen on a spiritual journey,
we lost sight of the star and drifted aimlessly for some years,
until we realised that the only sensible thing to do
was to get help.
So we went to our religious leaders,
and though they were rather confused themselves,
they put us back on the right track
and the old enthusiasm returned.
The last part of the journey went quickly:
suddenly we knew that we had found
what we had been looking for,
and it was like coming home, so that we went into the house,
fell on our knees and opened our treasures.
Thank you, Lord, for guiding us every part of the way.

Lord, it is strange how we become attached
to positions of privilege
    - as parents or teachers;
    - occupying a position in the church;
    - accepted as one of the better educated members of our little
    circle.
When people come forward
who are from a different background,
or who are asking new questions,
we are pertubed, as Herod was
when the wise men came to Jerusalem.
We reflect on what to say, and may even give them good advice,
but deep down our main concern is
that we should continue to feel secure where we are.
No wonder those whom we help do not come back to us
but return to their country by a different way.

Lord, for many centuries now the church has been European.
We thank you that in our day
people of other cultures are looking for Jesus

because they have seen a star out in the east.
Naturally, we are perturbed by all these foreigners,
and so is the whole of Jerusalem,
for they will bring changes to the whole church,
and we will lose our special status.
So, though we give them the right instructions,
we tell them that once they have discovered Jesus
they must come back and tell us exactly what they have found.
But you are guiding them, Lord, and when they come to Jesus
they will open the treasures of their own cultures.
Furthermore, you will reveal to them
that there is no need to come back to us,
and they will make their own way home.

Lord, we sometimes think that we must spend plenty of money
to make Jesus more attractive, or that we must be very learned
so that our preaching of him can draw many to him.
But wise men are looking for an infant king,
and the scriptures say that he will come from Bethlehem,
the least among the leaders of Judah,
because people are tired of great kings who dominate them.
But if they go into a simple house
and see the child Jesus with his mother Mary,
even as they fall on their knees and do him homage
they will feel comfortable to open their treasures
and offer him gifts of gold, frankincense and myrrh.

Lord, we look today for instant results
and for the 'quick fix' in all things,
so that we end up looking for instant spiritual growth as well.
But before we can see Jesus
and fall on our knees and do him homage
we have to make a long journey from the east.
We have to follow a star,
lose it and discover it again many times,
until finally it halts over the place where he is.

The Baptism of the Lord

Gospel reading: Matthew 3:13-17

13*Jesus came from Galilee to the Jordan to be baptised by John.* 14*John tried to dissuade him. 'It is I who need baptism from you' he said 'and yet you come to me!'* 15*But Jesus replied, 'Leave it like this for the time being; it is fitting that we should, in this way, do all that righteousness demands.' At this, John gave in to him.* 16*As soon as Jesus was baptised he came up from the water, and suddenly the heavens opened and he saw the Spirit of God descending like a dove and coming down on him.* 17*And a voice spoke from heaven, 'This is my Son, the Beloved; my favour rests on him.'*

The story of Jesus's baptism is told in all four Gospels – an indication that the early Christians considered it an important event in the life of Jesus.

There are two aspects to the event:
- verses 13 to 15: something happened between Jesus and John the Baptist;
- verses 16 and 17: something happened to Jesus.

Verses 13 to15

Jesus' baptism by John the Baptist seems to have caused much soul searching among the early Christians – how could the sinless Jesus subject himself to John's 'baptism of repentance'? The soul searching can be inferred from the way the successive gospel accounts tell the story:
- Mark (the earliest) is straightforward: Jesus was baptised by John.
- Matthew (a little later) agrees with Mark that Jesus was baptised by John, but adds a dialogue showing that both men were aware that there was a problem.
- Luke (still later) refers to the baptism but only as an introduction to the voice from heaven, and in any case makes no reference to John.
- John (the latest) makes no mention of the baptism.
Parallel texts are not directly a concern in lectio divina, since

the method requires that we focus on the text before us – St Matthew's in this case. However, parallels with other texts can give us an insight into the text, and for this reason we may want to refer to them (although it is never necessary to do so).

In today's meditation we are free to focus either on Jesus or on John the Baptist. In either case, awareness of the soul-searching behind the text reminds us that from time to time we too have to make choices which can be misunderstood. As happened with Jesus' baptism, our communities may need time to clarify misunderstandings; we can be confident that once we do 'what righteousness demands,' later 'evangelists' will explain our actions to those who come after us.

a) Jesus: We can see a progression of thought from Mark to Matthew in explaining how Jesus came to 'appear' on the banks of the Jordan. Whereas St Mark says that Jesus came from Galilee 'and was baptised', Matthew says he came from Galilee 'to be baptised'. St Matthew stresses therefore that Jesus sought baptism by deliberate choice; he chose to leave his familiar surroundings and join the rest of the population in the national renewal movement.

He explains his position to John by saying, 'We should do all that righteousness demands.' This is biblical language which must be interpreted. 'Righteousness' means more or less the same as 'salvation', so Jesus is saying in effect, 'There is an important work of salvation taking place in our country at this moment, and here and now ('for the time being') I cannot stand aloof but must be part of it.' He is accepting fully the consequences of the Incarnation, the Word has truly become flesh and he must dwell among his brothers and sisters. He was to continue making this choice right through his life – the model of leaders who lead not 'from above' but by 'being with.'

b) John the Baptist: John the Baptist becomes aware that he is ministering to someone greater than himself but still goes ahead with his ministry – 'He gave in to him.' This is an experience that we have from time to time as parents, teachers, spiritual guides, community leaders. We become aware of our unworthiness and that we are the ones who 'need baptism'. The result is that we accept our responsibility but with greater humility – it is only 'for the time being'. This was the response required of St

Joseph when he was told, 'Do not be afraid to take Mary home as your wife' (cf 4th Sunday of Advent).

Verses 16 and 17: Jesus' experience
Jesus' baptism was a turning point in his life. Up to then he was a carpenter at Nazareth, now he would begin his ministry as an itinerant preacher of the kingdom. The baptism therefore fits into the biblical pattern by which a call to do God's work is preceded by a deep religious experience (cf Isaiah, Jeremiah, Gideon in the Old Testament, Mary and Zechariah in the New). Many saints of the church had similar experiences before embarking on a new stage in their lives, e.g. St Augustine, St Ignatius of Loyola, St Teresa of Avila and St Margaret Mary.

This shows us that God does not invite people to do his work without first assuring them of his undying love. We can recognise this truth from experience – ours and that of people who have touched our lives. God's way of acting is a model for all who invite others to work with them – parents, spouses, community leaders.

'My favour rests on you' says that God's love is permanent. We are reminded of Jesus's words at the Last Supper: 'As the Father has loved me so I have loved you, remain in my love' (John 15:9). St Matthew says that the experience came 'after he came up from the water'. It was the fruit of his humility, 'he who humbles himself is exalted.'

Jesus's experience was first in symbols and then in words.
a) Verse 16 – symbols.
- 'The heavens opened' – this is the 'negative' aspect, the barrier between God and humanity is removed, they can now communicate freely. We remember similar experiences of reconciliation with God: we thought that the heavens were closed to us, then 'suddenly' (i.e. unexpectedly) they were opened.
- The Spirit of God descends like a dove and comes down on him. This is the positive aspect, an expereicne of God's presence, real but gentle, not possessive or dominating.
b) Verse 17 – words ('a voice from heaven'). The words echo two Old Testament texts both in the context of a call to service:
- 'This is my son' echoes Psalm 2:7, 'You are my son, today I have become your father'.

- 'The Beloved, my favour rests on him' echoes Isaiah 42:1, 'Here is my servant whom I uphold, my chosen one in whom my soul delights.' Both are 'feeling words' communicating intimacy and permanence.

* * *

'I am a shepherd who with his people has begun to learn a beautiful and difficult truth – our Christian faith requires that we submerge ourselves in the world.' Archbishop Romero in his acceptance speech when he was awarded an honorary doctorate by the University of Louvain.
Lord, we pray that your church may always, like Jesus,
choose to go from Galilee to the Jordan to be baptised by John.

'Between the silence of God and the silence of my own soul stands the silence of the souls entrusted to me.' Thomas Merton
Lord, in our different vocations, you call us to minister to others
as parents, church ministers, friends, spiritual guides,
but every once in a way we find ourselves
in the position of John the Baptist with Jesus.
People come to us to be ministered to
when it is we who would need to be ministered to by them:
    - one of our children is more courageous than we are;
    - holy people confess their sins to us;
    - someone we admire greatly comes to us for advice;
    - we are asked to pray for someone from a different religion
    who is more spiritual than we are.
Our first response is to try and dissuade them,
but then we realise that we must leave it like this
for the time being,
since this is what your saving will demands,
and so we give in to them.

Lord, often in life moments of grace come after great trials.
We remember a time when we felt overwhelmed with troubles,
and it was as if we were drowning.
Somehow we survived, and as we came up from the water
the heavens opened
and we felt your love descending on us gently like a dove.
We knew that we were your beloved,
and that your favour rested on us.

*'The church herself knows how richly she has profited by the history
and development of humanity.'* Vatican II, Document on the Church in
the Modern World
Lord, in our time you have given humanity
some important new insights
into the evils of racism, of sexism, of individualism.
We sometimes think that as a church we do not need conversion.
Teach us to be humble like Jesus,
to leave our comfortable Galilee and make our way to the Jordan
to be baptised like everybody else by John the Baptist.

*'God communicates himself to all persons, redeems them and stamps
their being with an orientation towards sharing his life.'* Karl Rahner
Lord, the role of the church in society today is to proclaim
that every human being is one for whom the heavens opened
and the Holy Spirit descended.
Lord, we remember with gratitude times when we had a deep
experience:
    - at the end of a retreat;
    - at the Easter vigil liturgy in our parish;
    - in the sacrament of reconciliation celebrated after many
    years.
As we came out, the heavens opened
and we felt your Spirit descending upon us,
and we knew that your favour rested on us.

*'Faith like a canoe at evening coming in,
like a relative who is tired of America,
like a woman coming back to your house.'*
Derek Walcott, Caribbean poet
Lord, we thank you for the gift of faith,
the kind we experience quite suddenly
coming out of the sea one day
when we know that the heavens have opened,
that your Spirit has come down upon us
and your favour rests on us.

'Proud as I was, I dared to seek that which only the humble can find.'
St Augustine

Lord, we thank you for the times when you gave us the grace
to humble ourselves before you.
As soon as we did this and were coming up from the water,
suddenly the heavens opened and we saw your Spirit
descending like a dove and coming down on us,
and we heard a voice that spoke from heaven,
telling us that we were your Beloved
and that your favour rested on us.

First Sunday of Lent

Gospel text : Matthew 4:1-11

¹Jesus was led by the Spirit out into the wilderness to be tempted by the devil. ²He fasted for forty days and forty nights, after which he was very hungry, ³and the tempter came and said to him, 'If you are the Son of God, tell these stones to turn into loaves.' ⁴But he replied, 'Scripture says: Man does not live on bread alone but on every word that comes from the mouth of God.' ⁵The devil then took him to the holy city and made him stand on the parapet of the Temple. ⁶'If you are the Son of God' he said 'throw yourself down; for scripture says: He will put you in his angels' charge, and they will support you on their hands in case you hurt your foot against a stone.' ⁷Jesus said to him, 'Scripture also says: You must not put the Lord your God to the test.' ⁸Next, taking him to a very high mountain, the devil showed him all the kingdoms of the world and their splendour. ⁹'I will give you all these' he said, 'if you fall at my feet and worship me.' ¹⁰Then Jesus replied, 'Be off, Satan! For scripture says: You must worship the Lord your God, and serve him alone.' ¹¹The devil left him, and angels appeared and looked after him.

Like all who see their lives as a grateful response to God's call, Jesus must make the basic choice to trust God, whatever the circumstances he finds himself in. In this story, under very great pressure, Jesus makes his choice. Who does he remind you of at this moment of decision?

The story is told as a journey in three stages:

- verse 1: Identify the wilderness into which you – or someone you know, or your community – have been led by the Spirit. Note that it is the Spirit – God's love – who leads him there. What does that say about true love? Deuteronomy 8:1-5 will help you to answer this question. Ask yourself also, do we sometimes go into the wilderness but not led there by the Spirit? What happens then?

- verses 3 to 10: The three temptations are three aspects of the one temptation not to trust God, or, stated in positive terms, to follow the way of achievement rather than that of trust. Repeat Jesus' three responses to yourself many times until you can identify with them. From that perspective you will understand the temptations. Thank God for the great people who continue to respond like Jesus. How is Satan tempting them? How is Satan tempting the church?

- verse 11: This is the moment when an individual (or a community) who has remained faithful through a long temptation experiences the love and care of God for that person (or cause) to whom he or she has been faithful. Who are the angels God sends to look after his faithful ones?

* * *

'Walk the dark ways of faith and you will attain the vision of God.'
St Augustine
Lord, it is risky to let ourselves be led by the Spirit.
So often he leads us into the wilderness
to be tempted by the devil.
We make an act of trust in you today,
letting ourselves be guided by you,
confident that the devil will eventually leave us
and angels will appear to look after us.

Lord, sometimes we go into the wilderness
because we are hurt or angry or resentful of others.
Teach us that we are only safe in the wilderness
if the Spirit leads us there.

'Understanding can follow only where experience leads.' St Bernard
We pray for parents and all those who guide others;
help them to be like you:
    - not to be over-protective;
    - to let their sons and daughters be led by the Spirit into the wilderness, because it is only there that they will experience angels appearing and looking after them.

'In prison you learn the value of self-discipline, you stand outside of yourself and see your weaknesses.' Nelson Mandela
Lord, we think of all those who are in the wilderness
at this moment,
those who have been there forty days and forty nights
without eating, and are very hungry –
hungry for love, for security, for recognition, for ordinary food.

The tempter has certainly come
and said to them that they can turn the stones before them
into loaves.
We pray that they may reply in the words of scripture,
that we do not live on bread alone
but on every word that comes from your mouth.

We pray for the youth of today.
They see the kingdoms of the world and their splendour;
but to be given all these
they must fall at the feet of the devil and worship him.
We pray that they may repeat the words of scripture
worshipping you, the Lord their God, and serving you alone.

*'The heart of the Christian message is that the most salvific moment in
the history of the world was when one man was pinned to a cross, unable to do anything for anyone about anything.'* Thomas Cullinane,
Benedictine monk
Lord, our church community has been led
by the Spirit into the wilderness,
the wilderness of falling numbers,
of failure, of uncertainty, of criticism, of scandal.
We remember that the Spirit
always leads your people into the wilderness
to be tempted by the devil.
Help us to refuse the easy solutions,
    - to turn stones into bread,
    - to throw ourselves from the parapet of the temple in order
    to prove that you will support us on your hands in case we
    hurt our feet against a stone,
    - to fall at the devil's feet and worship him.
We renew our trust in you, confident
    - that we can live on every word that comes from your
    mouth;
    - that we need not put you to the test;
    - that we worship you as our God and serve you alone.

Second Sunday of Lent

Gospel text : Matthew 17:1-9

¹Jesus took with him Peter and James and his brother John and led them up a high mountain where they could be alone. ²There in their presence he was transfigured: his face shone like the sun and his clothes became as white as the light. ³Suddenly Moses and Elijah appeared to them: they were talking with him. ⁴Then Peter spoke to Jesus. 'Lord,' he said 'it is wonderful for us to be here; if you wish, I will make three tents here, one for you, one for Moses and one for Elijah.' ⁵He was still speaking when suddenly a bright cloud covered them with shadow, and from the cloud there came a voice which said, 'This is my Son, the Beloved; he enjoys my favour. Listen to him.' ⁶When they heard this, the disciples fell on their faces, overcome with fear. ⁷But Jesus came up and touched them. 'Stand up,' he said 'do not be afraid.' ⁸And when they raised their eyes they saw no one but only Jesus. ⁹As they came down from the mountain Jesus gave them this order, 'Tell no one about the vision until the Son of Man has risen from the dead.'

The three apostles experience the glory of Jesus in a wonderful way that will affect for ever their relationship with him (see 2 Peter 1:16-18). When did you, or someone you know, experience glory that until then had been hidden? In Jesus? In the church community? In a friend or a member of your family? In a Bible passage? In nature?

The story is told as a journey with different stages, and as you meditate on it you will find yourself recognising these stages from your experience:

Verse 1: To experience the transfiguration the apostles must entrust themselves to Jesus and let him lead them up a very high mountain where they can be alone.

Verses 2 and 3: They see not merely Jesus in glory but conversing with his great fore-runners who have been heroes to them.

Verse 4: Identify with Peter who would like to remain there forever.

Verse 5: Jesus is experienced as beloved Son of God, to be listened to with reverence, but this time through 'a voice from the cloud', a totally inner experience, a 'blessed assurance'.

Verses 6 to 8: A very tender passage; Jesus gentle with the apostles, helping them to make the transition back to seeing him as he normally is, but now quite different because of the transfiguration experience. Who was Jesus in your life who did this for you?

Verse 9: The apostles return to ordinary living, but with a memory so deep that they know they cannot share it with others for the indefinite future.

* * *

'There are three phases of prayer: me and Him; Him and me; just Him.'
Anglican Bishop Stephen Verney
Lord, we thank you that in this season of Lent
you will take with you many of your disciples and lead them
up a high mountain where you can be alone with them;
then, in their presence you will be transfigured,
your face shining like the sun
and your clothes becoming as white as the light.
We thank you that not only you, but Moses and Elijah
will appear to them, talking with you.
Surely they will cry out in their joy:
'Lord, it is wonderful for us to be here.
If you wish, we will make three tents,
one for you, one for Moses and one for Elijah.'
We pray that you will lead them
beyond what they can see and feel;
that a bright cloud will cover them with shadow
and from the cloud a voice may come, saying:
'This is my Son, the beloved; he enjoys my favour, listen to him.'

'The traveller cannot love because love is stasis and travel is motion.'
Derek Walcott
Lord, we are afraid to get close to people,
to let them lead us up a high mountain where we can be alone.
And so they cannot be transformed in our presence
and we cannot hear the voice from the cloud
telling us that they are your sons and daughters, your Beloved,
that they enjoy your favour and that we must listen to them.

We pray for the church in the world.
Help us that when people fall on their faces before you,
overcome with fear,
we may come up and touch them, and say to them:
'Do not be afraid.'

'We ought not to learn silence from speaking but rather by keeping
silent we must learn to speak.' St Gregory
Lord, help us to be content that
when we raise our eyes from a deep experience
we see only those who we are called to live with
and we come down from the mountain with them.

Lord, we thank you for those beautiful moments
on the mountain,
so deep that as we came down we knew
that we must tell no one about the vision
until the Son of Man had risen from the dead.

Third Sunday of Lent

Gospel Reading: John 4:5-30

⁵*Jesus came to the Samaritan town called Sychar, near the land that Jacob gave to his son Joseph.* ⁶ *Jacob's well is there and Jesus, tired by the journey, sat straight down by the well. It was about the sixth hour.* ⁷*When a Samaritan woman came to draw water, Jesus said to her, 'Give me a drink.'* ⁸*His disciples had gone into the town to buy food.* ⁹*The Samaritan woman said to him, 'What? You are a Jew and you ask me, a Samaritan, for a drink?' – Jews, in fact, do not associate with Samaritans.* ¹⁰*Jesus replied, 'If you only knew what God is offering and who it is that is saying to you: "Give me a drink," you would have been the one to ask, and he would have given you living water.'* ¹¹*'You have no bucket, sir,' she answered 'and the well is deep: how could you get this living water?* ¹²*Are you a greater man than our father Jacob who gave us this well and drank from it himself with his sons and his cattle?'* ¹³*Jesus replied: 'Whoever drinks this water will get thirsty again;* ¹⁴*but anyone who drinks the water that I shall give will never be thirsty again: the water that I shall give will turn into a spring inside him, welling up to eternal life.'* ¹⁵*'Sir,' said the woman 'give me some of that water, so that I may never get thirsty and never have to come here again to draw water.'* ¹⁶*'Go and call your husband,' said Jesus to her, 'and come back here.'* ¹⁷*The woman answered, 'I have no husband.' He said to her, 'You are right to say, "I have no husband";* ¹⁸*for although you have had five, the one you have now is not your husband. You spoke the truth there.'* ¹⁹*'I see you are a prophet, sir,' said the woman.* ²⁰*'Our father worshipped on this mountain, while you say that Jerusalem is the place where one ought to worship.'* ²¹*Jesus said: 'Believe me, woman, the hour is coming when you will worship the Father neither on this mountain nor in Jerusalem.* ²²*You worship what you do not know; we worship what we do know: for salvation comes from the Jews.* ²³*But the hour will come – in fact it is here already – when true worshippers will worship the Father in spirit and truth: that is the kind of worshipper the Father wants.* ²⁴*God is spirit, and those who worship must worship in spirit and truth.'* ²⁵*The woman said to him, 'I know that Messiah – that is, Christ – is coming; and when he comes he will tell us everything.'* ²⁶*'I who am speaking to you,' said Jesus 'I am he.'*

27*At this point the disciples returned, and were surprised to find him speaking to a woman, though none of them asked, 'What do you want from her?' or 'Why are you talking to her?'* 28*The woman put down her water jar and hurried back to the town to tell the people,* 29*'Come and see a man who has told me everything I ever did; I wonder if he is the Christ?'* 30*This brought people out of the town and they started walking towards him.*

This Sunday's reading is very long; I suggest that you use the shorter version for your meditation (verses 5 to 30).

Jesus leads the woman along a wonderful journey towards a deeper, more human life. You can enter into the story from the perspective of the woman – when have you (or someone you know) made a similar journey in your relationship with God, with others, with your own self? Recognise the woman's resistance to growth, her complacency, her evasions, and her eventual acceptance, partial though it was, of Jesus.

You can enter the story with Jesus, the ideal leader, parent, teacher or spiritual guide. Notice how he meets the woman where she is, needing her assistance; how he is patient with her but also challenges her to grow to what she is capable of.

The story is in two sections:

Verses 2 and 3: At first the woman is content with the water she draws from the well. Jesus very gradually leads her to search for another kind of water which has two characteristics: when you drink it you do not get thirsty again, as it comes from a spring inside of you. Enter into the metaphor so that you can recognise the spiritual journey it evokes for you. When have you experienced Jesus guiding others in this way?

Verses 15 to 24, and 29: Here the journey is the woman coming to trust Jesus as Messiah because he leads her to self-knowledge: 'He told me everything I ever did.' Recognise spiritual growth as that kind of journey, with Jesus as guide.

Situate the story in the context of Lent, thinking of all those who will experience conversion and growth at this season, those who will be received into the church community on Holy Saturday night, or who will take part in Lenten missions.

* * *

'The task of the educator is not to cut down jungles but to irrigate deserts.' C. S. Lewis

Lord, the world is thirsting for living water.
So many people are content with water which,
when they drink it, leaves them thirsty for more:
- in personal relationships they look for security and domination;
- in positions of authority they enjoy lording it over others;
- they sacrifice precious things for the trappings of power;
- compromise their principles for popularity.

Send them Jesus who will lead them to ask for another kind of water:
- trust in relationships;
- service in authority;
- sincerity and truth rather than power;
- integrity at whatever cost;

the kind of water which they will drink
and need never be thirsty again,
water that they do not have to go to a well for
because it comes from a spring inside them
and wells up to eternal life.

'One does not seek to find a master, neither does one find a master. When the disciple and master meet they simply recognise each other.'
Mariella Robitaille, Canadian contemplative nun

We pray for teachers, parents,
community leaders, spiritual guides:
that like Jesus they may
- wait at the well where people gather,
- speak to them about down-to-earth realities they know,
- be patient when they are arrogant or mocking,
- challenge them to move beyond where they are,
- give them space until of their own accord
they put down the water jar that was so important to them
and hurry away.

Forgive us preachers of the gospel
for coming to others as superior,
- afraid to acknowledge that we are tired and thirsty;

- afraid to ask them for a drink;
- conscious that we are rabbis and they are women,
- that we are Jews and they are Samaritans.

'I would not have anyone think that I became a Catholic because I was convinced of the truth. I became a Catholic because I fell in love with the truth.' Eric Gill, English religious sculptor
Lord, we thank you for great people we have known
who in the eyes of the world appear to be needy,
but really are not:
- those who are in prison but in reality are free;
- those who have few possessions but are wealthy;
- those who live in small houses with place for many;
- those who have no power and yet influence thousands.
It seems at first that they are thirsty and we have access to wells .
We soon realise that we are the ones
who should be asking for living water
and they have it to give us. Thank you, Lord.

Lord, forgive us for running away from the important questions;
we argue whether we should worship on this mountain
or in Jerusalem,
forgetting that you are Spirit,
and those who worship must worship in spirit and truth.

We thank you for those who have led us
to understand ourselves better;
it was as if they told us everything we ever did,
so that we had a fleeting experience of meeting the Christ.

Fourth Sunday of Lent

Gospel Reading: John 9:1-41

[1]As Jesus went along, he saw a man who had been blind from birth. [2]His disciples asked him, 'Rabbi, who sinned, this man or his parents, for him to have been born blind?' [3]'Neither he nor his parents sinned,' Jesus answered 'he was born blind so that the works of God might be displayed in him. [4]As long as the day lasts I must carry out the work of the one who sent me; the night will soon be here when no one can work. [5]As long as I am in the world I am the light of the world.' [6]Having said this, he spat on the ground, made a paste with the spittle, put this over the eyes of the blind man [7]and said to him, 'Go and wash in the Pool of Siloam' (a name that means 'sent'). So the blind man went off and washed himself, and came away with his sight restored. [8]His neighbours and people who earlier had seen him begging said, 'Isn't this the man who used to sit and beg?' [9]Some said, 'Yes, it is the same one.' Others said, 'No, he only looks like him. The man himself said, 'I am the man.' [10]So they said to him, 'Then how do your eyes come to be open?' [11]'The man called Jesus,' he answered, 'made a paste, daubed my eyes with it and said to me, "Go and wash at Siloam"; so I went, and when I washed I could see.' [12]They asked, 'Where is he?' 'I don't know,' he answered. [13]They brought the man who had been blind to the Pharisees. [14]It had been a sabbath day when Jesus made the paste and opened the man's eyes, [15]so when the Pharisees asked him how he had come to see, he said, 'He put a paste on my eyes, and I washed, and I can see.' [16]Then some of the Pharisees said, 'This man cannot be from God: he does not keep the sabbath.' Others said, 'How could a sinner produce signs like this?' And there was disagreement among them. [17]So they spoke to the blind man again, 'What have you to say about him yourself, now that he has opened your eyes?' 'He is a prophet,' replied the man. [18]However, the Jews would not believe that the man had been blind and had gained his sight, without first sending for his parents and [19]asking them, 'Is this man really your son who you say was born blind? If so, how is it that he is now able to see?' [20]His parents answered, 'We know he is our son and we know he was born blind, [21]but we don't know how it is that he can see now, or who opened his eyes. He is old enough: let him speak for himself.' [22]His parents spoke like this out of fear of the Jews, who had already agreed to expel from the syna-

gogue anyone who should acknowledge Jesus as the Christ. ²³This was why his parents said, 'He is old enough; ask him.' ²⁴So the Jews again sent for the man and said to him, 'Give glory to God! For our part, we know that this man is a sinner.' ²⁵The man answered, 'I don't know if he is a sinner; I only know that I was blind and now I can see.' ²⁶They said to him, 'What did he do to you? How did he open your eyes?' ²⁷He replied, 'I have told you once and you wouldn't listen. Why do you want to hear it all again? Do you want to become his disciples too?' ²⁸At this they hurled abuse at him: 'You can be his disciple,' they said 'we are disciples of Moses: ²⁹we know that God spoke to Moses, but as for this man, we don't know where he comes from.' ³⁰The man replied, 'Now here is an astonishing thing! He has opened my eyes, and you don't know where he comes from! ³¹We know that God doesn't listen to sinners, but God does listen to men who are devout and do his will. ³²Ever since the world began it is unheard of for anyone to open the eyes of a man who was born blind; ³³if this man were not from God, he couldn't do a thing.' ³⁴'Are you trying to teach us,' they replied 'and you a sinner through and through, since you were born!' And they drove him away. ³⁵Jesus heard they had driven him away, and when he found him he said to him, 'Do you believe in the Son of Man?' ³⁶'Sir,' the man replied, 'tell me who he is so that I may believe in him.' ³⁷Jesus said, 'You are looking at him; he is speaking to you.' ³⁸The man said, 'Lord, I believe', and worshipped him. ³⁹Jesus said: 'It is for judgement that I have come into this world, so that those without sight may see and those with sight turn blind.' ⁴⁰Hearing this, some Pharisees who were present said to him, 'We are not blind, surely?' ⁴¹Jesus replied: 'Blind? If you were, you would not be guilty; but since you say, "We see", your guilt remains.'

Once again, like last Sunday, we have a long passage. However, you must read it in its entirety because, with great artistry, St John has woven three stories into one, each interacting with the others and shedding light on them like the different colours in a painting. In your meditation follow up one story at a time, the one that happens to touch you right now.

Verses 8 to 38: This is the story of the man born blind who gradually comes to the point where he worships Jesus (verse 38). It is the long, often painful, journey of a person who is called to see life in a new way and as a result makes a new commitment.

The story is told in four stages: verses 8 to 12; 13 to 17; 24 to 34; and 35 to 38. You will notice (and recognise from your own experience) how he sees more and more clearly at every stage that this is a call from God which he can trust. He also experiences more and more opposition and rejection, until the moment when he is lost, the same moment when he is found by Jesus.

Verses 13 to 40: The Pharisees (called 'the Jews' in the last part of the passage) make an opposite journey, becoming more and more blind. Trace the stages of their journey: verses 13 to 17; 18 to 23; 24 to 34, coming to the pathetic climax in verse 40. Recognise from your experience, and with great humility, how religious people can become complacent that they know God's will, and in the process become more and more intolerant and violent towards those who oppose them. Notice at every stage the contrast between them and the man born blind.

Verses 1 to 5 and 39 to 41: Jesus is the leader who has 'come into this world' to accompany the humble on their journey to sight and, on the other hand, to expose the blindness of the arrogant. Discover in him the ideal for all in authority, and also for the church in its relationship with the wider community. His own humble trust in the Father and his compassion are beautifully expressed in verses 1 to 5, his clarity of purpose in verses 39 to 41. Who does he remind you of?

* * *

Lord, we remember with great gratitude
the times when you opened our eyes to see that we needed to change:
>   - to relate at a deeper level with you, with members of our
>   family, with friends;
>   - to give ourselves more fully to the service of the poor;
>   - to turn away from a relationship that had us in bondage;
>   - to live more simply.
We remember the long journey you led us on,
>   - those first days when all we knew was that something important was happening to us;
>   - how it became clearer that it was you who were calling us;
>   - the painful time when, as we became more confident,
>   we faced opposition, ridicule and rejection.

We remember that beautiful moment
- when we were lost but knew that you had found us;
- when we felt certain that you were speaking to us;
- when very easily and spontaneously we worshipped you.

'This is the test of human knowledge of God, that he does not know God.' St Thomas Aquinas
Lord, we thank you for coming into our lives
so that we who were without sight would see.

'When we love the other, we obtain from God the key to our under- standing of who he is and who we are.' Thomas Merton
Lord, forgive us church people
for letting ourselves become Pharisees:
- confident that we know what is your will, who is from you and who is not;
- unwilling to accept that people should come to the light outside of our ministry;
- hiding from the evidence before us and taking refuge in pious words;
- violent to those who challenge our wisdom.
We ask you Lord to work a miracle for us this Lent:
that we may go and wash in some Pool of Siloam,
and come away with our sight restored.

Forgive us, Lord,
for taking for granted that when people are poor
it is because they or their parents have sinned.
Send us Jesus to remind us that every single person was born
so that the works of God might be displayed in them.

'If we take care of the means we are bound to reach the ends sooner or later.' Gandhi
We pray for those who are worried about the future.
Help them to accept that the night will soon be here
when no one can work.
Teach them that as long as the day lasts
they must carry on the work of the one who sent them,
and that as long as they are in the world
they are called to be the light of the world.

'The saving of the world from impending doom will come, not through the complacent adjustment of the conforming majority, but through the creative maladjustment of a non-conforming minority.'
Martin Luther King
Be with your church, Lord,
so that she may bring your judgement into the world
and lead the humble to the light,
showing those who think they see that they have become blind.

Fifth Sunday of Lent

Gospel text : John 11:1-45

¹*There was a man named Lazarus who lived in the village of Bethany with the two sisters, Mary and Martha, and he was ill.* ²*It was the same Mary, the sister of the sick man Lazarus, who anointed the Lord with ointment and wiped his feet with her hair.* ³*The sisters sent this message to Jesus, 'Lord, the man you love is ill.'* ⁴*On receiving the message, Jesus said, 'This sickness will end not in death but in God's glory, and through it the Son of God will be glorified.'* ⁵*Jesus loved Martha and her sister and Lazarus,* ⁶*yet when he heard that Lazarus was ill he stayed where he was for two more days* ⁷*before saying to the disciples, 'Let us go to Judaea.'* ⁸*The disciples said, 'Rabbi, it is not long since the Jews wanted to stone you; are you going back again?'* ⁹*Jesus replied: 'Are there not twelve hours in the day? A man can walk in the daytime without stumbling because he has the light of this world to see by;* ¹⁰*but if he walks at night he stumbles, because there is no light to guide him.'* ¹¹*He said that and then added, 'Our friend Lazarus is resting, I am going to wake him.'* ¹²*The disciples said to him, 'Lord, if he is able to rest he is sure to get better.'* ¹³*The phrase Jesus used referred to the death of Lazarus, but they thought that by 'rest' he meant 'sleep', so* ¹⁴*Jesus put it plainly, 'Lazarus is dead;* ¹⁵*and for your sake I am glad I was not there because now you will believe. But let us go to him.'* ¹⁶*Then Thomas – known as the Twin – said to the other disciples, 'Let us go too, and die with him.'* ¹⁷*On arriving, Jesus found that Lazarus had been in the tomb for four days already.* ¹⁸*Bethany is only about two miles from Jerusalem,* ¹⁹*and many Jews had come to Martha and Mary to sympathise with them over their brother.* ²⁰*When Martha heard that Jesus had come she went to meet him. Mary remained sitting in the house.* ²¹*Martha said to Jesus, 'If you had been here, my brother would not have died,* ²²*but I know that, even now, whatever you ask of God, he will grant you.'* ²³*'Your brother,' said Jesus to her, 'will rise again.'* ²⁴*Martha said, 'I know he will rise again at the resurrection on the last day.'* ²⁵*Jesus said: 'I am the resurrection. If anyone believes in me, even though he dies he will live,* ²⁶*and whoever lives and believes in me will never die. Do you believe this?'* ²⁷*'Yes, Lord,' she said 'I believe that you are the Christ, the Son of God, the one who was to come into this world.'* ²⁸*When she had said this, she went and called her sister Mary,*

saying in a low voice, 'The Master is here and wants to see you.' ²⁹*Hearing this, Mary got up quickly and went to him.* ³⁰*Jesus had not yet come into the village; he was still at the place where Martha had met him.* ³¹*When the Jews who were in the house sympathising with Mary saw her get up so quickly and go out, they followed her, thinking that she was going to the tomb to weep there.* ³²*Mary went to Jesus, and as soon as she saw him she threw herself at his feet, saying, 'Lord, if you had been here, my brother would not have died.'* ³³*At the sight of her tears, and those of the Jews who followed her, Jesus said in great distress, with a sigh that came straight from the heart,* ³⁴*'Where have you put him?' They said, 'Lord, come and see.'* ³⁵*Jesus wept;* ³⁶*and the Jews said, 'See how much he loved him!'* ³⁷*But there were some who remarked, 'He opened the eyes of the blind man, could he not have prevented this man's death?'* ³⁸*Still sighing, Jesus reached the tomb; it was a cave with a stone to close the opening.* ³⁹*Jesus said: 'Take the stone away.' Martha said to him, 'Lord, by now he will smell; this is the fourth day.'* ⁴⁰*Jesus replied, 'Have I not told you that if you believe you will see the glory of God?'* ⁴¹*So they took away the stone. Then Jesus lifted up his eyes and said:* ⁴²*'Father, I thank you for hearing my prayer. I knew indeed that you always hear me, but I speak for the sake of all these who stand round me, so that they may believe it was you who sent me.'* ⁴³*When he had said this, he cried in a loud voice, 'Lazarus, here! Come out!'* ⁴⁴*The dead man came out, his feet and hands bound with bands of stuff and a cloth round his face. Jesus said to them, 'Unbind him, let him go free.'* ⁴⁵*Many of the Jews who had come to visit Mary and had seen what he did believed in him.*

As on last Sunday, we have a long passage in which several stories are interwoven.

Jesus brings Lazarus out of the tomb; this is experienced as a liberation from bondage – 'Unbind him and let him go free.' Identify with Lazarus from your experience. He symbolises those who have been written off (by others but also by themselves) as dead – people? communities? a country or a civilisation?

Verses 3 and 36; 15; 39; 41 and 42: Faced with the bondage of the tomb, Jesus is armed with love (verses 3 and 36), trust in the Father (verses 15, 39, 41 and 42), and deep compassion (verses 33, 35, 38). Enter into the dramatic confrontation in which these forces are victorious over death.

Verses 25-26, 29 and 40: Jesus leads Martha (and to a lesser extent Mary) to a new insight into the power of faith over death by his teaching (verses 25 and 26) and by commanding her to take the stone away (verses 29 and 40). Recognise this journey from your own discovery of the power of faith over the forces of death and whatever keeps us in bondage. Where is Jesus teaching us this by word and example?

Verses 9 and 10: Jesus returns to Judaea, the place of death, in perfect freedom, because of his own faith which is an inner light that keeps him from stumbling.

The disciples decide to accompany Jesus in his journey to death, which turns out to be a place of new life and freedom. When did you or your community take such a risk and experience a similar surprise?

Since we are approaching Holy Week, interpret the story of the crucifixion of Jesus in the light of this story: there too, faith and love prove victorious over the forces of death and darkness.

* * *

Lord, we remember today the times when we were like Lazarus in the tomb, rejected, discouraged, in despair, feeling that life was not worth living, overwhelmed by guilt so that we wanted to hide ourselves away from the world.
We thank you for sending Jesus to us as we lay in the tomb
– a friend, a parent, uncle or aunt,
some member of our church community –
and this Jesus loved us,
reached out to us in the tomb,
and in a loud, confident voice, called us to come out.
Thank you, Lord.

'Christianity is not about opposing evil. It is a call to live in contrast to the prevailing mode of fragmentation and despair.' Derrick Wilson, founder of the ecumenical Corrymeela Centre in Northern Ireland
Lord, there are many who are Lazarus in our country,
seeming alive but really in the tomb:
- those who are letting themselves be killed by alcohol or drugs,
- those who are cynical, who have no energy or enthusiasm.

We ask you to send them Jesus
- someone who will be a friend to them as Jesus was to Lazarus,
- someone who will not be afraid to remove the stone that is closing them in,
- someone who will ignore us when we protest that they are already four days in the grave and will smell,
- someone who will call them to come out, and set them free.

'How much better to carry relief to the poor rather than sending it.'
John Wesley
Lord, we thank you for Jesus' great distress, for the tears he shed,
for the sighs that came straight from the heart.
We come to you today with our own grief,
our anger in the face of death, hatred, cynicism and despair.
Teach us, like Jesus, to leave ourselves in your hands,
remembering that you always hear our prayers,
if we only believe we will see your glory,
and through our faith we can call Lazarus from the tomb,
unbind him and set him free.

*'All the doctrinal work of the church is focused in only one direction,
serving human beings in their every condition, in their every ailment,
in every way. The church has proclaimed herself the handmaid of
humanity.'* Pope Paul VI
We pray for your church, in our country and in the world,
that we may be Jesus in the world,
walking without stumbling because we are walking in your
light;
not afraid to go to Judaea even when we know we could be put
to death there;
that we may let ourselves be led to where Lazarus is lying in a
tomb,
so that we can share in the grief of the world and in its sighs.
Fill your church with the love of Jesus for Lazarus,
and with his trust in you,
so that she may call him out of the tomb and set him free.

Palm Sunday

Gospel Reading: Matthew 21:1-11

1When they were near Jerusalem and had come in sight of Bethphage on the Mount of Olives, Jesus sent two disciples, 2saying to them, 'Go to the village facing you, and you will immediately find a tethered donkey and a colt with her. Untie them and bring them to me. 3If anyone says anything to you, you are to say, "The Master needs them and will send them back directly".' 4This took place to fulfill the prophecy: 5'Say to the daughter of Zion: Look, your king comes to you; he is humble, he rides on a donkey and on a colt, the foal of a beast of burden.' 6So the disciples went out and did as Jesus had told them. 7They brought the donkey and the colt, then they laid their cloaks on their backs and he sat on them. 8Great crowds of people spread their cloaks on the road, while others were cutting branches from the trees and spreading them in his path. 9The crowds who went in front of him and those who followed were all shouting: 'Hosanna to the son of David! Blessings on him who comes in the name of the Lord! Hosanna in the highest heavens!' 10And when he entered Jerusalem, the whole city was in turmoil. 'Who is this?' people asked, 11and the crowds answered, 'This is the prophet Jesus from Nazareth in Galilee.'

The gospel reading for this Sunday is St Matthew's version of the passion of Jesus. The story of his triumphant entry into Jerusalem, which is read during the ceremony of palms, is not merely a highly significant event in the life of Jesus, it gives us the key to interpreting all that subsequently happened to him. Meditating on this story is therefore an excellent start to Holy Week.

To understand this event it is essential to read two passages from the Old Testament:

- Psalm 118, a song of thanksgiving as a victorious pilgrim enters Jerusalem and the temple;

- Zechariah 9:9, 10, where the prophet paints a picture of God's chosen one coming to save his people.

Verses 1 to 3 of Matthew's text show us that Jesus made a deliberate choice to enter Jerusalem according to his own value system, and he was conscious that he was in line with Zechariah's vision.

You can meditate on the story from the point of view of Jesus: when have you experienced someone – perhaps yourself – making the choice that Jesus made? You can focus on the crowds instead: how does it feel to welcome someone (an experience or a reading) that clearly comes 'in the name of the Lord'?

The climax to the story in verses 10 and 11 is significant too: this is the kind of thing that happens when God's messenger enters a city.

* * *

'We must develop absolute patience and understand the fears of others.'
Nelson Mandela
Lord, we thank you for the great public figures of our time
who have chosen the way of nonviolence,
    - Gandhi and his successors in India,
    - Dorothy Day and the Catholic Worker Movement,
    - Nelson Mandela,
    - Caribbean people who resisted slavery and colonialism by
    peaceful means.
They have been for the modern world
Jesus entering Jerusalem on a donkey.
Like him they fulfilled the prophecy of Zechariah,
coming to the children of Zion with humility,
banishing chariots and horses and all the bows of war
and proclaiming peace to all.
It is through people like these
that your empire will stretch from sea to sea,
from the River to the ends of the earth.

'Forgive us, Lord, that we speak more of your death and ours, instead of the life and victory you have won for us all.'
Archbishop of Khartoum, 1994
Lord, we thank you for the times that you sent us someone who transformed our lives:
    - a great leader emerged in our nation or church community;
    - our family life was disintegrating and a counsellor brought
    us all together;
    - we read a great book;
    - a friend gave us back our courage.

We felt a great joy,
like the people when they saw Jesus entering their city,
we welcomed this messenger who came in the name of the Lord,
and cried out 'Hosanna in the highest heavens!'

Lord, give us the gift of final perseverance,
that like Jesus we may come to the end of our lives
faithful to what you have called us to be,
and enter Jerusalem as he did,
knowing that we come in your name
and welcomed by all the saints.

Lord, we pray for nations that are suffering from civil war.
Send them leaders who will come to them humbly as Jesus did,
banishing chariots and horses and the bows of war
and proclaiming peace for their nations,
so that their people may come out in great crowds
to celebrate and shout with all their hearts,
'Blessings on the one who comes in the name of the Lord!
Hosanna in the highest heavens!'

*'God does not want to be an idol in whose name one person kills other
people.'* Closing message of the African Synod, 1994
Lord, we pray for the church.
Often we are tempted to enter the modern world
with the methods that prevail there,
putting our trust in money or advertising or threats.
Help us, like Jesus, to deliberately choose our way,
concerned only that we are fulfilling the prophecies
and that we seek the blessings of those who come in your name.

Lord, we thank you that in many countries today
the church is taking a radical stand,
rejecting horses and chariots
and all the apparatus of earthly power
and identifying rather with the lowly.
Naturally the whole nation is in turmoil,
but when people ask, 'Who is this?'
the crowds can answer truthfully,
'This is the prophet Jesus from Nazareth in Galilee.'

Easter Vigil

Gospel Reading: Matthew 28:1-10

^{1}*After the sabbath, and towards dawn on the first day of the week, Mary of Magdala and the other Mary went to visit the sepulcher.* ^{2}*And all at once there was a violent earthquake, for the angel of the Lord, descending from heaven, came and rolled away the stone and sat on it.* ^{3}*His face was like lightning, his robe white as snow.* ^{4}*The guards were so shaken, so frightened of him, that they were like dead men.* ^{5}*But the angel spoke; and he said to the women, 'There is no need for you to be afraid. I know you are looking for Jesus, who was crucified.* ^{6}*He is not here, for he has risen, as he said he would. Come and see the place where he lay,* ^{7}*then go quickly and tell his disciples, "He has risen from the dead and now he is going before you to Galilee; it is there you will see him." Now I have told you.'* ^{8}*Filled with awe and great joy the women came quickly away from the tomb and ran to tell the disciples.* ^{9}*And there, coming to meet them, was Jesus. 'Greetings,' he said. And the women came up to him and, falling down before him, clasped his feet.* ^{10}*Then Jesus said to them, 'Do not be afraid; go and tell my brothers that they must leave for Galilee; they will see me there.'*

Each gospel tells the story of the resurrection in its own way. Enter therefore into the details of the passage before you, and identify with one of the characters involved.

There are several characters in the story. First of all Jesus himself. Your meditation will lead you to recognise how he continues to lie in the tomb and then rise again: an experience of God, a biblical word, a cause, a holy person.

The story of the women is in three distinct stages:
- In verse 1 they are the faithful ones who go to the tomb although the cause seems lost.
- In verses 3 to 6 they experience the resurrection.
- In verses 7 and 8 they receive the commission to announce the good news.

The angel is the typical messenger of God; he acts in his name by rolling away the stone and he delivers his message to the women.

The guards represent the folly of trying to contain God's chosen one in a tomb.

* * *

Lord, today we remember people
who once gave themselves with enthusiasm to a project:
   - they got married with the dream of founding a true Christian family;
   - they joined a religious congregation;
   - they started a political party that would be different;
   - a youth group was going to change things in a parish.
Today their hopes have been shattered and they are grieving;
for them remembering the past is like going to visit a sepulchre.
Lord, send them someone
who will be like an angel descending from heaven
and who will tell them that in life,
when we set out in search of a noble dream, it is never lost.
It may lie in the tomb for three days,
and we can go to see where it lay.
But the dream itself is not there,
it is risen, and so we must not delay at the tomb,
but we must go and tell those who shared it with us
that we can return to Galilee where it all started
knowing it is alive and we will see it again.

'We have seen immense changes taking place throughout Eastern Europe. Those who bravely nourished the roots of faith in wintry days now rejoice in heaven and on earth at signs of springtime.'
Archbishop Runcie of Canterbury, Message to the people of Russia, 1989
Lord, we thank you for the fall of oppressive regimes
in Eastern Europe.
It was as if all at once there was a violent earthquake
and your angel descended from heaven
and rolled away the great stone
that had kept whole populations imprisoned
for over forty years.
Those in authority were badly shaken,
so frightened that they were like dead men.

But the common people knew that they need not be afraid,
the spirit of freedom had risen as they always knew it would,
and filled with awe and great joy
they ran to tell the world the good news.
We remember with gratitude those who did not lose hope,
like Mary Magdala and the other Mary going to visit the sepulchre of Jesus.

*'Some would consider our hopes utopian. It may be that these persons
are not realistic enough and that they have not perceived the dynamism
of a world which in spite of its mistakes is, even unaware, taking slow
but sure steps towards its creation.'*
Pope Paul VI, *Populorum Progressio*
Lord, we pray for church leaders,
that they may always bring hope to the world.
Where others see darkness, may they show that dawn is near,
and what others experience as the end of an era
may they see as the first day of a new one.

*'History shows us that penalties do not deter men when their conscience
is aroused, nor will they deter my people.'*
Nelson Mandela at his trial in 1962
Lord, how foolish tyrants are.
They think they can imprison the human spirit in a tomb,
make the tomb secure by their threats,
put seals on the tombstone and mount a guard over it.
But the human spirit is your presence in the world,
and so the day must come when you will roll away the stone
and the ridiculous guards will be shaken and frightened;
while their prisoners are alive and free,
they will be like dead men.

Lord, you sometimes leave us in a hopeless situation
from which only your direct intervention can rescue us;
and yet you want us to wait there
like the women at the tomb of Jesus,
so that when your angel descends from heaven
and rolls away the stone
we are there to receive the good news and run to tell it to others.

'God's work comes out of silence and brings us to silence.'
Maggie Ross, a modern hermit
Lord, we church people talk so much about Jesus
that we end up thinking we have him under our control:
  - we understand his message perfectly;
  - we can judge who are his disciples;
  - we know how he will act in the future.
Help us to be silent before his mystery,
like Mary of Magdala and the other Mary,
so that we can be open to the unexpected message of the angel
telling us that he has escaped
from the narrow confines of our church language,
that we must come away from the tomb in which we laid him,
because he is alive and going before us into the world,
and it is in the daily activities of ordinary people
that we will see him.

Second Sunday of Easter

Gospel Reading: John 20:19-31

¹⁹*In the evening of the same day, the first day of the week, the doors were closed in the room where the disciples were, for fear of the Jews. Jesus came and stood among them. He said to them, 'Peace be with you,'* ²⁰*and showed them his hands and his side. The disciples were filled with joy when they saw the Lord,* ²¹*and he said to them again, 'Peace be with you. As the Father sent me, so am I sending you.'* ²²*After saying this he breathed on them and said: 'Receive the Holy Spirit.* ²³*For those whose sins you forgive, they are forgiven; for those whose sins you retain, they are retained.'* ²⁴*Thomas, called the Twin, who was one of the Twelve, was not with them when Jesus came.* ²⁵*When the disciples said, 'We have seen the Lord,' he answered, 'Unless I see the holes that the nails made in his hands and can put my finger into the holes they made, and unless I can put my hand into his side, I refuse to believe.'* ²⁶*Eight days later the disciples were in the house again and Thomas was with them. The doors were closed, but Jesus came in and stood among them. 'Peace be with you' he said.* ²⁷*Then he spoke to Thomas, 'Put your finger here; look, here are my hands. Give me your hand; put it into my side. Doubt no longer but believe.'* ²⁸*Thomas replied, 'My Lord and my God!'* ²⁹*Jesus said to him: 'You believe because you can see me. Happy are those who have not seen and yet believe.'* ³⁰*There were many other signs that Jesus worked and the disciples saw, but they are not recorded in this book.* ³¹*These are recorded so that you may believe that Jesus is the Christ, the Son of God, and believing this you may have life through his name.*

Today's gospel reading, like all of St John's gospel, is an interweaving of several themes. It is not possible to follow up all the themes together; we must focus on one at a time, going deeply into it and allowing it to reveal some deep truth about Jesus, about ourselves and about life.

In this reflection I invite you to focus on the apostle Thomas; this is in accord with the church's liturgical tradition for the Second Sunday of Easter. Therefore, although the reading includes two of Jesus' resurrection appearances – both of them deeply moving – we stay with the second, the dialogue between

Jesus and Thomas, and let the earlier appearance provide the context. We are free to identify either with Thomas or with Jesus, but not with both at the same time.

We need to be clear on how we understand Thomas. The popular interpretation puts him in a bad light, as 'doubting Thomas'. This, however, is not the movement of the text which culminates in Thomas' admirable act of faith, the most explicit in the New Testament – 'My Lord and my God'. We are more in accord with the spirit of the text, therefore, when we look at Thomas as a model of faith. He was right to insist that before he could believe in Jesus' resurrection, he must see the holes the nails made in his hands, put his finger into the holes and his hand into the great wound made by the centurion's lance.

Thomas then teaches us the important lesson that we must not separate the resurrection from the cross, since we are called to be followers of Jesus. He also teaches us the truth of the church and of our individual spiritual growth. We cannot live the life of grace, the 'risen life', authentically unless we bear in our bodies the wounds of the cross. This means being conscious that we develop the capacity to love and to be loved only by dying to ourselves. Our wounds are also a constant reminder of our frailty and that it is God's grace that raises us up to new life.

St Paul's epistles show that the first Christians needed the corrective of Thomas' faith. They tended to relate with the risen Jesus without reference to his crucifixion. They forgot that they were called to be 'followers of Jesus crucified,' choosing to die with him so that they could rise with him (see especially 1 Corinthians 1).

We Christians fall into the same error today when our lives and our teachings proclaim an abstract 'disembodied' Jesus, dispenser of graces and teacher of morality; we forget the historical person who was put to death for proclaiming the kingdom of God.

Thomas professes the true faith of the church. We too must insist that the Jesus we follow is the true Jesus, the one whose risen body bears the wounds of Calvary.

Jesus is the model leader and spiritual guide. He is pleased to give Thomas the assurance he is looking for, and then challenges him to look forward to the day when he will believe without seeing – always in the Jesus who passes through death to resurrection.

The blessedness of believing without seeing came from the experience of the early church. Jesus is not moralising but inviting Thomas (and us) to celebrate great people of faith – in our communities and worldwide – who take up their cross with confidence in the resurrection.

As always in our meditation we must not limit ourselves to personal relationships. We celebrate the resurrection faith lived by communities, nations and cultures.

* * *

'*You who remain ever faithful even when we are unfaithful, forgive our sins and grant that we may bear true witness to you before all men and women.*' Pope John Paul II, Service of Forgiveness, March 2000
Lord, we thank you for the moments of grace
of this Lenten season
when, as individuals and as a church community,
we walked in the footsteps of Jesus
by passing from death to new life.
We thank you in particular for the great day
when our church publicly asked forgiveness
from other religions and cultures.
We thank you for Pope John Paul who,
like Jesus with St Thomas,
invited us to see the holes
that the nails of arrogance and self-righteousness
made into the body of Christ,
and to put our fingers into the holes,
to put our hands into the huge wound
which the lust for power made in his side,
so that we would recognise how,
just as you raised Jesus from the dead,
you do not allow his Body, the church, to remain in the tomb,
but always raise her up to new life.

Lord, we thank you for the times
when reconciliation emerged triumphantly
from the tomb of conflict:

    - the spirit of dialogue between our church and Jews, Muslims, Hindus and African traditional religions;
    - the European Union created by former enemies;
    - the Good Friday Agreement in Northern Ireland;
    - the peace process in the Middle East.
Do not let us forget the terrible legacy of hatred and resentment
which had to be overcome;
invite us to put our fingers into the holes made by the nails,
our hands into the great wound made by lances,
so that we can recognise with awe and wonder
the spark of your divine life that is within us all.
Remind us too of those who worked for peace
during the long years of conflict
when they seemed to be working in vain.
How blessed were they who did not see
and yet continued to believe
in your power to bring new life into the world.

'Whoever sees anything of God, sees nothing of God.' Meister Eckhart
Lord, lead us to the blessedness of not seeing and believing.

'Go for broke, always try to do too much, dispense with safety nets, aim for the stars.' Salman Rushdie
Lord, we thank you for friends, leaders and spiritual guides
who challenge us as Jesus challenged Thomas.
When we commit ourselves to a cause
because we have tested its reality,
they invite us to experience the blessedness
of believing without seeing.

'Beware of the seduction of leaving the poor to think about them.'
Jean Vanier
Lord, forgive us for wanting to help those in need
without sharing their pain;
we look for their resurrection
but do not want to see their wounds:
    - young people have been deeply hurt and we serve them with pious exhortations;
    - we become impatient with those who continue to mourn the death of a spouse or a child;

- we think we can restore a broken relationship by merely saying we are sorry;
- we propose reconciliation between warring factions without acknowledging past wrongs;
- we pray for peace in the world and do not agonise over its terrible injustices.

We thank you for people like Thomas
who will not let us away with easy solutions;
they insist that we must see the holes
nails have made in the hands of victims,
put our fingers into the holes
and our hands into wounds lances have made in their sides;
and only then will we believe that they have within them
the capacity to rise to new life.

'We admitted to God, to ourselves, and to another human being, the exact nature of our wrongs.' Step 5 of the Twelve Step Method of Alcoholics Anonymous
Lord, when we are converted from an addiction
– to alcohol, drugs, power, or sex –
we are so anxious to make a new start
that we forget the hurt which was at the root of our problem,
    - the loneliness of our childhood,
    - the sense of racial inferiority,
    - our disability,
    - the fear of failure.
We thank you for sending us friends who insist
that we must face the reality of the past.
We pray that, like Jesus welcoming Thomas,
we will invite them to put their fingers into the holes
the nails have made
and their hands into our sides,
so that they can walk with us in our new life.

Third Sunday of Easter

Gospel Reading: Luke 24:13-35

[13]*That very same day, the first day after the sabbath, two of them were on their way to a village called Emmaus, seven miles from Jerusalem,* [14]*and they were talking together about all that had happened.* [15]*Now as they talked this over, Jesus himself came up and walked by their side;* [16]*but something prevented them from recognising him.* [17]*He said to them, 'What matters are you discussing as you walk along?' They stopped short, their faces downcast.* [18]*Then one of them, called Cleopas, answered him, 'You must be the only person staying in Jerusalem who does not know the things that have been happening these last few days.'* [19]*'What things?' he asked. 'All about Jesus of Nazareth,' they answered, 'who proved he was a great prophet by the things he said and did in the sight of God and of the whole people;* [20]*and how our chief priests and our leaders handed him over to be sentenced to death, and had him crucified.* [21]*Our own hope had been that he would be the one to set Israel free. And that is not all: two whole days have gone by since it all happened,* [22]*and some women from our group have astounded us; they went to the tomb in the early morning,* [23]*and when they did not find the body, they came back to tell us they had seen a vision of angels who declared he was alive.* [24]*Some of our friends went to the tomb and found everything exactly as the women had reported, but of him they saw nothing.'* [25]*Then he said to them, 'You foolish men! So slow to believe the full message of the prophets!* [26]*Was it not ordained that the Christ should suffer and so enter into his glory?'* [27]*Then, starting with Moses and going through all the prophets, he explained to them the passages throughout the scriptures that were about himself.* [28]*When they drew near to the village to which they were going, he made as if to go on,* [29]*but they pressed him to stay with them. 'It is nearly evening,' they said, 'and the day is almost over.' So he went in to stay with them.* [30]*Now while he was with them at table, he took the bread and said the blessing; then he broke it and handed it to them.* [31]*And their eyes were opened and they recognised him; but he had vanished from their sight.* [32]*Then they said to each other, 'Did not our hearts burn within us as he talked to us on the road and explained the scriptures to us?'* [33]*They set out that instant and returned to Jerusalem. There they found the Eleven assembled together with their companions,* [34]*who said to them,*

'Yes, it is true. The Lord has risen and has appeared to Simon.' [35]*Then they told their story of what had happened on the road and how they had recognised him at the breaking of bread.*

It is Easter morning, and Jesus leads the two disciples along the slow, painful journey to wisdom. God is inviting us to remember with gratitude times when he led us along a similar journey to the stage where we understood what was happening in our lives. We celebrate the teachers who did for us what Jesus did for the two disciples.

The story unfolds in several stages:

Verses 13 to 16: The disciples walk aimlessly along, unable to make sense of the events of Good Friday. Jesus the teacher is discreet, patient and content to walk silently alongside them.

Verses 18 to 24: Jesus invites them to tell their story, a long one, with many ups and downs, great hopes all dashed. Jesus listens in respectful silence. What a teacher!

Verses 25 to 27: Jesus' long silence bears rich fruit – as always happens with great teachers. Now fully in tune with the experience of the disciples, he takes up the dialogue, showing that the teaching of the scriptures is not complete until it is experienced in the reality of their lives. As he teaches, what had seemed senseless to the disciples now appears not only meaningful, but in accordance with age-old laws of life.

Verses 28 to 32: What Jesus taught them on the road now becomes a reality in the context of a community meal.

Verses 33 to 35: This is a crucial part of the story: as a result of the encounter with Jesus and the wisdom they have gained, the disciples are able to return to their community with a new heart.

* * *

Lord, there have been times when we were totally discouraged.
We walked aimlessly along the road, our faces downcast,
as we remembered the sad events of previous days:
    - a project which we thought would change our country had
    failed;
    - we were disappointed in a relationship that had seemed
    destined to fulfill all our longing;

- a church community we had hoped would be a true body of
  Christ was torn apart by conflict.
Then, quite suddenly, unexpectedly,
you sent your son Jesus to walk with us,
even though we did not recognise him.
He came in the guise of a friend,
a spiritual guide, a grandparent,
who listened in silence as we told our story once more.
Then, when the moment was right,
that Jesus whom you sent showed us how foolish we were,
how slow to believe the full message of the prophets;
he explained the passages throughout the scriptures
that were about ourselves
while we listened in silence, our hearts burning within us.
We remember with gratitude
how we were able to set out that instant
and return to Jerusalem.

Lord, our contemporaries are walking the road,
their faces downcast, unable to make sense of their lives.
Forgive us, church people, that we come arrogantly to them
labelling them materialistic, or unbelievers, or atheists,
and telling them our own stories.
Help us rather to be like Jesus,
to walk alongside them
so discreetly they don't even recognize who we are;
to ask them what matters they are discussing as they walk along;
to invite them to relate their stories,
even if they are impatient with our questions;
to listen respectfully for as long as their stories last.
How else will we be able to explain
the scriptures at work in their lives
so that they can return to Jerusalem,
their hearts burning within them?

Lord, send us Bible teachers like Jesus
who will make our hearts burn within us
as they talk to us on the road
and, starting with Moses and going through all the prophets,
explain the passages throughout the scriptures
that are about ourselves.

We thank you for those special Eucharists
that we experience from time to time,
when we recognise your presence in the breaking of bread
and feel no need to linger there,
but return to the Jerusalem of our daily occupations,
our hearts burning within us.

Lord, we would prefer to grow in wisdom
quickly and painlessly
by taking courses or reading many books.
But there is no way to wisdom
except by going through times
when we cannot understand what has happened to us;
only when we have told our story many times over,
experiencing again and again how senseless it is
will we reach down into the roots of our traditions
and discover with surprise
that what we have gone through is nothing new
but the fulfillment of ancient prophecies.

Lord, we get to know you through teachers and preachers,
and we thank you for them.
But it is only in a community of sharing and trust
that we can experience your presence in the world.
How true it is that we recognise you in the breaking of bread.

Fourth Sunday of Easter

Gospel Reading: John 10:1-10

[1]Jesus said, 'I tell you most solemnly, anyone who does not enter the sheepfold through the gate, but gets in some other way is a thief and a brigand. [2]The one who enters through the gate is the shepherd of the flock; [3]the gatekeeper lets him in, the sheep hear his voice, one by one he calls his own sheep and leads them out. [4]When he has brought out his flock, he goes ahead of them, and the sheep follow because they know his voice. [5]They never follow a stranger but run away from him: they do not recognise the voice of strangers.' [6]Jesus told them this parable but they failed to understand what he meant by telling it to them. [7]So Jesus spoke to them again: 'I tell you most solemnly, I am the gate of the sheepfold. [8]All others who have come are thieves and brigands; but the sheep took no notice of them. [9]I am the gate. Anyone who enters through me will be safe: he will go freely in and out and be sure of finding pasture. [10]The thief comes only to steal and kill and destroy. I have come so that they may have life and have it to the full.'

According to the liturgical tradition, the gospel reading on the fourth Sunday of Easter speaks about Jesus as shepherd, which is the theme of chapter 10 of St John's gospel. This theme is dealt with in several sections or 'movements', as is often the case in this gospel. One movement is read on this Sunday each year of the three year cycle; this year we read the first movement.

Shepherd is one of the biblical titles for a leader, a memory of the days when the Jews were sheep-rearing nomads. The passage therefore invites us to celebrate people who have 'shepherded' us by touching our lives, some through direct contact, others from reading about them or hearing their stories.

We remember, too, great world leaders, in modern times or in the past, and recognise that they were the presence of Jesus in the world, 'shepherding' the human family.

The passage can also be an examination of conscience on how we are fulfilling our vocation as parent, teacher, guide, friend, leader in the church community.

Actually, the shepherd theme (or 'parable', as it is called in

85

verse 6) is only in verses 1 to 5. In verses 7 to 10 Jesus speaks of himself as 'the gate'.

The special characteristic of good shepherds is brought out in the passage in the relationship of trust between them and the sheep. They are trusting and in turn they inspire trust in those whom they lead. This wonderful quality – so rare in our experience – is expressed in a series of images, each of which can touch us deeply.

The shepherds 'enter the sheepfold through the gate', they are not devious; they 'call the sheep by name' – no haranguing; they 'go ahead of the sheep' – no looking back to see if they are being followed. The sheep 'know the voice' of the shepherd; their relationship is almost instinctive, of the heart.

The image of the gate is not as well known as that of the shepherd and is more difficult to enter into, but if we make the effort it can be very touching. Leaders who are like a gate are the opposite of possessive; they are content to be the humble instruments through which others can 'go freely in and out', making their own way to 'life to the full'. A wonderful picture indeed of great parents, teachers, community leaders and friends.

* * *

Lord, we remember with gratitude
the great people we have known,
in the world and in our country:
    - teachers, fellow workers, community leaders,
    - parents, grandparents, uncles or aunts, elder brothers or
    sisters.
We remember how they came to us openly, without pretence,
passing through the open gate.
We knew immediately it was someone who understood us,
a voice we had always longed to hear.
We felt we were being called one by one, each by name.
They said what they had to say and went ahead,
not looking back suspiciously to make sure we were following,
and we did follow
because we knew we were not with a stranger.

Lord, we ask you to bless leaders
in our country and in the world.
Give them today the grace to look into their hearts
and ask themselves are they real shepherds of the flock.
Have they come openly through the gate like shepherds,
or deviously like thieves?
Have they come to give life or to steal, kill and destroy?
Do they speak a foreign language
that the sheep cannot recognise
so that they naturally run away from them?
Do they take the trouble to know their sheep
so that they can call them out one by one, by their own names?
Is their relationship with people one of trust,
freeing them to go ahead of the flock,
or must they always be looking back,
wondering if they are being followed?

Lord, we ask you today to send us
many good priests and religious,
men and women who will be like a gate to a sheepfold,
without the slightest trace of possessiveness,
happy to be a passageway
through which many will pass freely and live life to the full.

Lord, we pray for the church
as it emerges among the ancient cultures
of Asia, Africa and Latin America,
as it exists side by side with other faiths.
We pray that we may not be envious of things
that others have and we don't,
that we may never be destructive
or the cause of people or institutions dying,
but rather that we may be true shepherds
whose only concern is that people may have life to the full.

Fifth Sunday of Easter

Gospel Reading: John 14:1-12

¹*Jesus said to his disciples, 'Do not let your hearts be troubled. Trust in God still, and trust in me. *²*There are many rooms in my Father's house; if there were not, I should have told you. I am going now to prepare a place for you *³*and after I have gone and prepared you a place, I shall return to take you with me; so that where I am you may be too. *⁴*You know the way to the place where I am going.' *⁵*Thomas said, 'Lord, we do not know where you are going, so how can we know the way?' *⁶*Jesus said: 'I am the Way, the Truth and the Life. No one can come to the Father except through me. *⁷*If you know me, you know my Father too. From this moment you know him and have seen him.' *⁸*Philip said, 'Lord, let us see the Father and then we shall be satisfied.' *⁹*'Have I been with you all this time, Philip,' said Jesus to him, 'and you still do not know me? To have seen me is to have seen the Father, so how can you say, "Let us see the Father"? *¹⁰*Do you not believe that I am in the Father and the Father is in me? The words I say to you I do not speak as from myself: it is the Father, living in me, who is doing this work. *¹¹*You must believe me when I say that I am in the Father and the Father is in me; believe it on the evidence of this work, if for no other reason. *¹²*I tell you most solemnly, whoever believes in me will perform the same works as I do myself, he will perform even greater works, because I am going to the Father.'*

On the 5th and 6th Sundays of Easter time, it is traditional to read extracts from the long discourse which St John tells us Jesus had with his apostles at the Last Supper, and which he recounts from chapter 13, verse 31 to the end of chapter 17.

This is a very deep teaching of Jesus, and therefore you must make a real effort to discover that it is also down-to-earth, to be experienced by us personally.

It is useful to remember that the teaching was given on a specific occasion: Jesus was facing a great crisis in his own life and in the life of the little community he had founded. In your meditation, remember a similar moment in your own life, or in the life of your community, or in the history of a country or even a civilisation. Who was Jesus in that situation, speaking as Jesus did in these passages? Looking back on those experiences, what words of Jesus can you see were fulfilled?

This Sunday's passage is rather long, and you must divide it up so that you can meditate on one section at a time.

Verses 1 to 3: Jesus sees himself at this point in his life as having to make a painful journey alone. He knows that as a result of this journey he will go to a beautiful place, with plenty of space so there is freedom for all. Because of his journey, he will be able to lead his followers to that place as well. Recognise that moment is the life of every person, the church, any great movement of history.

Verses 4 to 6: Thomas is struggling with the desire, which is in all of us, to know exactly the destination before we set out. Jesus invites him to make an act of faith and to take one step at a time.

Verses 7 to 11: Philip too must make a journey which we can recognise. He wants to experience God directly. Jesus shows him that he has been experiencing God all the time by involving himself in the works which Jesus has been doing.

Verse 12: Jesus sees himself on a journey to the Father, trusting that the work will continue because it is not his but the Father's.

* * *

Lord, there was a time
when the teaching of Jesus meant nothing to us.
We were drifting,
we could not accept the values which had guided us in the past.
Then one day, almost miraculously,
we knew you were with us again.
It was like coming home;
in fact, we felt an inner freedom and security
such as we had never known before.
Looking back on that journey,
we see that our hearts need not have been troubled;
you had left us on our own for a while,
but only to prepare this wonderful place for us to be.

Lord, as parents, teachers, community leaders,
preachers of the gospel
we try to guide our charges
along a road we have not travelled ourselves.
That is not the way of Jesus.
Teach us that we must make our own journey,
painful though that may be;
only then can we come back and share it with others,
so that where we are they also may be.

Lord, we pray today for those
who are facing death or some terrible crisis.
We pray that their hearts may not be troubled.
They are making a lonely journey, but you will come back
and take them where they can be at home with you forever.

Lord, we are at a crossroads in life, and before we set out
we would like to know where you are leading us.
Help us to give ourselves to the present moment,
trusting that if we enter into the truth of our situation,
it will lead us to life.

Lord, we remember when we tried to meet you directly,
remaining alone, withdrawing from others.
We thank you for sending us a teacher
who invited us to become involved
    - in working with the poor;
    - in building communities;
    - in caring for those who are neglected by society.
Then to our surprise we found that you were working with us
and that we were in your presence.

Lord, we pray for those who have started great projects
here in our country and in the world.
They are often anxious about what will happen
when they move on.
Remind them that they are not alone,
that they are part of humanity making its way to you.
There will be followers who will do the same work
and will perform even greater works.

Sixth Sunday of Easter

Gospel Reading: John 14:15-21

15Jesus said to his disciples, 'If you love me you will keep my commandments. 16I shall ask the Father, and he will give you another Advocate to be with you forever. 17This is the Spirit of truth whom the world cannot receive because it neither sees him nor knows him. You know him, because he abides with you, and he will be in you. 18I will not leave you orphaned; I am coming to you. 19In a little while the world will no longer see me, but you will see me; because I live, you also will live. 20On that day you will know that I am in my Father, and you in me, and I in you. 21They who have my commandments and keep them are those who love me; and those who love me will be loved by my Father, and I will love them and reveal myself to them.'

Like last Sunday's passage, this reading will seem abstract to you at first, but situate it in the context of the Last Supper and you will recognise the movement of Jesus' thought from your own experience and from the lives of great people you have known or read about. As always, it may be helpful to divide the passage and meditate on one section at a time.

Verses 15 to 17: Jesus makes a difference between the way he has been present to the disciples until then and the way he will be present to them after he leaves them. Read it from the point of view of a teacher or a parent who must leave children, or from your memories of any teaching that was outside yourself and then became part of you.

Verses 18 and 19: The same movement expressed in a new metaphor – being orphaned and then realising that we are not lost after all.

Verse 20: This is a precious verse. It describes the moment when we read the story of Jesus in the gospels and discover that it is not the story of someone outside ourselves, but our own story, and that therefore our stories are really sacred. Great teachers can promise their followers that one day they will experience something similar.

Verse 21: Jesus describes the process of getting to know him, starting from a different point – the person follows his teaching and then enters into a deep relationship with him.

* * *

Lord, we thank you for calling us
to be leaders in our community.
At present things are going well:
there is trust among us, we share many things,
and we are working together.
But we know that this will not last forever,
and so we pray that the values we have grown to believe in
may become part of us,
so that even though the majority of people around us
do not accept them,
we may continue to live by them,
and even though outwardly we will no longer be a community,
we may remain one because of that inner bond that unites us.

Lord, from time to time you send us a wonderful person
who guides and inspires us;
when they die or leave us we feel orphaned.
But then we discover that they are still with us.
Others – even our friends – cannot understand this,
but we know that this person is alive,
and we know that our lives are fuller because of this.

Lord, forgive us for always wanting to see things:
    - we have become so dependent on external stimuli;
    - we must be listening to the radio or watching the television;
    - we need to hear sermons or read spiritual books.
Teach us to quieten ourselves
so that we may listen to our inner rhythms:
    - the memories we have, both painful and happy;
    - the deep longings of our hearts;
    - the instincts of our nature.
Remind us that Jesus prayed for us
that you would make your presence known to us
within the truth of ourselves.

Lord, we thank you for those wonderful moments of grace
when we knew that our lives were sacred.
We had read the story of Jesus,
but it was the story of someone else
– the story of the saints, of extraordinary people.
Then we experienced that we too are living Jesus lives,
and we are your presence in the world.

Lord, we thank you for people we have known
who are not Christians
but who love the teachings of Jesus and keep them.
We know, Father, that you love them as we love them,
and we pray that you may continue to show yourself to them.

Feast of the Ascension

Gospel Reading: Matthew 28:16-20

16*The eleven disciples set out for Galilee, to the mountain where Jesus had arranged to meet them.* 17*When they saw him they fell down before him, though some hesitated.* 18*Jesus came up and spoke to them. He said, 'All authority in heaven and on earth has been given to me.* 19*Go, therefore, make disciples of all the nations; baptise them in the name of the Father and of the Son and of the Holy Spirit,* 20*and teach them to observe all the commands I gave you. And know that I am with you always; yes, to the end of time.'*

When we think of the Ascension of Jesus, the account given us in chapter 1 of the Acts of the Apostles naturally comes to our minds. In fact, some may find that this passage from St Matthew's gospel is not an ascension story at all. This moment in the life of Jesus was significant from several points of view, however, and each account stresses some aspects over others.

We can identify three main aspects:
- At the end of his earthly life, and especially of his passion, Jesus makes his triumphant entry into heaven, to sit forever at the right hand of the Father.
- The time for forming his little community has come to an end, and Jesus sends his disciples out into the world.
- From now on Jesus and his followers must relate with each other differently.

All these aspects are present in the text. But do not look for them; just enter deeply into the story and you will discover for yourself how it presents the mystery of the Ascension.

In verse 16 the disciples (depleted since they were supposed to be twelve) make their way back to Galilee, the place where the whole adventure began.

Let verse 17 speak to you deeply; the scene is very touching. Ask yourself why some hesitated.

The commission of Jesus in verses 18 and 19 is in three waves:
- a statement of his own authority;
- a three-fold command,

- and a promise.
Each section is worth meditating on by itself.

* * *

'Mr Minister, I must remind you that you are not God, you are just a
man. One day your name shall be merely a faint scribble on the pages of
history, while the name of Jesus Christ shall live forever.' Archbishop
Tutu to a government minister who had threatened the church
Lord, when we have committed ourselves to a noble cause
we experience something of what the eleven felt
when they were reunited with Jesus on the mountain in Galilee.
We may have been defeated,
let one another down as they had let down Jesus,
our group depleted, as theirs without Judas.
But we are here together on this mountain
and we know that no power in heaven or on earth
will conquer what we stand for.
We can go into the world
teaching all nations to respect the values we believe in;
whatever happens to us, now or in the future,
our cause will live for ever.

Lord, we pray for those who at one time
were touched by your grace:
- they turned away from drugs, alcohol, or a wrong relationship;
- forgave a deep hurt;
- began to pray again.
Now they have strayed again , and they feel helpless,
without the energy to make a new start.
Teach them to do as the apostles did when, reduced to eleven,
they set out for Galilee.
Tell them that there is a mountain somewhere
where you have arranged to meet them again,
because once you have entered our lives
you will be with us always,
yes, even to the end of our lives.
Lord, we pray for those of us who are in positions of authority –
parents, teachers, leaders in the church or the state.
Don't let us become possessive of those in our charge.

Help us rather to be like Jesus,
to let them go, when the time comes,
to whatever part of the world you call them to,
and to do so without regrets,
trusting that whatever true or good they have learned from us
they will teach others to observe,
and wherever they are, we will always be with them.

'But when Carnival come and pass
People does go back to race and class.'
Earl Lovelace, *The New Hardware Store*
Lord, for us here in Trinidad and Tobago,
Carnival is a special time of togetherness.
Other nations have similar times.
We pray that we may not live these moments in isolation,
as if on some mountain far away from the rest of life.
Tell us, as Jesus told his disciples,
that we have seen possibilities for ourselves,
that we must go out and teach all nations to observe
what we have learned about humanity during these days,
– something that will be with us always.

Lord, we sometimes have regrets for the church of the past.
We feel like the eleven setting out for Galilee.
From time to time we meet that church again
and feel very happy,
as they did when they were reunited with Jesus
on the mountain.
But part of us quite rightly hesitates:
we know well that we cannot bring back the past,
that we must go in new directions,
discovering new disciples among the nations.
We need not be afraid:
Jesus promised that he will be with us always,
even when we come to the end of a time.

Lord, forgive us as a Church for limiting our horizons.
Let Jesus speak to us again
of the many nations who could be his disciples,
people ready to be baptised
and to observe all the commands he gave us.

Pentecost

19In the evening of that same day, the first day of the week, the doors were closed in the room where the disciples were, for fear of the Jews. Jesus came and stood among them. He said to them, 'Peace be with you,' 20and showed them his hands and his side. The disciples were filled with joy when they saw the Lord, 21and he said to them again, 'Peace be with you. As the Father sent me, so am I sending you.' 22After saying this he breathed on them and said, 'Receive the Holy Spirit. 23For those whose sins you forgive, they are forgiven; for those whose sins you retain, they are retained.'

The Mass of Pentecost has two accounts of the sending of the Holy Spirit, one from the Acts of the Apostles and one from St John's gospel. Don't combine the two accounts in your meditation. Each in its own way is true, in the sense that it helps us recognise moments when God sent his Spirit into us, as individuals or as a community. Sometimes it happens in extraordinary ways, and at other times it happens in quite ordinary ways.

I am inviting you to meditate on the gospel account. It is less spectacular than the one in the Acts, but no less true.

In verse 19 try to imagine how the disciples felt as they gathered in the room on that Easter Sunday evening; you will feel then the drama of Jesus' entry. Read it as a sending of the Spirit.

In order to interpret verse 20 let your memories explain for you the meaning of Jesus' showing his hands and his side.

Verse 21 has very little for the imagination, so you must make an effort to enter into it. It speaks of two sendings:

- Jesus sent by the Father, which we know from the New Testament;

- us sent by Jesus, which we know from experience.

Let the two shed light on each other.

Read verse 22 by itself, entering into the symbolism of Jesus' breathing on the disciples.

Verse 23 in our church tradition evokes memories of the sacrament of reconciliation. You might like to remember other times when we have forgiven or retained one another's sins.

Lord, we celebrate today our personal Pentecosts:
we were going through a difficult time:
  - a relationship had broken down;
  - a movement we had given ourselves to disintegrated because of internal conflicts;
  - our prayer life was totally dry.
We turned in on ourselves,
afraid to meet others lest we would have to relate with them.
Then quite suddenly something happened:
  - friends came and shared their journey with us;
  - we went on a retreat and had a deep sense of being loved;
  - we were invited to join a group who shared our values.
It was as if Jesus had come
through the closed doors of the room we were in,
stood with us and said, 'Peace be with you.'

*'The moment we cease to hold each other, the moment we break faith
with one another, the sea engulfs us and the light goes out.'*
James Baldwin
Lord, humanity today is deeply divided.
Groups of people have cut themselves off,
afraid to mix with others lest they lose their identity.
Send us people like Jesus
who will pass through the locked doors,
stand among others, share their own humanity,
and say 'Peace be with you.'

*'Why can't Christians see the poor wounded part inside themselves?
Can they not see Jesus there?'* Carl Jung
Lord, we spend so much energy denying our hurts,
hiding the marks of the nails in our hands
and the deep wounds in our sides.
Give us the grace to look with compassion
at the truth of ourselves,
like the disciples letting Jesus show them his hands and his side,
so that we may be at peace.

'It is not as if we had a high priest who was incapable of feeling our weaknesses with us; but we have one who has been tempted in every way that we are, though he is without sin.' Hebrews 4:15

Lord, you sent your Son Jesus as one of us.
He shared the weaknesses of the human condition,
he knew uncertainty and anxiety about the future,
he was limited to living in one culture
and in one period of history.
Help us, Lord, to accept that as you sent Jesus so he sends us.

Lord, the modern world knows
many ways of influencing others:
   - advertising;
   - the power of weapons;
   - aggressive argumentation which forces others to agree.
Forgive us, Lord, that we followers of Jesus
use these methods in preaching his message.
Teach us to trust in his power –
love, gentle as breath,
the kind that leaves others free and creative,
and comes from the very depths of our selves.

One day St Catherine of Siena had a strange experience: Jesus came to her and removed her physical heart saying: 'I am giving you my heart so that you can go on living with it forever.'

Lord, lead us to deep union with your Son Jesus,
let him breathe into us,
so that when we breathe he is breathing in us,
and when we love, he is loving in us.

Lord, we remember with gratitude
the times when a priest of the church forgave our sins
and we knew that they were forgiven.

Lord, we remember parts of the world that are torn by civil strife
– the Middle East, Northern Ireland, Sudan.
So many sins of the past are being retained
because they are retaining them.
We pray that they may forgive one another
 and so their sins may be truly forgiven.

Trinity Sunday

Gospel Reading: John 3:16-18

16At that time, Jesus said to Nicodemus: 'God loved the world so much that he gave his only Son so that everyone who believes in him may not be lost but may have eternal life. 17For God sent his Son into the world not to condemn the world, but so that through him the world might be saved. 18No one who believes in him will be condemned; but whoever refuses to believe is condemned already, because he has refused to believe in the name of God's only Son.'

The feast of the Trinity is classed in the church's calendar as a 'solemnity'. I have sometimes heard it called 'the climax of the liturgical year'. This is an unfortunate expression which betrays a misunderstanding of liturgy – and of our relationship with Jesus.

As I pointed out last week the focus of the church's liturgy (and of our lives as Christians) is always Jesus, not primarily as a teacher but as a person who like us lived in particular historical circumstances and responded to particular challenges as he met them.

This is why the church's main liturgical feasts are also the main events of Jesus' life:
- his birth and childhood at Advent and Christmas;
- his preaching in Lent;
- his passion and death at the Sacred Triduum;
- his resurrection culminating in the ascension and the sending of the Spirit, at Easter.

These events, as I also showed last week, are not particular to Jesus; they are 'mysteries' – like the mysteries of the rosary. This means that he now lives them in his followers and in the church, so that we do not merely look at or admire them, but 'celebrate' them as stories of Jesus, recognising them from our own experience (or the experience of others) and letting them lead us to become ever more like him. We apply to liturgical feasts the words of the popular prayer at the end of the rosary; 'we imitate what they contain and hope to obtain what they promise'.

In the liturgy then, 'doctrinal feasts' like the Trinity are always subordinate to 'events-feasts' like Christmas, the Sacred Triduum and Easter. The Vatican II Decree on the Liturgy made this clear: 'The minds of the faithful should be directed primarily to the feasts of the Lord, whereby the mysteries of salvation are celebrated throughout the year' (No 108).

The doctrine of the Trinity emerged in the church very gradually after several centuries of meditation on the life of Jesus. We do not need to make that journey again – the Trinity is now a doctrine of our faith. It remains true however that the best way to approach the Trinity is by meditating on Jesus, how he faced life and related with people.

This is how we approach today's feast, and the gospel reading. We meditate on Jesus responding to a concrete situation – he converses with Nicodemus who has come to him 'by night' because he is afraid of the Jews. Our meditation reveals him as a totally free person, his freedom rooted in his relationship with the Father and the Holy Spirit, the fact that he was a 'Trinitarian person' – as we too are called to be.

The reading comprises several 'themes' which are intertwined and run through the entire passage. We can identify three such 'themes'.

Jesus sees his mission as bringing 'eternal life' and 'salvation' to those who are 'lost'. These are traditional expressions, almost clichés. We must make a real effort to let them come alive through meditation.

'Eternal life' is in contrast with 'temporary life'. It means a life that can survive every form of death, failure in relationships or the work place, defeat and humiliation, the loss of a loved one. We remember people (ourselves included) being 'lost' – insecure, adrift, without guidance – and then moving to being 'saved' (safe) – the feeling of security, the tremendous relief of finding one's way after having drifted for a long time.

The next two themes answer the question, how did Jesus keep his mission truly 'life-giving' and 'saving'? The first answer is that he was conscious of his mission not originating in himself – he was the ' son' who had been 'given to the world' by the 'Father', a loving gift, as precious as an only child to its parents. Our meditation must make the expression 'only son' come alive. It means 'very dear son', conjuring up memories of only children, of how their parents dote on them, and how they grieve over them when they die prematurely.

Jesus' sense of himself as 'beloved son' (a 'sent person' as in many other gospel passages) keeps him focused on his mission. It removes any possessiveness; he loves selflessly.

Then there is the theme of 'condemning'. It is not an expression we like; for us it connotes self-righteousness and writing off people. On the other hand it is a theme (like God's anger) that is central to the Bible. If we ignore it (throwing out the baby with the bath water) the message of Jesus loses its 'muscle', becomes an innocuous, take-it-or-leave-it affair. We must keep the theme of 'condemning' therefore, just making sure that we purify it of wrong interpretations. The following are some conclusions.

a) Jesus (like his followers to the extent that they are true to him) is conscious that he poses a challenge to the world, one that requires a response. Those who refuse to accept him (to 'believe in the name of God's only Son') must also accept the consequences – 'condemnation'.

b) We human beings are not responsible for 'condemning'. When we take on that responsibility, we inevitably find ourselves condemning, not in the name of God but of our prejudices and narrow-mindedness. It is highly significant then that Jesus says he was sent 'not to condemn'.

c) Because God has created us free we ourselves are the only ones who have the right to condemn. It is the consequence of God's breathing his Spirit on us. A practical example – if Nicodemus is afraid to come in the daylight, as far as Jesus is concerned he is free to come at night. Note that this freedom has another side – we are not in bondage to the judgement of others. (cf St Paul 1 Cor 4:3: 'Not that it makes the slightest difference to me whether you or indeed any human tribunal find me worthy or not.')

The feast is the occasion for us to pray for the grace of a 'Trinitarian spirituality' for the church and for us as individuals:
- awareness of God as Father so that we stand in his presence with awe and never think we can possess or control him;
- consciousness that in Jesus we are sons and daughters of God, sharing in his divinity, so secure in ourselves that others feel 'safe' in our presence;

- awareness of the Spirit at work in others so that we will respect the freedom of each person, especially those who disagree with us or are different from us.
Truly we need to 'celebrate' the Trinity.

* * *

*'God is gracious and so graciously does he seize our hearts in order to
draw them on, that he in no wise impairs the liberty of our will. '*
St Francis of Sales
Lord, we thank you for sending us into the world
as parents, teachers, managers,
community leaders, ministers in the church community.
We thank you for the times when we feel secure in your love,
as secure as an only child is secure in the love of its parents,
so that we feel no desire to condemn,
are only concerned that those whose lives we touch
do not feel lost,
but feel safe and can live their lives to the full.

*'I am disarmed of the will to overcome, to justify myself at the expense
of others, I am no longer on the alert jealously guarding my riches.'*
Patriarch Athenagoras
Lord, forgive us as members of your church,
that we are quick to condemn those who are different from us
    - in race or ethnicity
    - in mores
    - in faith or religion.
Remind us that like Jesus you want us to be a saving presence
in your world that you love so much,
not condemning but at the same time
challenging our contemporaries
to make the choice for life rather than condemnation.

*'You know when you have met a saint; instead of feeling inferior you
feel enormously affirmed.'*
Margaret Hebblethwaite, meeting Cardinal Arns
Lord, we thank you for the great people
you have sent into our lives,
who touched us so deeply

that we felt that you had given us a precious gift.
We sometimes refuse to accept the values they teach us,
but they leave us free.

'It is not for me to win you round, I have only to say no to you.'
Jean Anouilh
Lord many people in our world are lost,
feel they are going nowhere,
that life is not worth living:
    - drug addicts wandering aimlessly through the streets;
    - once successful businessmen who have lost their jobs and
    sit at home doing nothing;
    - families suddenly orphaned;
    - a community floundering under corrupt leadership.
Forgive us that as Jesus' followers
we leave them in their lostness
and at times add to their lostness by condemning them.
Remind us that you gave us to them as your gift,
given out of your great love for them,
and your will is that we should befriend them
so that they can begin to feel safe again and live to the full.

'No one possesses the truth, we all seek it.'
Bishop Pierre Claverie. Dominican Bishop murdered in Algeria
Lord, help your church to recognise truth
as your beloved possession, your only child,
which you have entrusted to the world
so that we may not be lost but may have eternal life.

The Body and Blood of Christ

Gospel Reading: John 6:51-58

51 *Jesus said to the Jews: 'I am the living bread which has come down from heaven. Anyone who eats this bread will live for ever; and the bread that I shall give is my flesh, for the life of the world.'* 52*Then the Jews started arguing among themselves, 'How can this man give us his flesh to eat?'* 53*Jesus replied to them, 'In all truth I tell you, if you do not eat the flesh of the Son of man and drink his blood, you have no life in you.* 54*Anyone who does eat my flesh and drink my blood has eternal life, and I shall raise that person up on the last day.* 55*For my flesh is real food and my blood is real drink.* 56*Whoever eats my flesh and drinks my blood lives in me and I live in that person.* 57*As the living Father sent me and I draw life from the Father, so whoever eats me will also draw life from me.* 58*This is the bread which has come down from heaven; it is not like the bread our ancestors ate: they are dead, but any- one who eats this bread will live for ever.'*

Earlier in this same chapter of St John's gospel, Jesus presented himself to the people as 'bread come down from heaven'. Here he pushes the metaphor further: he gives them his flesh to eat and his blood to drink.

You may find the metaphor strange, but you should try to enter into it so that it becomes part of your prayer. Remember that in Bible meditation it is not sufficient to get the message of a passage; you must get into the words themselves and grow to love them so that you feel moved to repeat them many times.

The metaphor has its origins in 'flesh and blood', a biblical expression that means the reality of a human being with special stress on his or her weakness or limitations. For example, when in Matthew 16 Peter made his act of faith, it did not come from 'flesh and blood,' but as a gift from God. So too St Paul warned the Ephesians that their struggle was not merely against 'flesh and blood', but against heavenly forces.

Therefore, when Jesus says that he gives his flesh to eat and his blood to drink, he is saying three things.

- The first is that he gives himself totally to others; every part of his being is at their service; it is the same as saying, 'This is my body, given for you.'

- Secondly, he is inviting people to deep union with himself, to 'have his spirit coursing through their souls so that they can know the passion of his love for every one,' as we sing in the hymn 'To be the Body of the Lord.'

- Thirdly, he wants them to unite their weakness and their sufferings with his, so that they can experience his strength and his courage. As he would say to them at the Last Supper, 'In the world you will have trouble, but be brave, I have conquered the world.' When we eat his flesh and drink his blood, our own flesh and blood are ennobled. St Paul says in 2 Corinthians: 'We carry with us in our body the death of Jesus so that the life of Jesus too may always be seen in our body.'

The passage is therefore a meditation on Jesus as teacher, leader and guide. In all three roles he does not stand outside of people, he wants to share their lives and to have them share his.

Now this tells us something about God; whereas we tend to imagine God in heaven looking down on us but not getting involved in the movement of our history, Jesus shows God entering into flesh and blood with us.

But the passage also tells us about human relationships. In your meditation remember with gratitude people who have been Jesus for you – a parent, a spiritual guide, a friend, a national leader. Naturally you will feel the passage calling you to growth in your relationships.

Finally a good meditation on this passage will help you to appreciate the Eucharist. It will show you why Jesus chose to be present in the church under the form of bread and wine.

To meditate deeply on this passage, take one section at a time and enter into it, letting it speak to your experience. I suggest the following divisions:

Verses 51 and 52: the people are questioning the very possibility of someone giving himself totally, as Jesus claims to do. Their response is cynical, but is it not typical of the way many would respond today?

Verse 53 invites us to think of people who have no life in them, and to go to the root cause: they have never experienced, or perhaps never let themselves experience, the kind of selfless love that Jesus gives.

Verse 54 introduces a theme that appears several times in this chapter: deep relationship with God in Jesus lifts us up beyond the limitations of time and history.

In verse 55 we remember that there is false food and drink and to recognise them we can look by contrast at what relationship with Jesus does to us.

Verse 56 teaches us the effect of love, the love of Jesus, as well as of all those who love selflessly.

In verse 57 we see another effect of selfless love. Here, as frequently in St John's gospel, Jesus' relationship with his followers is similar to his relationship with his Father – 'As the Father has sent me so I am sending you; as the Father loves me so I have loved you.'

In verse 58 we see again the theme of the newness of Jesus' teaching.

* * *

Lord, we remember with gratitude
the day when we realised for the first time
that following Jesus meant eating his flesh
and drinking his blood.
Up to then it was a matter of believing abstract truths –
that Jesus was truly God and truly man,
that there were three persons in God and seven sacraments.
That kind of faith was not a source of life for us.
Then one day we knew that we had to lay down our lives
     - caring for a wayward child;
     - working for reconciliation in the work place and being at-
     tacked by both workers and employees;
     - forgiving someone who had hurt us deeply.
At that moment we knew
that Jesus on the cross was present within us,
and the strange thing was
that we felt an inner strength and freedom,
and we were certain that no matter how low we fell
he would raise us up.

Lord, self-centredness has become
like a first principle of living today.
People will argue with one another
that it is not possible for us to give our flesh to be eaten,
and yet there can be no life in the world without selfless giving,
not in nature, not in families, not in any society.

Lord, we pray for those who are mourning for a loved one.
Remind them that Jesus gave them his flesh to eat
and his blood to drink
and he will raise them up on the last day.

*'I should like to set down here my own belief. In so far as I am willing to
be made an instrument of God's peace, in that far have I already entered into eternal life.'* Alan Paton
Lord, we thank you for those who eat the flesh
and drink the blood of Jesus
and therefore already have eternal life.

*'We need the eyes of deep faith to see Christ in the broken bodies and
dirty clothes under which the most beautiful one among the sons of
men hides.'* Mother Teresa
Lord, help us to receive Jesus
when he comes to us in flesh and blood.

Lord, you give us food and drink
so that we might live more freely and creatively.
Yet we nourish ourselves with many things
that are not life-giving at all,
but rather clutter up our lives and keep us in bondage.
We pray that your Christ may be Jesus today,
giving the world real food and drink.

Lord, we thank you for the people who have touched our lives;
when we read the story of Jesus, we see them living in him,
and when we remember their stories,
we see Jesus living in them.
Truly they have eaten his flesh and drunk his blood.

Lord, we speak too much when we pray.
Teach us to remain silent
so that we become conscious of Jesus present within us
and the life he draws from you may well up in us too.

Lord, we think today of those
who see their spouses destroying themselves
with bitterness, envy and false pride.
With anguish in their hearts, they say to them,
as Jesus said to his followers,
'Unless you allow yourself to receive my selfless love,
you will not have life within you.'

Lord, we pray for the people of South Africa, Ireland,
Afghanistan, and East Timor.
For generations,
their ancestors have eaten the bread of suspicion,
fear and hatred, and they are dead.
We thank you for raising up new leaders in those countries,
and they, like Jesus, are offering their people
a different kind of nourishment,
based on reconciliation and sharing,
bread come down from heaven,
so that they can eat it and live.

Celebrating Ordinary Time

This coming Sunday we enter into the liturgical time that is known in our tradition as 'the Year' or more appropriately 'Ordinary Time'. One of the most important post-Vatican II reforms was to restore Ordinary Time as a distinctive period in the liturgical year, with its own spirit.

The name itself is significant: Ordinary Time means 'the time of the order', reminding us that in the early centuries before the emergence of Lent, Christmas and the other seasons, the church's liturgy followed its own 'order' which did not correspond to national festivals. Having no political power, the Christians of that time had no choice – they could not impose their festivals on the rest of society.

Ordinary Time is a living reminder therefore that the church existed – and even flourished – at a time when it was ignored by civil society. This is still the situation today in many parts of the world: where Christians are a minority group (as in much of Asia); where members of Christian churches are not allowed to practise their faith in public (as was the case in Socialist countries); or where society pursues different interests, as in the Western world during Advent ('Christmas shopping season'), Christmas ('party time' or even 'beginning of the Carnival season') and Easter ('long holiday weekend'). We face these situations calmly and confidently, as our ancestors in the faith did; during Ordinary Time, we remain faithful to our 'liturgical order' as a source of the energy we need to preserve our Christian values.

In the post-Vatican II liturgy the lectionary of Ordinary Time follows the ancient tradition called 'continuous reading *(lectio continua)*, that is to say that one particular book of the Bible is read from beginning to end, according to the order in which it was written. Passages are not chosen according to themes (as happens during the 'Seasons'). We receive them as they occur in the Bible text and welcome them as God's word for us, just as we welcome people and events as they come our way.

Continuous reading teaches us the important lesson that the

Bible is one unified book – the Word Made Flesh in a wide variety of circumstances, each of which brought its own unique perspective and added its own insight into the Word. The original Word, spoken in earlier texts, became clearer as time went on. We read the Bible 'historically' therefore, aware of the particular circumstances in which the Word was Made Flesh, and the stage of its evolution.

In our Catholic understanding of the Bible, the process continues. The biblical text remains sacred but each historical era – including our own – throws new light on it and is in turn illuminated by it. This is the essence of the *lectio divina* method.

The continuous reading of the gospels focuses on one section of the life of Jesus – his public ministry, starting after the temptations and ending before the passion, death and resurrection. It invites us to experience Jesus as a human being who carried out his life work within historical circumstances. This is part of the human condition and he accepted it fully. Continuous reading corrects the common tendency of experiencing Jesus as a disembodied 'voice' speaking to us 'from heaven' or some indeterminate place.

The Jesus of the gospels – at least as experienced in continuous reading – is a historical person. He has set a goal for himself – the kingdom of God. This is a biblical expression meaning God's plan for the world – the world as it would be if God were in charge. It is spelt out in some detail in various Old Testament texts as a world of harmony and abundance for all.

Jesus could not dictate how this goal would be lived out in practice. Like us, he had to adapt to circumstances he could not control. At times he was in control (e.g. in Galilee), at other times (e.g. on the cross) he had to accept circumstances which others imposed on him.

The Jesus we meet in continuous reading is therefore a living lesson that we too are called by God to live 'historically'.

- Like Jesus we are God's sons and daughters, made in God's image and likeness, endowed with freedom. We choose to set goals for ourselves and we are responsible for being faithful to them.

- Like him too we are limited creatures. We too must live out our goals within historical circumstances which we can influence, but only to some extent. We grow spiritually by 'living with' them. We combine idealism and realism and seek the 'wisdom to know the difference,' according to the well-known 'Serenity Prayer'.

During Ordinary Time we do continuous reading of the synoptic gospels. There are slight differences in the way each gospel tells its story, but one thing they all have in common – their 'one optic' – is that they divide Jesus' public ministry into three historical stages.

1. He started in Galilee. It was a triumphant period, great crowds followed him and hung on his words, but there were already rumblings of opposition, originating from the leaders in Jerusalem. The lectionary for this Year A – St Matthew's year – presents this stage from the Third to the Twenty-First Sundays.

2. At a certain point of the Galilean ministry, Jesus decided it was time for him to go to Jerusalem and confront the religious leaders. He journeyed there, on foot naturally, but continued his teaching, the difference being that he focused more on his disciples than on the crowds. This year Jesus is on his way to Jerusalem from the Twenty-Second to the Twenty-Fifth Sundays.

3. Jesus arrived in Jerusalem and ministered there, in an atmosphere of heightened opposition and impending crisis. This year we read the story of the Jerusalem ministry from the Twenty-Sixth to the Thirty-Third Sunday.

We start the Sundays of Ordinary Time in early January, and interrupt them for Lent. Several Sundays are replaced by feasts such as the Trinity and Corpus Christi.

Second Sunday in Ordinary Time

Gospel Reading: John 1:29-34

29Seeing Jesus coming towards him, John said, 'Look, there is the lamb of God that takes away the sin of the world. 30This is the one I spoke of when I said: A man is coming after me who ranks before me because he existed before me. 31I did not know him myself, and yet it was to reveal him to Israel that I came baptising with water.' 32John also declared, 'I saw the Spirit coming down on him from heaven like a dove and resting on him. 33I did not know him myself, but he who sent me to baptise with water had said to me, 'The man on whom you see the Spirit come down and rest is the one who is going to baptise with the Holy Spirit.' 34Yes, I have seen and I am the witness that he is the Chosen One of God.'

As happens each year, the lectionary remains with Christmas themes (and with St John's gospel) for one more week. It is as if the church is still enjoying Christmas and is reluctant to move on to Ordinary Time and St Matthew.

The passage has a double focus: Jesus and John the Baptist. John invites us to 'look' at Jesus; he reflects on his mission to proclaim Jesus to the world.

We are free to identify with either:
- to celebrate times when some John the Baptist (a person, a word or an event) invites us to take a fresh look at Jesus 'coming towards us';
- to celebrate our mission as parents, teachers, friends, community leaders, spiritual guides to 'proclaim' to the world (and often to ourselves) that those in our care are sacred.

1. John points to two aspects of Jesus:
a) He is the lamb of God that takes away the sin of the world (verse 29). We say these words at every Mass, and we have become so accustomed to them that they no longer strike us. We can take the opportunity of this Sunday's reading to let them come alive for us. We do this in the lectio divina way – linking text and experience and letting each throw light on the other:
- the words help us to appreciate those who have been for us 'lambs of God' who 'took away' the sin of our community;

- people who have touched our lives help us to understand the words.

The second part of the saying – 'he takes away the sin of the world' – states the purpose of the first, so we start with it. It tells us that Jesus is an activist; he does not merely oppose sin in theory, he 'takes it away'. He does not accept sin as inevitable, he wages war against it. As individuals and as a church we have tended to water down this aspect of Jesus' – and our – mission:

- we resign ourselves to accepting evil on the grounds that it is inevitable and in any case we are powerless to do anything about it; we say to ourselves – and to others – that this is how life is and we must accept it;

- we 'spiritualise' sin, saying things like 'we must hate sin but love the sinner', 'we pray for sinners', 'we are all sinners in our own way', etc. These are all important (and Christian) sentiments, but in practice they are used all too often to cover up the fact that we are not 'taking away' some evil in our community.

We celebrate the times when some John the Baptist (a person, an event, a scripture passage) challenged us to 'look again' at Jesus 'taking away' the sin of the world.

By using the singular – 'the sin of the world' – the text invites us to identify one particular 'sin' which marks our community or culture, e.g. individualism, racism, elitism. Once we have given it a name, we can celebrate the 'lamb of God' who 'takes it away'.

Jesus has a distinctive way of 'taking away sin'. He does it by being a 'lamb of God'. This is another image which we are accustomed to and find difficult to bring to life.

We can identify two problems (aside from familiarity):

- 'Lamb' gives an impression of someone who is passive, someone 'meek and mild'. Jesus was not that kind of person, however, and so we need to imagine (from experience) a 'lamb' who is powerful and energetic and effectively 'takes away' sin from our community. It is a biblical image, not one we are accustomed to using; we may have to turn to other Bible texts in order to enter into it.

The biblical tradition stresses two aspects of the lamb. First, his blood is shed as a source of life to others. The model is the lamb whose blood was sprinkled on the door posts on the night of the Exodus. Leaders are 'lambs' to the extent that they are ready to accept the sufferings involved in leadership. This is not to say that suffering is a value in itself (as Christians have often done); what it tells us is that true leaders do not stand aloof and are not afraid to make themselves vulnerable. They accept the suffering that goes with leadership: being criticised unfairly; being disappointed in people; the occasional failure.

- Secondly, the lamb is not violent. This is well expressed in Isaiah 53:7, 'Harshly dealt with he bore it humbly, he never opened his mouth, like a lamb that is led to the slaughter-house, like a sheep that is dumb before its shearers, never opening his mouth'. Leaders who are 'lambs' are prepared to suffer violence against themselves, but refuse to inflict violence on anyone, certainly on those whom they lead.

We must also focus on the words 'of God'. Jesus knows himself to be 'God's lamb'; he is self-confident, therefore, not self-pitying, he knows he is secure in the hands of God.

b) The second thing we notice when we 'look' at Jesus is that God's Spirit 'comes down on him from heaven and rests on him' so that he can 'baptise with the Spirit' (verses 32 and 33b).

The coming of the Spirit on Jesus (and on his followers) has two effects:

- he has a sense of himself; he does not get his identity from being a leader;
- he knows he is loved; he does not depend on the love of the people he leads.

2. John shares some reflections on his mission to proclaim Jesus.

We can identify four sayings which help us to understand our own mission to 'proclaim' those in our care (see above):

a) 'He comes after me but he ranks before me because he existed before me.' There are times when we feel awe before the people we minister to. Even if they 'come after us' in the sense that they depend on our assistance, we know that in another sense they 'existed before us', i.e. that there is a divine spark within them.

b) 'I did not know him and yet it was to reveal him to Israel that I came baptising with water.' We understand only gradually the greatness of the people in our care. We do not 'know' them and yet God sends them into our lives so that we can 'reveal' their greatness.

c) 'He who sent me to baptise with water said: the man on whom you see the Spirit come down and rest is the one who is going to baptise with the Holy Spirit.' We are not ready to minister to people until the voice of God (conscience) tells us that we will see the Spirit come down on them and realise that they will 'baptise with the Holy Spirit', i.e. complete what we have done for them. We think of the moment when parents realise that their children will do greater things than thet themselves did.

d) 'I have seen and I am the witness, he is the chosen one of God.' It is not enough to say with our lips that someone is sacred; we must 'see and bear witness' that this is the chosen one of God.

* * *

'The death of a single human being is too heavy a price to pay for the vindication of any principle, however sacred.' Dan Berrigan
Lord, forgive us for thinking that you want us to destroy people
in order to take away some evil from our community.
Send us John the Baptists
who will tell us to focus on the Jesus among us
who takes away the sin of the world not through violence
but as your precious lamb.

'I find it troubling that we say so readily, "Well, there aren't any alternatives, we have to do it the way we're doing it".' Bishop Thomas Gumbleton of Detroit, commenting on the US bombing of Afghanistan
Lord, we thank you for church leaders
who affirm the message of Jesus with conviction
so that people can have the experience of John the Baptist,
see Jesus coming into their community and say,
'Look, there is the Lamb of God
who takes away the sin of our world.'

'The Word of God is red-hot iron. And you who preach it, you'd go picking it up with a pair of tongs lest you burn yourself.'
George Bernanos, *Diary of a Country Priest*
Lord, forgive us for being afraid of being like Jesus,
lambs led to the slaughter house
as we take away the sins of the world.

Lord, forgive us that as leaders
we look to the members of our community
to give us our identity
so that we cannot risk being unpopular by telling the truth.
Send us John the Baptist to remind us of the day
when your Spirit came down from heaven and rested on us.

'A time will come when we will once again be called so to utter the Word of God that the world will be changed and renewed by it. It will be a new language, perhaps quite non-religious, but liberating and redeeming.' Dietrich Bonhoeffer
Lord, we pray that your church will be truly John the Baptist
saying to the world, 'Look, there is the Lamb of God
who transforms the world by taking away its sins.'

'The old man repeats the prayers he recited as a child, but now with the experience of a lifetime.' Hegel
Lord, we thank you that today we can look back on our lives
and say like John the Baptist, 'Yes, I have seen,
and I am the witness that Jesus is your Chosen One.'

'He is the unseen seer, the unheard hearer, the unthought thinker, the unknown knower. There is no other seer than he, no other hearer than he, no other thinker than he, no other knower than he.'
The Upanishads
Lord, fill us with a spirit of awe in our ministry.
When we minister to others help us to remember
that though they come after us they rank before us
because there is something within them which existed before us.

*'To understand the scriptures we must stop acting like mere specta-
tors.'* Karl Barth
Lord, send us John the Baptist
to remind us that we must see and be witnesses
that your Spirit came down from heaven
and rested on the sacred writers
and that the Bible is your chosen book.

'I don't like that man; I have to get to know him better.'
Abraham Lincoln
Lord, teach us to wait for one another.
When we don't know people,
say to us as you said to John the Baptist,
that we will see the Spirit come down from heaven
and rest on them,
and we will discover in them
the capacity to complete what we have done,
baptising with the Holy Spirit
where we only baptise with water.

Third Sunday in Ordinary Time

Gospel Reading: Matthew 4:12-23

12*Hearing that John had been arrested he went back to Galilee,* 13*and leaving Nazareth he went and settled in Capernaum, a lakeside town on the borders of Zebulun and Naphtali.* 14*In this way the prophecy of Isaiah was to be fulfilled:* 15*'Land of Zebulun! Land of Naphtali! Way of the sea on the far side of Jordan, Galilee of the nations!* 16*The people that lived in darkness has seen a great light; on those who dwell in the land and shadow of death a light has dawned.'* 17*From that moment Jesus began his preaching with the message, 'Repent, for the kingdom of heaven is close at hand.'*

This Sunday we begin the series of readings for the liturgical time called in our tradition 'Ordinary Time'. Ordinary Time actually began last week, but the church spends an extra Sunday celebrating the spirit of Christmas.

Today's passage then belongs to the beginnings of Jesus' ministry. It is a very significant time. John has been arrested and Jesus decides he must make his move. He is self-confident, determined; he knows what he is about – a role model for us all in our different vocations and also for the church in the world today.

Verse 12: St Matthew makes a clear link between John the Baptist's arrest and Jesus' decision to begin his ministry. The end of one time of hope becomes the beginning of a new and more glorious time.

Verses 12 to 16: Jesus was entering into a prophetic tradition. He was different – indeed, he was unique – but not totally new. We too, as individuals and as a community, are both unique and rooted in a tradition.

St Matthew also stresses the significance of Jesus's choice to start in Galilee. Galilee was situated at the extremes of the Holy Land; it was therefore a symbol of Jesus's vocation to bring God 'to the ends of the earth'.

Verse 17 is the formula used in all the synoptic gospels to summarise the content of Jesus' teaching. It comprises three statements, and it is best to start with the third.

- 'It is close at hand'. Jesus is aware that this is a moment of grace. When we enter into God's work we always have the sense that we are 'called', part of a movement that is greater than us, and that we are merely God's instruments. As we saw recently, John the Baptist experienced a similar awe when he began to preach.

- 'The kingdom of heaven' is St Matthew's version of the more common 'kingdom of God', reminding us that the Jews were reluctant to use the name of God. This biblical expression means God's plan for the world – 'the world as it would be if God were in charge.' The Old Testament spelled out God's plan in detail, for example in the Genesis description of creation before the fall; in Isaiah 11:6-9 and 65:19-25; in Amos 9:11-15. God's kingdom has two characteristics: harmony and abundance.

- 'Repent'. Jesus knows he is calling for a revolution in thinking. The sure sign that we understand God's kingdom is that we are – and encourage others to be – dissatisfied with the *status quo*.

We celebrate people who 'begin their preaching with this message.' Nowadays many of them are not members of our church and do not even share our Christian faith, but they challenge us, both as individuals and as a church.

* * *

'Without a revolution of the spirit, the forces which produced the iniquities of the old order will continue to be operative, posing a constant threat to the process of reform and regeneration.'
Aung San Suu Kyi, Myanmar leader
Lord, we remember with gratitude
the great liberation movements
which have been your blessing for our time:
- the Declaration of Human Rights,
- the affirmation of women's dignity and right to equal treatment,
- the struggle for independence in former colonies,
- sharing of gifts between different churches, religions and faiths,
- the breakdown of all forms of racial discrimination,
- the recognition of the rights of children.

All these movements arose
at a time when their leaders were imprisoned
in one way or another,
but new life emerged in unexpected places.
It was like when John the Baptist was arrested
and Jesus returned to Galilee
and began preaching that a new era of grace was at hand.

Lord, we remember turning points in our lives
    - we started working with the poor;
    - we joined a religious community;
    - we entered public life.
A path we had followed previously was leading nowhere,
and we knew we had to move to a new place,
not to Nazareth, the place where we were comfortable,
but to a border country,
so that people who lived in darkness would see a great light,
and on those who dwelt in the land and shadow of death
light would dawn.

*'Inter-religious dialogue has taken on new and immediate urgency in
the present historical circumstances.'* Pope John Paul II
Lord, we thank you that the church today has decided,
like Jesus, to go and settle in the border country,
between races and religions, on the far side of the Jordan,
where the nations meet.

Lord, we pray today for those who are feeling lost
    - rejected by family and friends,
    - overwhelmed by remorse,
    - having failed an important examination.
We pray that some Jesus may go and sit with them,
so that the prophecy of Isaiah may be fulfilled,
and they who now live in darkness will see a great light,
and on them who dwell in the land and shadow of death
a light will dawn.

'By sharing in the cross of the Salvadoreans, the church becomes Salvadorean and credible.' Jon Sobrino
Lord, we thank you that, in many countries,
the church, like Jesus, has left centre-stage
and gone back to the margins,
settling where people live in darkness
and in the shadow of death.

'I have to teach my people that together we can build the people's church, a true church. Not just a hierarchy or a building, but a real change inside people.' Roberta Menchu
Lord, we thank you that Jesus is still preaching his message
that your kingdom is within our grasp
and we must change our values.

Fourth Sunday in Ordinary Time

Gospel Reading: Matthew 5:1-12

¹Seeing the crowds, Jesus went up the hill. There he sat down and was joined by his disciples. ²Then he began to speak. This is what he taught them:

³'Happy are the poor in spirit; theirs is the kingdom of heaven.

⁴Happy the gentle; they shall have the earth for their heritage.

⁵Happy those who mourn; they shall be comforted.

⁶Happy those who hunger and thirst for what is right; they shall be satisfied.

⁷Happy the merciful; they shall have mercy shown to them.

⁸Happy the pure in heart: they shall see God.

⁹Happy the peacemakers: they shall be called sons of God.

¹⁰Happy those who are persecuted in the cause of right: theirs is the kingdom of heaven.

¹¹Happy are you when people abuse you and persecute you and speak all kinds of calumny against you on my account. ¹²Rejoice and be glad, for your reward will be great in heaven; this is how they persecuted the prophets before you.'

On this Sunday the 'continuous reading' of St Matthew's gospel leads us to the Sermon on the Mount, Jesus' long discourse which runs from chapters 5 to 7 and has always been recognised as a summary of all his teaching.

If the Sermon on the Mount summarises the teachings of Jesus' public ministry, the Sermon itself is summed up in the beatitudes. Today's reading therefore launches us on the journey to a deeper understanding of the public ministry, a journey which the church invites us to make during Ordinary Time.

Doing lectio divina on the beatitudes is a different exercise from reading a book on them. There have been many excellent books on the beatitudes in recent years. No matter how helpful they are, reading them is not the same as doing lectio on the beatitudes. A book can help us to grasp the message of the beatitudes. In lectio divina we focus on the text, we get to love it (perhaps for the first time) and let it lead us to love the beatitudes. As a result the text engages us. Our response to it is not merely

'What a beautiful message!' but 'What a beautiful text!' and 'It has touched me deeply!'

The Jerusalem Bible version introduces each beatitude with the word 'happy'. This is an unfortunate translation which the New Jerusalem Bible has corrected by returning to the traditional 'blessed'. Even with 'blessed' we need to give it its full biblical meaning. It includes being 'happy' (an aspect which was neglected in the past) but adds the notions of 'specially chosen by God' and 'a blessing for others'.

The beatitudes are 'wisdom teaching', a biblical literary form that our church has tended to neglect in recent centuries. Jesus is reporting facts, not moralising. At no point does he say, 'you should do this.' He says simply, 'people like this are blessed' and lets us draw our conclusions. We respond by entering into the truth of the passage – not 'Jesus is telling me to do this', but 'this teaching is true.' The wisdom is celebratory and our meditation must be the same. Each beatitude begins with an exclamation – 'How blessed!' So let me correct myself: our response is not 'This teaching is true' but 'How true it is!' and even, 'How wonderful that it is true!'

Wisdom is universal by definition. The beatitudes are teachings in human living, valid not for Christians only (still less for Catholics only) but for 'all men and women of good will', an expression used by all recent popes in their social teaching. We must make sure that our meditation leads to universal conclusions – 'all gentle people have the earth for their heritage', 'all who are pure of heart see God', and so forth.

As always with lectio divina, the text is intended to be in dialogue with our experience. The beatitudes throw light on our experience and our experience explains the beatitudes. Our response is not merely 'this is true' but 'this helps me to understand this parent, friend or teacher who touched my life very deeply' and in turn, 'this person helps me understand the beatitudes.'

Referring to concrete experience is specially important with the beatitudes which are expressed in biblical language that is foreign to us, e.g. 'poor in spirit', 'hunger and thirst for what is right', 'pure of heart', etc. With them especially we will start with our experience of people and let them explain the meaning of the beatitude, e.g. 'my mother was the kind of person to whom the kingdom of heaven belongs, so being poor in spirit means being like her.' Jesus himself is the prime example of the beatitudes in practice. We should apply them to him, basing ourselves on some incident reported in the gospels.

The beatitudes constitute a whole. They are seven (in the Bible, the number indicates perfection) aspects of the model human being – for us Christians, the Jesus way of being human. There is a movement between the seven so that the full picture of the ideal human being unfolds gradually, one beatitude leading spontaneously to another, until we grasp the entire teaching in its complex harmony.

It would be a mistake to look for these connections too quickly however; our reflection would end up 'heady' rather than 'celebratory'. We take one beatitude at a time (any one), stay with it for as long as we are comfortable and then allow the connections with others to emerge in our consciousness, so that they are all contained in the one.

This will take time and we shouldn't hurry the process. At any one stage in our lives we will find that one beatitude is particularly dear to us. We must be in no hurry to move to another. Perhaps one lifetime is not long enough to love them all – and in any case when we go to the Father we will see them as one.

In the Bible (as in all great religious traditions) we enter wisdom through paradox. Things that are usually opposed are reconciled at a higher level, giving us new insight – and new joy. The beatitudes are paradoxes and we must make an effort to read them as such; this is difficult because they have become familiar and no longer surprise us. If a beatitude does not surprise us, even shock us, it means that we have lost its meaning.

Each paradox is in two 'movements', like the movements of a symphony; a main section brings together two 'opposites':
- 'poverty of spirit' and 'possessing the kingdom';
- 'gentleness' and 'having the earth for one's heritage';
- 'mourning' and 'being comforted', etc.

The bringing together is simultaneous. We weaken the beatitudes when we make the second a 'reward' for the first.

The bringing together must be based on experience. The question in each case is, 'When have I seen these two things combined in one person?'

Having seen the combination, we exclaim 'How blessed!' (in the wide sense explained above).

The beatitudes are generally interpreted as a teaching on the interior life, and so they are. This must be correctly understood however. According to biblical spirituality, our inner dispositions are reflected outwardly, not merely in one-to-one relationships but in every area of human living, including public life, international relations, etc.

Some commentators make a distinction between 'inward looking' beatitudes: poor in spirit, mourn, pure in heart; and 'outward looking' ones: gentle, hunger and thirst for righteousness, merciful, peacemakers, being persecuted.

We must not make too much of this distinction however. All the beatitudes speak of inner dispositions which are reflected outwardly. What we must do is give the beatitudes their full scope, seeing them as ideals of human behaviour at every level:

- our relationship with God;
- one-to-one relationships, as parents, friends, teachers, spiritual guides;
- leadership style in church or secular communities;
- relationships between communities within nations and nations within the human family.

Verses 1 and 2 give the setting of the sermon. They remind us that every gospel passage, even a long discourse like this one, is a story. It is never a text book reading, a disembodied 'voice' speaking to us from an indeterminate place. We read it as a story then, asking ourselves (from our experience, as always) who has been the Jesus who 'began to speak' to us in this vein.

Verses 3 to 12 can be divided:

a) 3-10: a main section which proclaims the 'blessedness' of the Jesus way;

b) 11-12: a small section outlining its negative aspects.

Verse 3:

This first Beatitude summarises them all. We will experience this by seeing how it is lived in each of the others.

The two sides of the paradox are

a) 'Poor in spirit' means not being attached to anything less than the absolute;

b) 'theirs is the kingdom of heaven' means attaining the absolute. We can give this as wide a meaning as we are attracted to, e.g. union with God, a wonderful human relationship, a harmonious community. etc.

Verse 4:

a) We must make sure to relate 'gentle' to concrete experience; e.g. it must include being 'non-violent' in one form or another.

b) The 'earth' can be taken literally, giving the beatitude an ecological meaning, but we can also interpret it as of a community.

Verse 5:

With this beatitude especially we must not pose a time lag between the two aspects of the paradox. Jesus' teaching is that only those who know how to mourn will experience true comfort.

Verse 6:

'What is right' is an unfortunate translation. The traditional 'righteousness' is better. It means God's plan of harmony for ourselves as individuals and for all communities, including the entire human family.

Verse 7:

We can interpret 'have mercy shown them' of the response of others, 'people will show them mercy'. Or we can take it as a Jewish way of saying, 'God will show them mercy'. In either interpretation it is a 'paradoxical' statement. We often think that the way to have people on our side is by inspiring them with fear, and believers tend to think that God is pleased when they are hard-line.

Verse 8:

We give a wide interpretation to both sides of the paradox. 'Pure of heart' means being free from every form of ego-centredness. 'See God' means being conscious of the divinity in every person and situation.

Verse 9 is paradoxical for the same reason as verse 7.

In verse 10 again 'right' is better translated as 'righteousness'.

Verses 11 and 12:

Here again we must give a correct interpretation to the future tense. The contrast is not between present and future but between the inner peace of believers and the turmoil which surrounds them.

'When I was, he was not, now he is, I am not.' Hindu sage
Lord, how true it is that when we are poor in spirit,
your kingdom is ours.

'I can be saved only by being one with the universe.'
Teilhard de Chardin
Lord, forgive us for looking on the earth as an enemy
to be conquered.
Teach us to be gentle
so that we will experience the earth as a precious heritage
that we come home to.

'If you love God the pain does not go away but you live more fully.'
Michael Hollings
Lord, forgive us for being afraid to mourn
and so not experiencing your comfort.

'The ideals which have lighted my way and time after time given me new courage to face life cheerfully have been kindness, beauty and truth. The trite subjects of life – possessions, outward success, luxury – have always seemed contemptible.' Einstein
Lord, forgive us that we no longer hunger and thirst
for your righteousness
and so are never satisfied.

'We don't possess the truth, we need the truth of the other.' Bishop Pierre Claverie, French Dominican Bishop killed by fundamentalist Muslims in Algeria
Lord, lead us to the blessedness
of looking at others with compassion
and then experiencing their compassion for us.

'Whether it is the surface of scripture or the natural form of nature, both serve to clothe Christ, two veils that mask the radiance of his faith, while at the same time reflecting his beauty.' John Scotus Eriugena

Lord, free your church from all that takes away
our purity of heart and clouds our vision:
- focusing on showing that we are superior to others;
- trying to be popular with our contemporaries;
- being concerned with increasing our numbers.

Lead us to purity of heart so that we may see you at work
in every person and every situation.

'Once you have rid yourself of the fear of the oppressor, his prisons, his police, his army, there is nothing they can do to you. You are free.'
Nelson Mandela

Lord we thank you for peace makers;
they are truly your sons and daughters.

'Truth must be protected at all costs but by dying for it, not by killing others.' Lactantius, 4th century

Lord, forgive us for being afraid of being abused and persecuted
and having calumny spoken against us.
Help us rather to rejoice and be glad
when these things happen to us,
and to know that we will have a great reward
and that this is how they persecuted the prophets before us.

Fifth Sunday in Ordinary Time

Gospel Reading: Matthew 5:13-16

13*Jesus said to his disciples: 'You are the salt of the earth. But if salt becomes tasteless, what can make it salty again? It is good for nothing, and can only be thrown out to be trampled underfoot by men.* 14*You are the light of the world. A city built on a hilltop cannot be hidden.* 15*No one lights a lamp to put it under a tub; they put it on the lampstand where it shines for everyone in the house.* 16*In the same way your light must shine in the sight of men, so that, seeing your good works, they may give the praise to your Father in heaven.'*

Following on the beatitudes, this Sunday's gospel adds some more insights into the qualities of the followers of Jesus. It does this through three images – salt, light (in two phases) and a city built on a hilltop.

It is a short passage which means that we can spend time on whichever of the images we are drawn to and go deeply into it. Even as we do this, we may find it necessary to refer to the others, as the three complement one another, painting the picture of a perfectly rounded person.

As always in the Bible, the images are not static and we must discover the movement within them, two movements in fact – one of sin and one of grace. We identify with both movements – repent of the sin and celebrate the grace. In each case we choose who we are identifying with:
- Jesus and his followers;
- the people whose lives they touch;
- Jesus teaching the crowds from the mountain.

The passage is a teaching of Jesus but also a personal testimony revealing to us the kind of person he was, and still is, living in the 'Jesus people' we meet. We celebrate them and allow them to challenge us both as individuals and as a church community.

Verse 13a: 'You are the salt of the earth'

Salt is an appropriate symbol of Christian living from different points of view; this text invites us to focus on one of these – it gives taste. Remember people who have brought sparkle to your life ('the earth'), at a time when it had become drab.

Apply the image at different levels:

- the arrival of a new born baby brings reconciliation to a family;
- a family in distress is cheered up by the visit of a kindly parent, grandparent, uncle or aunt;
- a manager or worker brings a new spirit of co-operation between management and labour.
- a newly elected leader injects idealism into public life.

We can apply the image to groups as well as to individuals:

- a new movement arises within a parish community or a neighbourhood;
- an NGO starts a community project which transforms a run-down neighbourhood;
- a new political party brings hope by campaigning against corruption or working for independence;
- the church is converted to the cause of the poor and becomes a force for radical change in society.

We think of Jesus being 'salt' for the Jewish religion of his time, bringing a humanity to it that was lacking. We remember him

- refusing to let the Pharisees intimidate his disciples;
- eating with sinners;
- so fond of feasting that he was accused of being a 'drunkard' and 'possessed'.

Remember when someone was Jesus for your community or family.

All these are stories of grace. The passage then raises another option, a story of sin: the salt becomes tasteless. The text evokes three aspects of the decline:

a) 'Nothing can make it salty again.' Feel the hopelessness – 'If this person or this community acts like this, what hope is there for the rest of us?'

b) 'It is good for nothing' – extreme pathos, 'They had so much potential, now look at them!'

c) 'It can only be thrown out to be trampled on by men'. Fallen heroes are looked down on in word and deed:

- a large church building once packed with worshippers is now empty;
- a great doctor is alone in his office;

- the seminary has a handful of students;
- the church is mocked because of clerical scandals;
- former nationalist leaders turned corrupt and now languish in prison.

We think of how the great Jewish religion became mean and narrow minded at the time of Jesus, a 'loss of savour' which would recur many times in the history of the church:

- the Crusades;
- theologians of the 16th century defending the ill-treatment of the Indians;
- Christian churches not speaking out against segregation in the Southern United States and apartheid in South Africa;
- church leaders blessing armies (today again in the 'war against terrorism').

We celebrate bishops of today who 'go up a hill and sit down' to challenge their fellow bishops to be 'salt to the earth' by taking a prophetic stance against their governments, for example Bishop Gumbleton in the US, and Archbishop Ncube in Zimbabwe.

Verse 14a: The image of light: 'You are the light of the world'

This image also presents a contrast, this time between 'the light' and 'the world', understood as a place of darkness. We remember good people coming into our lives, like day dawning after a long night, or a rescuer arriving with a light when we had been plunged in darkness.

Here the text does not spell out the image, so we can be guided by our experience. We remember our feelings:

- clarity: we had been lost and confused, then we saw a way forward;
- joy driving away sorrow;
- hope: we saw possibilities where before we had seen none.

Verse 14b: 'You are a city built on a mountain top.'

The text brings out one aspect of the image – such a city cannot be hidden.

We are free to imagine the reasons why someone would want to 'hide' it.

- From within, the community is afraid of publicity ('We will become an easy target'), or is over anxious ('Will our message get through?').

- From outside, an enemy fears the consequences; a tyrant says, 'If we let them get away with their freedom, others will want to follow.'

To all Jesus says 'You won't be able to stop it'. Remember when some person or event made you realise this (with fear or relief); that was Jesus speaking to you.

Verses 15 and 16: Second aspect of the image of light, more concrete than the first, a lamp hanging on a lampstand.

We choose who we want to identify with – the owner? the lamp? the people in the house?

- Verse 15a: The sin option: the owner can put it under a tub. Feel the sadness. Imagine why owners would want to do that. As with the previous image it could be the fear of publicity and the accompanying criticism in case of failure.

In this case, however, there is another possibility – selfishness. The owners hide the light under a tub because they want to keep it for themselves; they can impose charges or conditions on those who will use it. We think of

- the abuse of the notion of 'intellectual property';
- resources like water, light and minerals, kept in the hands of a few;
- the rules of international trade, preventing the free flow of natural goods.

Jesus' teaching is a radical critique of the modern capitalist system.

- Verse 15b: The grace option: it shines for everyone in the house. Feel the relief that the light is no longer hidden under a tub. Celebrate the people who hang it on the lampstand.

- Verse 16: Application of the image.

16a: Your light shines in the sight of all. The image must be interpreted in the light of the other images. Jesus is not advocating showiness or putting ourselves forward; this would go against the images of salt and the city on a mountain, top both of which affect others merely by being what they are. We celebrate people who live their values in public but are humble at the same time.

16b:They see your good works and glorify your Father in heaven. Be imaginative in interpreting 'glorify'. It does not necessarily refer to saying prayers. What it reminds us of is how good people dispel negativity, they make others (including those who belong to other churches and religions) feel happy and hopeful – 'life is worth living', 'there is a God!'. Celebrate the times when people (movements) had this effect on you.

* * *

'Be men and women of the world, but not worldly men and women.'
José Maria Escriva
Lord, we thank you for the people who have been as salt for us, bringing life and joy to our lives:
- families,
- neighbourhoods
- workplaces
- church communities.
Remembering them and their good works makes us glorify you, our Father in heaven.

Lord, we remember with immense sadness
people who have ruined their lives
with alcohol, drugs, fanaticism.
We see them lying on the side of the road,
no one can bring them to be
what we know they are capable of becoming;
people are trampling them underfoot.
Lord have mercy.

'The sons and daughters of the church must return with a spirit of repentance for the acquiescence given, especially in certain centuries, to intolerance and even the use of violence in the service of the truth.'
Pope John Paul II, *Tertio Millennio Adveniente*
Lord, we ask forgiveness for the times, both past and present, when your church did not reject the dominant values of its time and was not salt to the earth.
No wonder idealistic people have scorned us,
trampling your people underfoot as Jesus foretold.

'The truth cannot impose itself except by virtue of its own truth as it wins over the mind with both gentleness and power.'
Vatican II, *Declaration on Religious Freedom*
Lord, in our modern Western culture
groups spend much time, money and energy on public relations.
We pray that we may not follow this trend
in our efforts to attract more people to join us.
Help us to concentrate rather
on being true to the best of ourselves,
remembering that a city built on a mountain top
cannot be hidden.

'The world has enough to satisfy every person's need, not enough to satisfy every person's greed.' Gandhi
Lord, forgive us that many people nowadays
see their talents as opportunities for making money.
They hide them under a tub
so that they can ration them out to the highest bidder.
The result is that your abundant gifts are not being shared.
We pray that your church may be the voice of Jesus in the world,
reminding our contemporaries
that you have lit lamps in the world,
not to be hidden under a tub,
but so that they can be put on a lampstand
and shine on everyone in the house.

Sixth Sunday in Ordinary Time

Gospel Reading: Matthew 5:17-37

[17]*Jesus said to his disciples: 'Do not imagine that I have come to abolish the Law or the Prophets. I have come not to abolish but to complete them.* [18]*I tell you solemnly, till heaven and earth disappear, not one dot, not one little stroke, shall disappear from the Law until its purpose is achieved.* [19]*Therefore, the man who infringes even one of the least of these commandments, and teaches others to do the same, will be considered the least in the kingdom of heaven; but the man who keeps them and teaches them will be considered great in the kingdom of heaven.* [20]*For I tell you, if your virtue goes no deeper than that of the scribes and Pharisees, you will never get into the kingdom of heaven.* [21]*You have learnt how it was said to our ancestors: You must not kill; and if anyone does kill he must answer for it before the court.* [22]*But I say this to you: anyone who is angry with his brother will answer for it before the court.* [27]*You have learnt how it was said: You must not commit adultery.* [28]*But I say this to you: if a man looks at a woman lustfully, he has already committed adultery with her in his heart.* [33]*Again, you have learnt how it was said to our ancestors: You must not break your oath, but must fulfil your oaths to the Lord.* [34]*But I say this to you: do not swear at all.* [37]*All you need to say is 'Yes' if you mean yes, 'No' if you mean no; anything more than this comes from the evil one.'*

This Sunday we have the third of the extracts from the Sermon on the Mount. I would advise that you stay with the full passage for this Sunday, even though a 'shorter form' is allowed; we never know which section of a passage will touch us or the people with whom we are sharing.

The passage lends itself to moralising reading: 'Jesus is telling us to ...' We must therefore make a special effort to start from our experience, as always in *lectio divina*. We ask ourselves the question: when did I experience Jesus telling me these things? The reading then becomes a celebration of moments of grace, teaching through experience.

As always, you can remain with one section of the passage, or try to discover – with the heart, not the head – a thread running through the entire passage.

Like the whole Sermon on the Mount, this passage describes a conversion experience, 'going deeper than the virtue of the scribes and Pharisees'. We need therefore to retrace our spiritual journey, from a 'scribe and Pharisee' attitude to one that is 'deep' – from a 'single-issue' approach to one that is radical and holistic.

The rest of the passage celebrates the kinds of implications we become aware of when we experience radical conversion. Our spiritual journey will affect our commitment to Jesus and the church, but also our other commitments – to our families, neighbourhoods, social or political movements we may be involved in.

A recent statement by Pope John Paul II is an example of the church's conversion in its pro-life stance: 'To choose life involves rejecting every form of violence, the violence of poverty and hunger, the violence of armed conflict, the violence of criminal trafficking in drugs and arms, the violence of mindless damage to the natural environment.'

By giving a broad interpretation to the text, we experience it as wisdom teaching, as Jesus intended it to be.

As always in Jesus' teaching, the language is metaphorical, inviting us to enter it from experiences which we remember with emotion.

The sequence of thought may seem haphazard to our Western way of reasoning, but it has its own inner logic.

The passage can be divided as follows:

Verse 20 is the centre peice of the passage; it explains the verses which precede and follow it.

Verses 17 to 19 are an emotional celebration of 'the Law' (here, the term can be taken to mean any noble cause we feel committed to) and of those who uphold it.

Verses 21 to 26: a first series of implications, concerning those with whom we have quarrels.

Verses 27 to 32: a second series of implications, concerning marriage relationships.

Verses 33 to 37: a third series of implications, concerning the taking of oaths.

* * *

Lord, we thank you for those wonderful moments
when something we believed in half-heartedly
and from the surface of ourselves
suddenly touches us deeply.
We move from head to heart conviction,
feel passionately committed,
see the implications for every aspect of life.
Sometimes it is a teaching of Jesus:
    - we must forgive seventy times seven times
    - our neighbours and ourselves are linked in a common des-
    tiny
    - the gentle will inherit the earth
    - only those who mourn will be comforted.
At other times it is traditional wisdom:
    - the importance of family and friendship
    - love is more powerful than selfishness
    - we can trust the future.
At other times we recognise the full implications
of a cause we had given ourselves to:
– democracy, feminism, ecology, human rights, non-violence.
It is a conversion experience, sudden, unexpected.
We are touched, as Jesus was when, in a burst of emotion,
he celebrated the greatness of the Law of Moses,
exclaiming that not one dot, not one little stroke,
would disappear from the Law until its purpose is achieved.
Like him, we feel tremendous gratitude for the great people
who kept the vision alive and taught it;
we feel sad that anyone could think of infringing
one of the least of these commandments
and teach others to do so.

How sad it is, Lord, to see a noble, idealistic enterprise
fall into the hands of scribes and Pharisees
who follow the letter of the law but go no deeper,
so that the enterprise loses its savour,
is no longer a city built on a hilltop, ushering in your kingdom.
The sign of this happening
is that people start being content with the minimum,
playing it safe, avoiding evil rather than doing good,

concerned mainly with being respectable
and making a good impression.
In Jesus' day is was not killing, not committing adultery,
not breaking oaths;
but Moses' law, like all authentic renewal movements,
intended to do away with
    - anger and contempt in any form whatsoever,
    - calling one another fool or renegade,
    - looking at others lustfully,
    seeing them as objects of conquest
    who will satisfy our ambition,
    or compensate for our insecurities,
    - acting because we feel bound by an external force,
    in heaven, on earth, in some holy city, even in ourselves,
    rather than from our inner conviction, our own yes or no.

We remember when our virtue too went no deeper
than that of the scribes and Pharisees.
We thank you that we experienced a conversion,
and our priorities are now quite different from what they were.
We realise how much
we used to be concerned with external rituals.
Now, if brothers or sisters have something against us,
we leave our offering on the altar,
go and be reconciled with our brothers and sisters first,
and then come back and present our offering.
We feel a new urgency about living according to our beliefs,
it becomes a matter of life or death.
We are like litigants
who come to terms with their opponents in good time
when they are still on the way to the court,
for fear that they will be handed over to the judge
and be thrown into prison until they have paid the last penny.

We thank you that we feel fulfilled
and have no problems giving up
things we had thought we could not do without:
    - being popular or surrounded by a group of friends,
    - making a lot of money,

- having our name in the newspapers.
We had thought it would be painful to give up these goals,
almost like tearing out our right eye
or cutting off our right hand.
We thank you for the grace of seeing
that they were causing us to betray our integrity,
that we are better off without them
than having them and living empty lives,
like people having their bodies intact
and being thrown into hell.

Lord, we thank you for that person you sent into our lives,
that Jesus who brought us to conversion.
We pray that we in our turn
may bring his message of conversion
to those we live and work with – our church communities,
the great renewal movements of our time,
our families, neighbourhoods and schools.

Seventh Sunday in Ordinary Time

Gospel Reading: Matthew 5:38-48

38Jesus said to his disciples: 'You have learnt how it was said: Eye for eye and tooth for tooth. 39But I say this to you: offer the wicked man no resistance. On the contrary, if anyone hits you on the right cheek, offer him the other as well; 40if a man takes you to law and would have your tunic, let him have your cloak as well. 41And if anyone orders you to go one mile, go two miles with him. 42Give to anyone who asks, and if anyone wants to borrow, do not turn away. 43You have learnt how it was said: You must love your neighbour and hate your enemy. 44But I say this to you: love your enemies and pray for those who persecute you; 45in this way you will be sons of your Father in heaven, for he causes the sun to rise on bad men as well as good, and his rain to fall on honest and dishonest men alike. 46For if you love those who love you, what right have you to claim any credit? Even the tax collectors do as much, do they not? 47And if you save your greetings for your brothers, are you doing anything exceptional? Even the pagans do as much, do they not? 48You must therefore be perfect just as your heavenly Father is perfect.'

As always, it is important for us to stay with the words of the text we are given.

In this passage Jesus tells his disciples that they must be guided entirely by him and by his message, not by what is said in the culture at large. Jesus was aware of the problems of his followers. Some of these were personal, others were more general; others again were general defects of the culture. We too, in our time, must be aware of this as we make choices and decisions day by day.

Jesus starts with two sayings, or teachings – something that was 'said to our ancestors'. Both are well known to us: 'Eye for eye and tooth for tooth' and 'You must love your neighbour and hate your enemy.'

Jesus never wished to teach against the Old Testament. It is a point he makes quite clearly earlier in this sermon. 'Do not imagine that I have come to abolish the Law or the Prophets', he said. 'I have not come to abolish but to complete them. I tell you solemnly, till heaven and earth disappear, not one dot, not one little stroke shall disappear until its purpose is achieved'.

What Jesus was against was the fact that some people were misusing the law. He was anxious to change this for something better. He did not want 'to abolish' the law but merely to 'complete it' and he showed how his own interpretations would in fact 'complete' the law.

Let us look first at verses 38 to 42.

Jesus wants us first of all to reject the false notion that we must relate to others only as they treat us. This would go against what he taught us by words and by example.

He gives us some positive teachings on three situations:

'Offer the wicked man no resistance. If one hits you on the right cheek, offer him the other. If someone takes you to law and would have your tunic, let him have your cloak as well. If someone orders you to go one mile, go two. Give to anyone who asks and if anyone wants to borrow do not turn away.'

These are clearly difficult passages to interpret. We must however continue looking at them over and over again until they begin to make some sense to us.

To understand what this section means, we must therefore try and find out what is in the mind of the person who hates us. The question is what does he want, what is deep in his heart, what is his general attitude?

We then turn to the second half of the passage, verses 43 to 48.

Jesus starts off by saying that we need to go against the old commandment that we know and love. 'You have learnt how it was said …' The statement said, 'you must love your neighbour and hate your enemy'.

He gives three positive teachings to show how we can go against this.

The first is to 'Love your enemies and pray for those who persecute you.' In this way 'we will be sons and daughters of our Father in heaven'. The reason is obvious. He is kind to both people: 'The sun rises on bad as well as good,' 'His rain falls on all alike.'

He then goes on to ask the question. 'If you love those who love you, what right have you to claim any credit? Even tax collectors do as much, do they not? What about greetings for your brothers and sisters? Even the pagans do as much, do they not?'

Jesus' own conclusion is there, clearly stated. 'Be perfect as our Father in heaven is perfect.' God does not link his gifts to how people feel about him. So too we must do the same to one another.

* * *

'Walk the dark ways of faith and you will attain the vision of faith.'
St Augustine
Lord, we thank you for the great teachings
which Jesus left us in this passage.
They are in many ways opposed to what we hear all round us
and deep down we know they are true.

'Not all are called to be hermits but all need enough silence and solitude in their lives to enable the deep inner voice of our true self to be heard at least occasionally.' Thomas Merton
Lord, teach us therefore
to offer the wicked people we meet no resistance.
Remind us that when someone strikes us on one cheek
we need to ask why they did it,
and we may find that we can offer them the other cheek as well.
If they take us to court and would have our tunic
we ask why and then, if it is necessary,
we can let them have our cloak as well.
If they order us to go one mile,
we need to go through the matter ourselves
and then we may find that we can go two miles with them.
Help us Lord, that we may give to anyone who wants to borrow
and not turn them away.

'The essence of prayer is to be established in the remembrance of God and walk in his presence.' Theophane the Recluse
Lord, help us to strive for perfection,
knowing that our heavenly Father is perfect.
Remind us that this really is the same as loving our neighbour
and praying for those who persecute us,
so that we can truly be sons and daughters
of our Father in heaven,
he who causes his sun to rise on the bad as well as the good,
and his rain to fall on honest and dishonest alike.

Lord, if we love those who love us,
what right have we to claim any credit,
even the tax collectors do as much, do they not?
And if we save our greetings for our brothers
are we doing anything exceptional?
Even the pagans do as much, do they not?

Eighth Sunday in Ordinary Time

Gospel Reading: Matthew 6:24-34

24Jesus said to his disciples: 'No one can be the slave of two masters: he will either hate the first and love the second, or treat the first with respect and the second with scorn. You cannot be the slave both of God and of money. 25That is why I am telling you not to worry about your life and what you are to eat, nor about your body and how you are to clothe it. Surely life means more than food, and the body more than clothing! 26Look at the birds in the sky. They do not sow or reap or gather into barns; yet your heavenly Father feeds them. Are you not worth much more than they are? 27Can any of you, for all his worrying, add one single cubit to his span of life? 28And why worry about clothing? Think of the flowers growing in the fields; they never have to work or spin; 29yet I assure you that not even Solomon in all his regalia was robed like one of these. 30Now if that is how God clothes the grass in the field which is there today and thrown into the furnace tomorrow, will he not much more look after you, you men of little faith? 31So do not worry; do not say, 'What are we to eat? What are we to drink? How are we to be clothed?' 32It is the pagans who set their hearts on all these things. Your heavenly Father knows you need them all. 33Set your hearts on his kingdom first, and on his righteousness, and all these other things will be given you as well. 34So do not worry about tomorrow; tomorrow will take care of itself. Each day has enough trouble of its own.'

The first issue raised in this passage is stated in verse 24. The text reminds us that we need to make a choice in life between loyalty to the God we believe in and loyalty to money. We cannot be loyal to both. As we look at our own world today we see that this is indeed the choice we need to make for ourselves. Money is necessary if we are to pursue the goals we set for ourselves – raising a family, providing our children with educational opportunities, helping our friends, contributing in various ways to the life of our community. But how much importance do I give to money, and how much money do I really need?

The second part of the passage is also about making choices, this time between the presence of God and my sense of security; here the issue is one of implicit trust.

We look at the birds in the sky as an example – they do not sow or reap or gather into barns: the heavenly Father feeds them. And are we not worth much more than they are?

Therefore we need not worry. Our Father knows what our needs are. We must simply set our hearts on two things: the first is the very fact of God's kingdom, and the second is 'his right-eousness' and what this means for us. Once we can focus on these things, everything else will be given to us.

* * *

'Non-aggressive physically, but dynamically aggressive spiritually.'
Martin Luther King
Lord, we thank you for putting before us our double loyalty,
to you or to money.
Help us, Lord, to keep our values straight
so that we can make the right decisions.

'You must wait for the eye of the soul to be formed in you. Religious truth is reached, not by reasoning but by inward perception. Any one can reason; only disciplined, educated, formed minds can perceive.'
John Henry Newman
We thank you for what you have done for us.
We think of the birds of the air and the grass in the fields.
We thank you that tomorrow will take care of itself
and that each day has trouble of its own for us to worry about.

'Whether it is the surface of scripture, or the natural form of nature, both these things serve to clothe the Christ. They are both veils that mask the radiance of the faith while at the same time reflecting his beauty.' John Scotus Eriugena
Lord, we thank you
for the words your Son spoke to his disciples on the Mount;
we pray that they will always reveal to us
the greatness of his teaching
on how we are to live our lives and relate with one another.

'The hand on which the Eucharist is carried is not to be stained by the blood of the sword.' St Cyprian
Lord teach us to value what is the important thing in our lives.
Help us to recognise what really counts for us
as we venerate your Body and Blood here among us.
Help us discover what truly counts
in our relationship with one another and with the world
and then what we now know counts for nothing at all.

Ninth Sunday in Ordinary Time

Gospel Reading: Matthew 7:21-27

[21]Jesus said to his disciples: 'It is not those who say to me, 'Lord, Lord' who will enter the kingdom of heaven, but the person who does the will of my Father in heaven. [22]When the day comes many will say to me, 'Lord, Lord, did we not prophesy in your name, cast out demons in your name, work many miracles in your name?' [23]Then I shall tell them to their faces: I have never known you, away from me, you evil men! [24]Therefore, everyone who listens to these words of mine and acts on them will be like a sensible man who built his house on rock. [25]Rain came down, floods rose, gales blew and hurled themselves against that house, and it did not fall: it was founded on rock. [26]But everyone who listens to these words of mine and does not act on them will be like a stupid man who built his house on sand. [27]Rain came down, gales blew and struck that house, and it fell, and what a fall it had!'

For the past seven Sundays we have been reflecting on various parts of the Sermon on the Mount; here we have a truly good conclusion to it all. You may want to take some time to look back over the previous weeks and come to some understanding of what it has meant to you.

This passage is in two sections – verses 21 to 23, and verses 24 to 27. In the first section Jesus speaks of the effects of his teachings and of their serious implications for our destiny, both in this life and in the next. Entry into God's kingdom, both in heaven and here on earth, is reserved to those who make up their minds to follow what Jesus taught, and to live it in all the different dimensions of their lives – in daily life, in their relationships with themselves and with others, in public life, and in the wider world. This is a conscious decision that we make and our final destiny is determined by it.

Verses 24 to 27 describe two kinds of people. There are those who listen to his words and 'act on them'. Jesus likens them to sensible people who decided to build their house on something solid, like rock. When troubles came – 'rains came down, floods rose and gales blew' – their house did not fall, for it was founded on rock.

As for those people who 'do not listen to these words of mine' and 'do not act on them', they are like stupid people who build their house on loose foundations, 'like sand'. When troubles came, this house fell, and the writer exclaims with anguish, 'And what a fall it had!'

There is a great sense of wonder at what happened. We are reminded of an earlier part of the sermon (on the Fifth Sunday) when Jesus said of those who heard his words but did not put them into practice that they will be like salt which has become tasteless and can never be made salty again. It is now 'good for nothing and can only be thrown out to be trampled underfoot by others'. This is truly the lot of those who will not put his teachings into practice.

* * *

'At the Council, the church has been concerned not just with herself and her relationship of union with God, but with humanity as it is today.' Paul VI, Final Speech at the end of the Vatican II Council
Lord, we thank you for this wonderful text
with its many lessons for us.
We thank you that we now have something we can use
to challenge the world
and to say clearly how far it has strayed from your message.

'Every effort should be made to make artists feel that they are understood by the church in their artistic work and to encourage them while enjoying ordered freedom to enter into happier relations with the Christian communities.' Vatican Document, Gaudium et Spes
Lord, we thank you for showing us
the importance of teaching in language
that suits those who want something better for people.
Help us to remain true to this concern.

'The secular school explains things and creates knowledge, the religious school teaches how to contemplate things and creates wonder.'
Anthony de Mello
Lord, we thank you for the greatness of all you have made.
Help us to appreciate the wonder of your creation.
Help us also to appreciate the greatness of your teaching
and to put it into practice.

'We seem to be losing the sense of who we are, of the purpose of our own enterprise, of the essential unity of our honesty, experience and culture and the lightness of our people.'
President Cheddi Jagan, former president of Guyana
Lord, we thank you
for those who have truly lived your message.
Teach us to be true to them,
so that what we build is built on solid foundations,
and when rain comes down, floods rise and gales blow
our house can stand firm because it is built on rock.

Tenth Sunday in Ordinary Time

Gospel Reading: Matthew 9:9-13

9As Jesus was walking on he saw a man named Matthew sitting by the customs house, and he said to him, 'Follow me'. And he got up and followed him. 10While he was at dinner in the house it happened that a number of tax collectors and sinners came to sit at the table with Jesus and his disciples. 11When the Pharisees saw this, they said to his disciples, 'Why does your master eat with tax collectors and sinners?' 12When he heard this he replied, 'It is not the healthy who need the doctor, but the sick. 13Go and learn the meaning of the words: What I want is mercy, not sacrifice. And indeed I did not come to call the virtuous, but sinners.'

The passage is in two very distinct sections:
- verse 9 tells the story of the call of Matthew;
- verses 10 to 13 are a teaching in dialogue form on a specific aspect of Jesus' message: the basis of communion is our common need.

The sections are different in method and content and we are free to meditate on them separately. It would be more in accord with the intention of the text however to link them and see the second section as the central message of the passage – a teaching on the 'new' understanding of religion which Jesus called Matthew to adopt, and Jesus-people continue to call their contemporaries to adopt. It also shows us the logic of why Jesus chose followers like Matthew (see below).

1. The call of Matthew (verse 9)

The very brief but very touching account of Matthew's call relates one particular historical event; it is also the story of every call to follow Jesus, and indeed to move to any higher quality of life. The call can be of two kinds:
- major, one that makes a radical difference to one's life – turning away from one way of life and adopting another;
- minor, recognising that we have been lacking in one aspect of our lives, e.g. being self-righteous in our relationship to someone.

We can read the story from two points of view:

- Jesus is the person who calls an individual (or a community such as the church for example) to adopt new attitudes. Note that Jesus-leaders aren't content to give instructions, they teach by example – 'follow me'. The story is also a call to conversion, reminding us of our prophetic role as individuals and as a church.

- Matthew is the person who takes the decision for conversion. The details of the story remind us that conversions (minor or major) often occur 'naturally' i.e. within the normal routine of our lives:

- Jesus 'walks on' from where he was, and he 'sees' Matthew;
- Matthew for his part is 'sitting by the customs house,' his normal environment.

At the same time conversions are transforming: to 'follow' Jesus, Matthew must 'get up' from where he is sitting.

2. The dialogue on eating with sinners (verses 10-13)
The dialogue method is frequent in the wisdom teaching of all religious leaders. It is dramatic teaching, inviting us to see the message in terms of a journey that we make from one position in the dialogue to another. In this case it is a journey from

- the Matthew stage where we follow Jesus without question,
- degenerating to the Pharisee stage, where we become complacent and mean-spirited,
- and then re-discovering the Jesus stage where we learn true humility.

We celebrate the Jesus people who lead us along the journey:
- one of our children,
- a friend,
- a Bible passage.

We also celebrate Jesus people who lead their communities:
- church leaders risk being criticised for praying with leaders of other religions;
- politicians mix with members of the opposition;
- someone who opposes what we stand for invites us to share a meal with them.

a) Setting (verse 10)

- Jesus at dinner in the house reminds us that conversion moments come when we are together with people, sharing their vulnerability – physically or mentally.
- The tax collectors and sinners who 'came to sit at table with Jesus and his disciples' remind us that everyone feels comfortable with Jesus people – a challenging lesson on holiness.

b) Dialogue (verses 11-13)

The teaching of this section (the central point of the whole passage, as explained above) is that Jesus' community (and every truly human community) is based on common vulnerability - all are in need of compassion. This value system is based on the understanding that the deepest thing in us human beings is our capacity to trust; when we trust we are at the deepest level of our humanity, the level at which our entire self is integrated. We are most human when we trust.

This understanding goes against the anthropology of modern Western culture, according to which we find our identity by affirming the ego – our capacity to accomplish things and so to become human by our accomplishments. The corollary of course is that when we can no longer accomplish, we have lost our humanity.

The passage tells us that true relationship with God affirms our capacity to trust. Pharisee religion does the opposite – it tells us that we must come before God with accomplishments to show. Today's gospel tells us further that at some time in our lives we pass through that stage and Jesus calls us back to the truth. This is why it was important for Jesus to call Matthew in his custom house – he wanted his followers to remember where they came from. This was St Paul's point in 1 Corinthians 1:26-31.

Jesus' teaching is expressed in three sayings:
- A secular common sense proverb: 'It is not the healthy who need the doctor but the sick.'
- A Bible saying, 'What I want is mercy not sacrifice', but we must 'go and learn its meaning'.
- Jesus' vision of himself: 'I did not come to call the virtuous but sinners.'

God continues to call us to conversion through the three kinds of 'words':

- the folk wisdom of our contemporaries ('signs of the times');
- a Bible text 'correctly understood'– we have to 'go and learn the meaning of it';
- the attitude of a great person.

Sayings 2 and 3 are typical of Bible teaching by hyperbole – 'not' in both sayings means 'rather than'. In saying 2 'mercy not sacrifice' means that our basic attitude before God is trust in his love rather than having things to give. In saying 3, the meaning is, 'our starting point in my community is that we are all sinners'.

This teaching is crucial in the context of what is happening in the church today, when we find ourselves 'eating with tax collectors and sinners'. In a community based on common trust we are free to put our energies into reaching out and forgiving – one another and ourselves. We can then make an honest appraisal of ourselves:
- we do not deny wrong doing,
- we are not paralysed by guilt feelings.

Both of these false attitudes prevent us taking a firm decision for restorative justice. We ask the Lord to send Jesus to our church at this time.

* * *

Lord, forgive us that we see you as distant,
situated in the heavens far away from us.
We thank you that in Jesus you have chosen to dwell with us,
as close as someone with whom we sit at table.

Lord, forgive us that the leaders of your church
have distanced themselves from people,
forgetting the example of Jesus
who was often at dinner in the houses of tax collectors.

Lord, we get all hot and bothered
about how we are going to touch the hearts
of those you have entrusted to our care.
Remind us that when the time of grace comes,
it happens very naturally and spontaneously.
It is like the day when Jesus was walking on from somewhere
and saw a man named Matthew and said to him,
'Come follow me,' and he got up and followed him.

Lord, we thank you for conversion experiences
when we got up and followed a new way.
We thank you for people like Jesus
who challenge us to enlarge our horizons,
to go beyond the ego
and enter the way of humility and compassion.

Lord forgive us for becoming complacent in our faith.
Remind us of our conversion,
how Jesus walked by and saw us at our work place.
It was a rather disreputable one,
not at all the kind where holy people are found,
but he did not let that deter him; he said to us, 'Come, follow me'
and we were so overwhelmed by the thought
that he believed in us that we got up immediately,
left our wrong ways and followed him.
Then one day we begin thinking that we own you;
we are resentful that you welcome into your company
those we consider to be tax collectors and sinners.
We hear the voice of the Pharisees within ourselves
saying to us, 'Why does he eat with them?'
Remind us that it is not the healthy who need the doctor
but the sick,
that what you want is mercy not sacrifice,
and that Jesus did not come to call the virtuous but sinners.

Lord, in the world of today, none of us can isolate ourselves;
we often find ourselves at dinner
with people whom our church members label
tax collectors and sinners
but who come to sit at the table with us.

Lord, we thank you for times
when we experience our vulnerability
as individuals and as a church.
At these times we go off by ourselves and learn the meaning
of Biblical teachings such as, 'What I want is mercy not sacrifice'.
We have read them many times,
now we understand them for the first time.

Eleventh Sunday in Ordinary Time

Gospel Reading: Matthew 9:36-37; 10:1-8

36When Jesus saw the crowds he felt sorry for them because they were harassed and dejected, like sheep without a shepherd. 37Then he said to his disciples, 'The harvest is rich but the labourers are few, so ask the Lord of the harvest to send labourers to his harvest.'

1He summoned his twelve disciples, and gave them authority over unclean spirits with power to cast them out and to cure all kinds of diseases and sickness. 2These are the names of the twelve apostles: first, Simon who is called Peter, and his brother Andrew; James the son of Zebedee, and his brother John; 3Philip and Bartholomew; Thomas, and Matthew the tax collector; James the son of Alphaeus, and Thaddaeus; 4Simon the Zealot and Judas Iscariot, the one who was to betray him. 5These twelve Jesus sent out, instructing them as follows: 'Do not turn your steps to pagan territory, and do not enter any Samaritan town; 6go rather to the lost sheep of the House of Israel. 7And as you go, proclaim that the kingdom of heaven is close at hand. 8Cure the sick, raise the dead, cleanse the lepers, cast out devils. You received without charge, give without charge.'

We are still with the 'continuous reading' of St Matthew's gospel. In this passage, Jesus is still in Galilee, but he comes to a new stage in his ministry – he sets up his foundation community of the twelve apostles and sends them on their mission. We celebrate similar turning points in our own lives, in the lives of great people we have known, in communities.

We can identify:
- with Jesus, the ideal leader, parent, teacher, spiritual guide, friend;
- with the apostles, celebrating moments (as individuals or communities, church communities in particular) when we discover our mission in the world – the modern process of working out a 'mission statement'.

The passage is clearly divided into sections:
- chapter 9, verses 36 and 37;
- chapter 10, verses 1 to 8.

Both sections are extremely rich, and we are free to take them separately or to look for a thread running through them.

Chapter 9, verses 36 and 37: two general statements indicating Jesus' attitude at this moment in his life; they complement, even correct, each other, with the metaphor of the harvest giving the correct interpretation of 'feeling sorry'. We often 'feel sorry' for people but in a condescending way which confirms our position of superiority. Jesus rejects all condescension; he wonders at the extraordinary potential of the people. What he 'feels sorry' for is that they are not being given the opportunity to fulfill this potential.

Chapter 10, verses 1 to 8 can be subdivided as follows:

a) a general statement on the mission of the disciples, verse 1;

b) the solemn naming of the apostles, verses 2 to 4;

c) a list of five 'instructions', or qualities, of those sent, verses 5 to 8.

Let us take the sections one by one:

a) Verse 1 must be interpreted in the light of experience. We must think of the 'unclean spirits' and the many 'kinds of diseases and sickness' which great people (or great communities) have 'power' to 'cast out' or to 'cure'.

b) Verses 2 to 4 show that Jesus does not go about his mission haphazardly but with a clearly defined plan:

(i) He is founding a new Israel, so he sets up a foundational community composed of twelve members, corresponding to the twelve tribes of the first Israel.

(ii) The fact that each member is 'named' is important. They are unique individuals, not mere numbers.

(iii) The inclusion of 'Judas Iscariot, the one who was to betray him,' is very touching. There is no covering up as community historians (in the church, too!) are inclined to do.

(iv) It is an 'apostolic' community, not turned in on itself, but with a mission to the wider community.

c) Each of the 'instructions' of verses 5b to 8 has its own metaphor which can be explored in the light of our experience:

(i) Verses 5b and 6 belong to the context of the life of Jesus and we must interpret them in the light of later history: good leaders know that the way to transform society is to start with their own communities.

(ii) Verse 7 is a summing up of the mission, somewhat like 9:37. The disciples of Jesus are always ready to discover the potential for the kingdom in the people they meet.

(iii) Verse 8a, like verse 1, must be interpreted from our experience of great people and great communities.

(iv) Verse 8b is deep and mysterious, haunting even, truly a gem among Jesus' sayings.

'Without charge' can refer to money, a radical challenge to our modern idea that what we give can always be calculated in financial terms. But it means much more: the 'charges' the text refers to include 'psychological' ones like 'you must be grateful to me,' 'you must admire me,' ' you must do what I say,' 'this is the only way to ensure your salvation,' 'this will bring me closer to God' etc.

The list is endless, as we know well from our experience and that of the church. We celebrate those who have given 'without charge'. Pre-eminent among them is God himself, although we often turn him into one who imposes 'charges'.

* * *

Lord, teach your church to look at the modern world
with the eyes of Jesus.
So often we look on the world as evil,
to be shunned as evil and dangerous.
Help us rather to look on our contemporaries with sympathy,
to see that their violence, greed, mindlessness, instability
are symptoms of a lack of meaning, of direction.
They have no reference points for their lives,
are harassed and dejected,
like sheep without a shepherd.
Help us, like Jesus, to recognise the graces of our modern world,
its insistence on:
- human rights
- the equality of all cultures
- the complementarity of men and women.
The world is an abundant harvest which you have sown,
send us more labourers to do the reaping.

Lord, every age has its own consciousness of sin.
Today, for example, we are sensitive
to the rape of the environment,
lack of respect for life, individualism,
making greed into a virtue.
We thank you that in this age, as in all ages,
you have sent us great men and women
to show us the power of nonviolence,
to teach us to re-discover that nature is your sacrament,
and that generosity is more powerful than self-interest.
Truly you have summoned disciples of your son Jesus
– many of them not members of our church –
and given them authority over the unclean spirits of our time,
with power to cast them out and to cure the different diseases
and sicknesses which afflict us.

Lord, we thank you for continuing to summon your church,
in cultures where it has never existed before,
giving your disciples names that are very different
from those which you gave to the twelve apostles;
they still include some who will betray you.

Lord, you know how, as a church,
we like to talk down to the rest of the world,
hiding from the truth of ourselves,
our own hidden racism, sexism and elitism.
We can understand why Jesus told the apostles
not to turn their steps to pagan territory
or to Samaritan towns
but to look at themselves as lost sheep of the House of Israel.
We speak to the world only when
within our church communities we cure the sick,
cleanse lepers and cast out devils.
Help us Lord to look at ourselves honestly but without cynicism
proclaiming to ourselves that your kingdom is within our grasp.

Lord, we pray that the soul of our church
may always be contemplative prayer,
the experience of your unconditional love,
so that we may recognise our accomplishments as your free gift.
Rooted in that experience that we have received without charge,
we will be able to give our service to the world without charge,
    - without demanding gratitude,
    - without looking to be protected
    from the obligations of ordinary people,
    - without requiring that those whom we serve
    become members of our communities.
We pray that in this way
we will be an example to the great nations of the world,
and they too will remember
that they have received their wealth as an inheritance
and having received without charge,
will give their aid to third world countries without charge.

Twelfth Sunday in Ordinary Time

Gospel Reading: Matthew 10:26-33

26Jesus said to his apostles: 'Do not be afraid. For everything that is now covered will be uncovered, and everything now hidden will be made clear. 27What I say to you in the dark, tell in the daylight; what you hear in whispers, proclaim from the housetops. 28Do not be afraid of those who kill the body but cannot kill the soul; fear him rather who can destroy both body and soul in hell. 29Can you not buy two sparrows for a penny? And yet not one falls to the ground without your Father knowing. 30Why, every hair on your head has been counted. 31So there is no need to be afraid; you are worth more than hundreds of sparrows. 32So if anyone declares himself for me in the presence of men, I will declare myself for him in the presence of my Father in heaven. 33But the one who disowns me in the presence of men, I will disown in the presence of my Father in heaven.'

With today's passage we are still with the 'continuous reading' of St Matthew's gospel, although it is not strictly continuous since last week's reading ended with verse 8 of chapter 10, and this week's starts with verse 26 of the same chapter. Jesus is still in Galilee, however, continuing to lay the foundation for his great work of transforming the ancestral religion of the Jews and eventually all religion.

The passage is a series of sayings, an opportunity to remember that according to the *lectio divina* method the sayings of Jesus, like all other bible passages, must not be read in a vacuum, hanging in midair as it were, but as historical events, 'fulfilled' in subsequent history. It is significant that the lectionary reading starts, not with the sayings themselves, but with 'Jesus said to his apostles ...' To be true to the text itself then, we must situate this event both in Jesus' context and in ours, asking ourselves where is he uttering these sayings today? to whom? why?

The sayings are in metaphorical language and therefore open to different interpretations. We are not free to interpret them as we like however; our interpretation must be guided by the original historical context.

The context here is that Jesus has just warned his disciples that they will be persecuted as he was (verses 24 and 25). We interpret the sayings, therefore, as words of encouragement addressed to those who are being unfairly condemned. In verse 26, for example, 'do not be afraid' means 'do not be afraid of those who are condemning you unfairly.'

Each saying has its movement which we must enter into.

Verse 26 is in two stages. In the first, the disciples are misunderstood because some truth about themselves is 'covered up' and 'hidden' e.g. the fact that they are being honest, are protecting someone's good name, are not sure what they should say.

The second stage is the moment of vindication – the truth is 'uncovered' and 'made clear.'

We celebrate:

- the Jesus people (including ourselves) who encourage others with words like this at times of discouragement,
- moments when we feel at peace because we trusted that the truth would be uncovered in God's good time.

In verse 27 the perspective changes. The passivity of the previous verse is gone; Jesus' disciples are now active, speaking out openly and self-confidently. 'What I say to you in the dark' and 'what you hear in whispers' can be interpreted in two ways.

They can mean:

- what many are saying in secret ('in whispers') because they are reluctant to speak out, will eventually come to the light;
- we come to deep truth (the kind worth preaching from housetops) only if we take time to hear what is said in 'whispers.'

Verse 28 can also be interpreted in two ways depending on the meaning of 'he who can destroy both body and soul in hell.'

- It can refer to God, in which case Jesus is saying our only concern is for God's judgement; we don't have to be afraid of human judgments.
- It can refer to people, in which case Jesus is warning us against those who can break our spirits, wear us down, erode our self-confidence or our determination.

When did we make the journey to this insight? Who is the Jesus who is saying this to the world?

Verses 29 to 31 become very touching if we enter into their movement.

- A first stage when people are feeling that no one (not even God) cares about what happens to them.

-A second stage when Jesus arrives on the scene and speaks these words.

Verses 32 and 33 are often misinterpreted. The secret of interpreting a Bible passage correctly lies in following a correct method – a good method leads to a good interpretation. This passage is therefore an opportunity to look at method.

I suggest four aspects to look at:

- The first criterion for knowing that we have read a passage right is Jesus' saying, 'by their fruits you shall know them.' If at the end of our reading we feel fearful or lacking in self-confidence, our interpretation has been wrong. So too if Jesus comes across as harsh and unforgiving.

- The language is poetry – imaginative, not rational, teaching. We must be guided by our feelings and get the 'feel' of the passage.

- As always with lectio divina, we start with experience. Jesus must remind us of a great person who touched our lives deeply, someone straight-forward but compassionate, who does not let us give in to self-pity but at the same time does not crush us – someone who lifts us so that we act from the best in us.

- The context here is still Jesus speaking a word of encouragement to those who are being unfairly treated. The passage then must mean something like: 'Don't worry what people are saying about you. As long as you are being true to your convictions you are being affirmed in the presence of God in heaven. On the other hand, don't hide behind the fact that you are being persecuted. Be honest with yourself, don't fool around with the truth.' Who has spoken to you (or to your community) like that? Who is speaking like that in the world today?

* * *

'As the setting sun brings out the stars, so great principles are found to shine out which are hailed by men and women of various religions when infidelity prevails.' Cardinal Newman

Lord, we often feel discouraged in our attempts to be good
and to make our country a more human place.
There is so much envy in the world and in ourselves,

so much lust, greed, desire for power,
whereas trust and selflessness are so rare and vulnerable.
Help us not to be afraid.
Teach us to trust people, ourselves and history,
to remember that true goodness is covered over by evil
and you will uncover it;
that love is hidden deep under all the selfishness
and you will bring it to light.

'The captains, merchant bankers, eminent men of many letters
Distinguished civil servants, chairmen of many committees
Industrial lords and petty contractors, all go into the dark.'
T. S. Eliot
Forgive us, Lord, for the times when we become self-righteous,
forgetting that we are covering up many sins
which will one day be uncovered,
and hiding impure motives
which will one day be brought to light.

'The surface of scripture and the form of nature both serve to clothe
Christ, they are two veils that mask the radiance of his faith while at the
same time reflecting his beauty.' John Scotus Eriugena
Lord, people are dazzled by great achievements,
large crowds and impressive buildings.
We pray that your church will be for our society
what Jesus was for his:
free enough to appreciate the true greatness
that is covered over in society,
the real virtue that is hidden because it meets with no success.

'To understand scripture, we must stop acting like mere spectators.'
Karl Barth
Lord, we pray for preachers of the gospel.
Don't let them become superficial in their preaching,
to look for the limelight or for quick results.
Teach them to be true to the dark aspects of life
for it is there that they will learn
what they must tell in the daylight.
Help them to be comfortable with silence,
because it is what they hear in whispers
that they must proclaim on the housetops.

Lord, we remember with gratitude
the great people we have known:
  - world famous figures like Gandhi, Martin Luther King and
    Archbishop Romero;
  - members of our families;
  - leaders in our communities.
We thank you that they were never afraid
of what could kill their bodies alone:
  - prison, torture or the assassin's bullet,
  - unpopularity, failure, or losing their jobs.
But they were mortally afraid of other things:
  - of insincerity,
  - of being unfaithful to themselves,
  - of whatever could destroy their souls.

'Hope is the thing with feathers that perches in the soul
And sings the tune without the words and never stops at all.'
Emily Dickinson
Lord, we remember today the many people
who are feeling that no one cares:
  - others only see their failures, not how hard they have tried,
  - people think they have no problems, when in fact they are
    heavily burdened.
They feel abandoned like a sparrow that has fallen to the ground
while a hundred others are flying overhead.
Send them someone who will be Jesus for them,
telling them that every hair on their heads
has been carefully counted.

'Every single thing we do, provided it has a good and constructive pur-
pose, is helping our world grow towards its common goal.'
Leonard Cheshire
Lord, when we take a stand on principle
we come across as impractical or foolish.
Help us to fear nothing so much as
to be disowned in your presence,
and keep as our goal the following of Jesus
rather than the approval of society.

Thirteenth Sunday in Ordinary Time

Gospel reading: Matthew 10:37-42

37Jesus said to his apostles: 'Anyone who prefers father or mother to me is not worthy of me. Anyone who prefers son or daughter to me is not worthy of me. 38Anyone who does not take his cross and follow in my footsteps is not worthy of me. 39Anyone who finds his life will lose it; anyone who loses his life for my sake will find it. 40Anyone who welcomes you welcomes me; and those who welcome me welcome the one who sent me. 41Anyone who welcomes a prophet because he is a prophet will have a prophet's reward; and anyone who welcomes a holy man because he is a holy man will have a holy man's reward. 42If anyone gives so much as a cup of cold water to one of these little ones because he is a disciple, then I tell you solemnly, he will most certainly not lose his reward.'

According to the liturgical practice of our church, when a teaching of Jesus is continued over several weeks, each Sunday's reading begins with a reminder of the context. Today's passage therefore begins, 'Jesus instructed the twelve as follows', or 'Jesus said to his apostles'. This practice reminds us that in our Catholic tradition we always read the Bible 'historically' – with the awareness that each book, indeed each passage, was composed in a certain historical context and is also to be read in a historical context.

Applying this principle to today's passage, we read it not as a list of commands (far less of threats) but as a 'story' – this is what Jesus said when he sent his disciples into their world. It is a living story so that in our meditation we ask the question, who is the Jesus who said (is saying) these things – to us? to the modern world? The passage also issues a challenge to us as individuals and as communities (as the church) – this is how Jesus wants us to be present in the world.

The passage is in two sections, very different both in content and in atmosphere:

- Verses 37 to 39 speak of the demands Jesus makes on people and wishes his followers to make on their contemporaries. We remember with gratitude the people who have made such de-

mands on us, lifting us out of mediocrity and giving us something for which we are willing to risk everything we hold dear.
Martin Luther King once said, 'People who haven't discovered
something they will die for, are not fit to live.'

Each verse ends with 'is not worthy of me'. This reminds us
that as followers of Jesus we have the option of watering down
his teaching in such a way that it is no longer 'worthy' of him.

'Prefer' in verse 37 is biblical language, and we must be careful to interpret it correctly. The Bible takes for granted that hurt-
ing 'father or mother', 'son or daughter' causes very deep pain;
we must read this verse then as part of the 'cross' which Jesus'
followers must 'take up' (verse 38), and of 'losing one's life'
(verse 39).

'Follow in my footsteps' in verse 38 shows that Jesus only imposes on others what he has imposed on himself.

Verses 37 and 38 can give the impression of Jesus' followers
as a surly lot, suffering from 'victim syndrome'; verse 39 corrects
such wrong interpretations – the overall effect of the following
of Jesus is positive, it calls for self-sacrifice as a way to fuller life.

The verse presents two sharply contrasting possibilities; we
stay with each one in turn, getting a feeling for both and letting
them play off each other like contrasting colours in a painting:
- on the one hand, there is complacency – 'I can relax now
that I have found what I was looking for'. We feel Jesus' sadness at mediocrity where there was immense potential;
- on the other hand we feel his exhilaration at people who
have taken risks (lost life) and discovered new vitality (found
life).

Verses 40 to 42 speak of the presence of Jesus in his community after he has left them. Many leaders want their followers to
be always referring back to them; Jesus is different, he sends his
followers out so selflessly and with so much trust that they feel
his presence long after they have gone on their own.

In accord with the original context of the passage, we focus
on ourselves sent into the world by Jesus with our different vocations – as parents, teachers, community leaders, church ministers etc.

Like all caring leaders Jesus is concerned that his missionaries
should be 'welcomed', a powerful image we need to spend time

on. We are 'welcomed' when we are invited to feel at home with others while at the same time being allowed to remain true to ourselves – a rare and very precious experience.

In verse 40 Jesus tells the twelve, 'Don't be afraid, I am so completely with you that when people welcome you they welcome me.' The secret of non-possessiveness is the sense of 'being sent' by a higher power; we find it easier to entrust our authority to others when we remember that it is not 'ours' but entrusted to us by God.

In verse 41, we need not make a distinction between 'prophet' and 'holy man'; they are different names for great people sent by God to a community. The verse brings out that Jesus' 'missionaries' (in the widest sense as explained above) and those who welcome them become one. Missionaries are not 'givers of objects' (not even 'spiritual objects'); they have had a deep experience and invite others to share in it. We remember times when we experienced that those who welcomed us shared in our blessedness.

In our preaching we tend to stress that God is 'offended' by our sins. The God whom Jesus reveals in verse 42 is not concerned about himself. Like a good parent, teacher or church minister, his concern is for the 'little ones' he has formed and sent into the world. He fusses over them (note 'certainly') and rewards generously anyone who looks after them. We think of parents who declare themselves 'eternally grateful' to a teacher for befriending their children.

The designation 'little ones' is very significant. Jesus does not want his missionaries to be overly concerned at being treated with honour or respect. In his eyes, they are (and must see themselves as) 'little ones'. As many have noted, one of the root causes of many of the recent clerical scandals is that we church leaders have encouraged the culture of elitism, forgetting that we were sent by the Lord as 'little ones' grateful for 'as much as a cup of cold water'.

We think too of the church's call to be a humble presence (a little one) in non-Western or non-Christian cultures.

* * *

'Only those are great whose faith lifts them higher than themselves and who give themselves entirely to this faith.' Yves Congar
Lord, we remember with deep gratitude those moments of grace
when we had an experience which changed all our values
and gave a new direction to our lives:
>   - we met someone whom we loved more than anyone else in the world;
>   - a new leader gave our community a new vision for itself;
>   - we read a book which changed our lives;
>   - a Bible passage touched us deeply.

The experience affected us so much
that we looked with new eyes
at those who up to then were very dear to us,
father or mother, son or daughter;
we were ready to give up things
that up to then were very precious to us.
It was the only attitude worthy of this new call we had received.
Looking back on that moment
we realise that had we not made the choice ,
we would have lost ourselves;
because we made it, we found ourselves.

Lord, your will is that the message of Jesus should bring life
to societies torn apart by racial and ethnic hatred.
Forgive us for watering down the message
allowing it to be second to father and mother, son and daughter.
Followers of Jesus are concerned
to protect their ethnic and class identity
but are in fact losing it,
whereas if they lost it for your sake they would find it.

Lord, we pray for the leaders of our country.
Don't let them impose burdens on others
which they have not borne themselves.
Teach them that, like Jesus, they must first take up their cross,
and only then invite others to follow in their footsteps.

Lord, we remember today
those who are taking an important new step in their lives:
    - getting married or becoming parents;
    - taking public office;
    - committing themselves to a new form of service.
Give them the courage to risk losing themselves,
for it is only then that they will find their true selves.

Lord, we thank you that in many countries of the world
your church has made an option for the poor,
    - preferring them to father and mother, son and daughter
    - risking everything for the sake of the gospel.
It has lost many of its privileges
but has found life as the church of Jesus.

'When I walk with Jesus, he always leads me to the poorest, the lowli-
est, and the lost so that I may open my heart to them.' Jean Vanier
Lord, many leaders today, even in the church,
are concerned only for the important members
of the community,
for their friends or for those who can help them.
We thank you for Jesus and all like him,
men and women who feel deeply
for the little ones in the community,
and are grateful to those
who give as much as a cup of cold water to them.

'The more faithfully you listen to the voice within you, the better you
will listen to what is sounding outside.' Dag Hammarskjold
Lord, we thank you for the holy men and women,
the prophets you send into our lives.
How true it is that when we welcome them
we share in their greatness.

Lord, we thank you for sending us into the world
as parents, teachers, community leaders, ministers in your church.
Don't let us be possessive of those you entrust to our care.
Help us like Jesus, to have a sense that you sent us,
so that when we have done all we have to do,
we can let ourselves live in those we have formed,
trusting that whoever welcomes them welcomes us
and in welcoming us welcomes you who sent us.

Lord, forgive us that the leaders of your church
have come to others with a sense of superiority.
We thank you for the times that life teaches them
that you have sent them as little ones
who are grateful for as much as a cup of cold water
to slake their thirst.

Fourteenth Sunday in Ordinary Time

Gospel Reading: Matthew 11:25-30

25At that time, Jesus exclaimed, 'I bless you, Father, Lord of heaven and of earth, for hiding these things from the learned and the clever and revealing them to mere children. 26Yes, Father, for that is what it pleased you to do. 27Everything has been entrusted to me by the Father; and no one knows the Son except the Father, just as no one knows the Father except the Son and those to whom the Son chooses to reveal him. 28Come to me, all you who labour and are overburdened, and I will give you rest. 29Shoulder my yoke and learn from me, for I am gentle and humble in heart, and you will find rest for your souls. 30Yes, my yoke is easy and my burden light.'

Today's passage is best understood as a wonderful summary of the 'Little Way' of St Thérèse of Lisieux. For those who are acquainted with the spiritual teaching of the saint, it is an opportunity to celebrate her and all she has meant to the church and to the world of our time.

Like all Bible passages, this one teaches by way of story. It records a moment of intense emotion in the life of Jesus, when he 'exclaims' i.e. utters a heartfelt prayer of thanksgiving.

The experience was particular to Jesus but as always with lectio divina we are invited to enter into it, recognising with gratitude that we and great people who have touched our lives have lived similar moments. They have been 'wisdom moments', moments that taught us some important lessons about human living.

Jesus reflects on three aspects of his life:
a) verses 25 and 26: the learned and the clever did not understand him but 'mere children' did;
b) verse 27: his relationship with his heavenly father;
c) verses 28 to 30: his ministry to those who are overburdened by the religion of his time.

We read the passage as one continuous flow, interpreting each section in the light of the other two.

Verses 25 and 26. The Jewish community which Jesus ministered to was divided into two categories: (a) those who knew

172

and practised the law and (b) those who did neither. Jesus experiences that those barriers are of no consequence – the experts in the law didn't understand him whereas the others did – and this moves him very deeply. Note the adjective 'mere' – they were considered of no consequence.

Jesus' overall response is positive; he is not concerned with those who don't understand, his entire focus is on the wisdom of the little ones. He is like Mary in the Magnificat celebrating the 'lowly lifted up' rather than rejoicing at 'the mighty cast down'.

We too have had moments when we became aware of the greatness of those we had previously looked down upon:
- men and women who never darken the doors of a church turned out to be 'holy' people;
- those with little formal education shared insights which we had never thought of;
- the children of dysfunctional families became wonderful parents.

We remember our feelings then – how wrong we had been! What good news that we had been wrong!

The 'mere children' need not be people. We can interpret them as aspects of ourselves that we tend to disown – our weak points, failures, jealousies, feelings of insecurity. One day we realise that in order to see reality more clearly we must see the world with the eyes of a child and renounce our need/desire to find security in power or status – being 'learned and clever'.

We celebrate moments when perhaps for the first time we appreciated:
- the beauty of nature,
- the greatness of others,
- the potential in a community.

The passage is a lived experience of Jesus' teaching that unless we are converted and become like little children we will never enter the kingdom of heaven.

In verse 27 Jesus remembers that he himself was a 'mere child' in the presence of his heavenly Father. The passage is recognised to be difficult. Many scholars read it as a testimony to Jesus' unique relationship with God the Father – in parallel with similar testimonies in St John's gospel. It therefore becomes a 'proof text' that he was truly God. But the 'law' of lectio divina

that I mentioned earlier above must apply to this verse in particular – the only way to understand a Bible passage is from personal experience.

Lectio reminds us that by the incarnation Jesus does not merely
reveal God, he reveals us to ourselves. He invites us to share his
unique experience, even though on a lower level.

Furthermore we approach the passage 'from below' remembering our deep human relationships, with a spouse, a col-
league, a 'soul friend'; the relationship then becomes a 'parable'
of our relationship with God.

The passage looks at two aspects of Jesus' relationship with
the Father,
- trust, in verse 27a,
- 'knowing' in verse 27b.

Verse 27a tells us that for Jesus (and for us) 'everything' in
the relationship is a gift, temporarily 'entrusted to us' by a loving Father. This is how 'mere children' relate with adults.

'Know' in 27b has the biblical meaning of 'have a very inti-
mate relationship' (in the Bible 'know' often means 'have sexual
intercourse with').

'No one knows except ... ' is also a biblical way of speaking.
It indicates the intensity of the relationship. 'I know you in a
way that no one in the world does.' It is like the passages which
speak of Israel as God's 'only' or 'first-begotten' son which
mean, 'my love for you is very special'. Parents will understand
this; they know about loving each of their children as an 'only
child'.

Verse 27c adds that Jesus has shared with others his intimacy
with the Father. The verse is saying two things:
- his ministry (like ours) consists in initiating people into intimacy with God;
- he 'chooses', in the sense that he puts the stamp of his freedom on the relationship he establishes: 'Life (the Lord) sent
you on my path, and I have turned what was a chance meeting into a personal choice.'

Verses 28 to 30 draw the conclusion from the first two sections: because Jesus has experienced life as a gift, his followers
are truly free.

In the time of Jesus (as in our time) religion had become a

matter of keeping commandments; people experienced it as 'labour'; they felt 'overburdened' by it. Jesus changed that; he made religion an experience of freedom. He challenged his followers to reach beyond their narrow concerns, but they experienced this 'yoke' as 'easy' and this 'burden' as 'light'. We celebrate people who did that for us.

We interpret 'gentle and humble of heart' in the light of the two previous sections. It means being able to accept weakness (being mere children) in the presence of God. Our interpretation will be based on personal experience – we think of people who made life's challenges easy to bear and recognise how they were gentle and humble of heart.

We can interpret the passage as a celebration of the teaching method of the great Brazilian educator, Paulo Freire, as taught in his famous work *Pedagogy of the Oppressed*. We can identify the three stages of the passage, starting with the third:

- teaching must not be a 'burdensome' transferring of facts (the 'banking method' of education) but an initiation to freedom;
- for true teachers knowledge is a sacred trust they grow into, side by side with their students;
- the sign of a good teaching method is that the lowly understand things hidden from the learned and the clever (including the teacher).

* * *

Heavenly Father, Lord of heaven and earth,
we thank you for hiding things from the learned and the clever
and revealing them to mere children;
yes, Father, that is what it has pleased you to do.

Lord, we always tend to form groups where we feel superior
to others and listen only to one another,
- as a church and as groups within the church;
- within ethnic groups and social classes;
- within our families and communities.
We thank you for those precious moments
when you break down the barriers we have set up,
surprising us by hiding things from us
and revealing them to those we considered mere children:

- someone we thought a sinner taught us true loyalty or love;
- a child we looked on as inferior said a word that brought
peace to our family;
- young people accomplished something we adults had not
been able to do;
- a group we had written off as unemployable organised
themselves into a co-op.
At that moment you were calling us to poverty of spirit
whereby we recognise you as Lord of heaven and earth.

Lord, we pray that our church may be a presence of Jesus
in our country:
- always on the lookout for those who are looked down upon
as mere children;
- grateful when you reveal things to them that have been hidden from the learned and the clever;
- and proclaiming your love to the world.

Lord, we thank you for moments of intimacy and sharing,
when friends opened themselves to us in trust,
letting us know them as no one knew them,
and we felt known as we had never been known,
and there was no worry about our trust being betrayed.
These were truly sacred moments
when we experienced your love and your trust.

We pray today for families,
that they may be living experiences of your Holy Trinity,
with trust between parents and children,
parents letting themselves be known by their children
and children letting themselves be known by their parents,
and children free to invite whoever they like
into that place of trust.

Lord, there are people in our society who are overburdened:
- society makes them feel responsible for the country;
- their sins appear more shameful than the sins of more respectable people;
- they are caught in a trap of poverty and lack the energy to
get out.

We pray that as a church we may not add to their burdens.
Help us on the contrary to come to them like Jesus,
    - with respect and trust and in a spirit of dialogue;
    - with humility and gentleness of heart,
so that they may feel themselves understood
and so find rest for their souls.

Lord, we pray today for those
who feel called to take up some burden:
    - to accept death or illness;
    - to forgive an enemy;
    - to let a loved one go;
    - to involve themselves in a struggle for justice.
Help them to trust you,
that you know how they labour and are overburdened,
that you are gentle and humble of heart,
and they will find the yoke easy and the burden light.

Heavenly Father, we thank you for moments of deep prayer
when we experience that everything is your gift entrusted to us.
Others misunderstand us, but we feel you understand,
and we say no one knows us except you;
we feel so close to you, we can say no one knows you except us;
so close to those we minister to,
we can say those whom we have chosen
to reveal you to also know you.

Lord, religion often becomes a matter
of keeping commandments, a heavy burden to bear.
We thank you for sending us teachers like Jesus,
so gentle and humble in heart that we find rest for our souls;
they lay a yoke on us but it is easy,
they ask us to bear a burden but it is light.

Lord we thank you for the gift of St Thérèse of Lisieux.
Truly you revealed things to this mere child
which you hid from the learned and the clever
among her contemporaries.

Yes, Father that is what it pleased you to do:
- she knew that whatever she had was entrusted to her by you,
- she felt herself known by you in a way that no one else knew her,
- she knew you as no one else knew you,
- she called to her all who felt religion as a labour and a burden and she gave them rest;
- we have learnt humility and gentleness of heart from her and we found rest for our souls;
- we found her yoke easy and her burden light.

Fifteenth Sunday in Ordinary Time

Gospel Reading: Matthew 13:1-23

*¹That same day, Jesus left the house and sat by the lakeside, ²but such crowds gathered round him that he got into a boat and sat there. The people all stood on the beach, ³and he told them many things in parables. He said, 'Imagine a sower going out to sow. ⁴As he sowed, some seeds fell on the edge of the path, and the birds came and ate them up. ⁵Others fell on patches of rock where they found little soil and sprang up straight away, because there was no depth of earth; ⁶but as soon as the sun came up they were scorched and, not having any roots, they withered away. ⁷Others fell among thorns, and the thorns grew up and choked them. ⁸Others fell on rich soil and produced their crop, some a hundred fold, some sixty, some thirty. ⁹Listen, anyone who has ears!'
¹⁰Then the disciples went up to him and asked, 'Why do you talk to them in parables?' ¹¹'Because,' he replied, 'the mysteries of the kingdom of heaven are revealed to you, but they are not revealed to them. ¹²For anyone who has will be given more, and he will have more than enough; but from anyone who has not, even what he has will be taken away. ¹³The reason I talk to them in parables is that they look without seeing and listen without hearing or understanding. ¹⁴So in their case this prophecy of Isaiah is being fulfilled: "You will listen and listen again, but not understand, see and see again, but not perceive. ¹⁵For the heart of this nation has grown coarse, their ears are dull of hearing, and they have shut their eyes for fear they should see with their eyes, hear with their ears, understand with their hearts, and be converted and be healed by me." ¹⁶But happy are your eyes because they see, your ears because they hear! ¹⁷I tell you solemnly, many prophets and holy men longed to see what you see, and never saw it; to hear what you hear, and never heard it. ¹⁸You, therefore, are to hear the parable of the sower. ¹⁹When anyone hears the word of the kingdom without understanding, the evil one comes and carries off what was sown in his heart: this is the man who received the seed on the edge of the path. ²⁰The one who received it on patches of rock is the man who hears the word and welcomes it at once with joy. ²¹But he has no root in him, he does not last; let some trial come, or some persecution on account of the word, and he falls away at once. ²²The one who received the seed in thorns is*

the man who hears the word, but the worries of this world and the lure
of riches choke the word and so he produces nothing. ²³*And the one who*
received the seed in rich soil is the man who hears the word and under-
stands it; he is the one who yields a harvest and produces now a hun-
dred fold, now sixty, now thirty.'

On this and the next two Sundays we have parables of Jesus for
our meditation so it would be good to remember the special
characteristics of parabolic teaching.

1. Parables are wisdom teaching. By reading them we get a
new insight into some aspects of life, such as parenting, friendship, leadership, spiritual guidance, etc.

2. They teach by way of paradox. Things that we thought to
be opposed turn out to be both true, and taken together reveal
the new insight. We must always be on the lookout for a surprise
in a parable – an unexpected turn of events, something being
praised that we would not normally consider praiseworthy. If
we follow this up, the parable ends up challenging our values or
the dominant values of our culture.

3. Parables are stories and we are invited to enter into their
movement. At a certain point the story comes to a climax – the
moment when we experience surprise. This moment will be different for different readers, and for us at different times in our
lives.

The parable of the sower is one of Jesus' greatest, not merely
for its content, but as a masterpiece of imaginative teaching. Our
meditation will lead us to exclaim 'What a deep teaching! What
a great teacher!'

The passage is in four sections:
- the parable in verses 4 to 9;
- a comment on teaching in parables in verses 10 to 15;
- a reflection on the grace of the present in verses 16 and 17;
- the parable interpreted in verses 18 to 23.

We are free to remain with one section only or to see a thread
running through the entire passage.

1. In meditating on verses 4 to 9 we are free to take a different
interpretation to that proposed in verses 18 to 23. Those verses
focus on the different kinds of soil, and this is generally how the
parable has been read in the church. We can read the parable

from the point of view of the sower, however, getting a feel of how free and generous of spirit he is – the fact that he is not overly concerned that some of the seed will not produce crop but continues to sow, trusting that eventually his work will bear abundant fruit.

This was probably Jesus' original perspective. We can imagine him telling the parable in response to the disciples' complaints, 'We're wasting our time', 'No one's listening'. He then points to a sower sowing seed in a nearby field and answers them, 'Let's learn from him that we have to continue sowing.'

We celebrate sowers, God himself first of all, generous both in nature and in the work of grace. We also celebrate people like Jesus who praise the approach of the sower and reject their critics who advocate being calculating in relationships.

We read the parable with hindsight in a spirit of thanksgiving: 'Thank God for sowers who continued working in hope'; or as a call to repentance for today: 'Forgive us, Lord, for being so calculating in our ministry.'

2. In verses 10 to 15, we take 'parables' in the wide sense of events (in human behaviour or nature) which become lessons about life. The passage reminds us that it is the way of teaching preferred by God and by all good teachers – parents, community leaders, church ministers, spiritual guides. We ask ourselves, why?

3. Verses 16 and 17 celebrate the experience of parabolic teaching bearing fruit – the 'Aha!' moment. We think of insights we take for granted today, whereas some years ago 'sowers' were attacked for preaching them – equality of races and sexes, democracy, the church's option for the poor.

4. Verses 18 to 23 belong to a different context from verses 4 to 9. The church has grown and become more settled. The question now arises, how come some remained faithful and others didn't? The parable answers, 'Look at the sower, you will see that it is the soil which determines whether seed bears fruit or not.'

We repent of times when we allowed obstacles to prevent seed from bearing fruit in our individual lives and our communities.

We also celebrate experiences of rich soil bearing abundant

fruit. We are free to focus on the fact that even when the harvest is abundant there are still differences – 'now a hundred fold, now thirty, now sixty.' What is the wisdom in being conscious of this?

The parable of the sower is perfectly fulfilled in the *lectio divina* method. The biblical word is a seed sown in us; personal experience is the soil in which it takes root; we can identify various factors which prevent the word from 'producing crop'; once we 'hear the word and understand it' (i.e. come to wisdom) it yields a rich harvest.

The parable is also a powerful teaching on development. If aid from rich to poor countries is to 'yield a rich harvest' it must be given as a seed which will take root in the local culture. Truly a call to repentance for those involved in globalisation today – and we all are!

*　*　*

Lord, in the world today we have become very calculating:
whatever effort we put out must bring maximum gain;
what does not bring results we omit altogether;
we even relate like that in our families, in our church community,
with our friends.
Teach us to look at the sower going out to sow,
to see in him how generous you are:
　　- you don't mind that some seeds fall on the edge of the path
　　　and birds come and eat them up;
　　- or that some fall on patches of rock where they spring up
　　　right away but as soon as the sun comes up the seedlings are
　　　scorched and wither away;
　　- or that some fall on thorns and are choked by the thorns.
You let all this happen because you know
that eventually seeds will fall on rich soil,
and will produce their crop,
some a hundred fold, some sixty, some thirty.

Lord, we thank you for our parents:
　　- they were generous with their love;
　　- they sowed the seeds of care, good advice and their own
　　　example.
Often they saw no results

as these seeds fell on the edge of the path,
on patches of rock, or among thorns.
But they sowed all the same,
and eventually the seeds fell on rich soil
and produced their crop.

Lord, forgive us for not giving Jesus' message
a chance to go deep into society:
    - we choke it with many compromises;
    - we imply that it wasn't really meant to work,
    - that it was only for children, youths or older people.
As a result, it never gets a chance to fall on rich soil,
to touch the generosity and idealism of people,
and so it does not produce
the crop it was meant to produce in society.

We pray today for those who work the land,
that they may sow like the sower in the parable,
    - not mean or calculating or arrogant,
    - but trusting the land and respecting its wildness
    so that it may produce abundant crops.

Lord, we look back on our journey to maturity.
We remember with gratitude
how at first we had only a glimmer of light;
we knew very vaguely
    - that we wanted to live a life of service;
    - that we needed a deep relationship with you;
    - that here was the kind of person we wanted to be with for
    the rest of our lives.
Then, as we needed more clarity, you gave us more,
and now we experience abundant peace within ourselves.
Help us to be content with the little faith you give us,
knowing that as we need more you will give us more,
and when it is time we will have more than enough.
Have mercy on those who cannot trust at all,
lest the little chance they may have be taken away.

Lord, help us to feel compassion
for those who cannot interpret your parables,
to understand that their ears are dull of hearing
and they have shut their eyes
for fear that they should see with their eyes
or hear with their ears,
or understand with their hearts;
for it they did, they would have to be converted
before they could be healed by you.

Lord, we thank you for the many wonderful things
that our eyes can see and our ears can hear:
- that you created men and women as equal partners;
- that the human family is called to live in harmony;
- that the church of Jesus Christ is the church of the poor;
- that all the baptised are fully members of the church.
We thank you for all the prophets and the holy people
who longed to see what we see,
but never saw it, to hear what we hear, but never heard it.

Sixteenth Sunday in Ordinary Time

Gospel Reading: Matthew 13:24-43

[24]*Jesus put another parable before the crowds: 'The kingdom of heaven may be compared to a man who sowed good seed in his field.* [25]*While everybody was asleep, his enemy came, sowed darnel all among the wheat, and made off.* [26]*When the new wheat sprouted and ripened, the darnel appeared as well.* [27]*The owner's servants went to him and said, 'Sir, was it not good seed that you sowed in your field? If so, where does the darnel come from?'* [28]*'Some enemy has done this,' he answered. And the servants said, 'Do you want us to go and weed it out?'* [29]*But he said, 'No, because when you weed out the darnel you might pull up the wheat with it.* [30]*Let them both grow till the harvest; and at the harvest time I shall say to the reapers: First collect the darnel and tie it in bundles to be burnt, then gather the wheat into my barn.'* [31]*He put another parable before them, 'The kingdom of heaven is like a mustard seed which a man took and sowed in his field.* [32]*It is the smallest of all seeds, but when it has grown it is the biggest shrub of all and becomes a tree so that the birds of the air come and shelter in its branches.* [33]*He told them another parable, 'The kingdom of heaven is like the yeast a woman took and mixed in with three measures of flour till it was leavened all through.'* [34]*In all this Jesus spoke to the crowds in parables; indeed he would never speak to them except in parables.* [35]*This was to fulfill the prophecy: 'I will speak to you in parables and expound things hidden since the foundation of the world.'* [36]*Then, leaving the crowds, he went to the house; and his disciples came to him and said, 'Explain the parable about the darnel in the field to us.'* [37]*He said in reply, 'The sower of the good seed is the Son of Man.* [38]*The field is the world; the good seed is the subjects of the kingdom; the darnel, the subjects of the evil one;* [39]*the enemy who sowed them the devil; the harvest is the end of the world; the reapers are the angels.* [40]*Well then, just as the darnel is gathered and burnt in the fire, so it will be at the end of time.* [41]*The Son of Man will send his angels and they will gather out of his kingdom all things that provoke offences and all who do evil,* [42]*and throw them into the blazing furnace, where there will be weeping and grinding of teeth.* [43]*Then the virtuous will shine like the sun in the kingdom of their Father. Listen, anyone who has ears!'*

We have three more parables this Sunday. The first is the parable about the wheat and the darnel in verses 24 to 30, with an interpretation in verses 36 to 43; this is one possible interpretation – feel free to let the parable lead you in other directions.

As always when reading a parable, be conscious of the perspective you are coming from: are you identifying with the wheat that a planter allowed to grow although some enemy had sown darnel alongside it? With the man who had the trust to let both grow together? Or with the servants who wanted to pull up the darnel, even though they might pull up the wheat with it? Be conscious also of whether the parable is
- bringing back memories from your past,
- giving you an insight into what is happening to you now,
- or inviting you to trust in the future.

The parable about the mustard seed in verses 31 and 32, and the one about the yeast in verse 33, are on the same general theme, but don't try to meditate on both together; rather, choose the one that appeals to you now.

Verses 34 and 35 are another summary about parables. Remember with gratitude when you understood one of life's parables and became aware that what you had learnt was an ancient truth.

* * *

Lord, we thank you for those
who educated or guided us from youth.
They saw that we had bad traits as well as good ones,
that darnel was mixed in with the good wheat they sowed in us.
There were people who wanted to weed out the darnel
but they said no, lest the wheat be pulled up also:
- if they did not let us mix freely with others, we might no longer be open and generous;
- if we were not allowed to make mistakes, we would never take risks;
- if we did not feel free to ask foolish questions, we would never learn.
We thank you for those who let wheat and darnel grow
till harvest time,
and now we have gathered the wheat
and can let the darnel be burned.

Lord, forgive us for writing off people
as if there is nothing to them but
  - their selfishness;
  - their insincerity;
  - their arrogance.
We forget that they are good seed that you sowed in the world.
The evil in them is only weeds that some enemy sowed
while others were asleep.
Those sins which colour our judgement about them
will be tied up in bundles and burnt,
while you gather them like precious wheat into your barn.

Lord, we thank you for the church today,
our own community and the worldwide church.
What a big tree it has become,
and so many birds of the air come and shelter in its branches.
We remember that it was once a mustard seed,
but people of faith took that seed and sowed it:
Jesus, the apostles, the first Christians,
the founder of our community.

We pray today for all those
committed to making the world more human:
  - those who are spreading the spirit of co-operation and com-
    munity;
  - human rights organisations;
  - those who uphold the ideal of chastity.
They often feel that the seed they are sowing in the world
is the smallest of all seeds,
but they do it in trust that it will be a big shrub,
and will eventually become a tree
and birds of the air will come and shelter in its branches.

Lord, we thank you for mothers:
  - endlessly correcting and reproving,
  - repeating the old sayings and proverbs,
  mixing them into the daily lives of the family,
  so that today we recognise that their teaching has touched
  every part of our society.

Seventeenth Sunday in Ordinary Time

Gospel Reading: Matthew 13:44-52

44Jesus said to the crowds: 'The kingdom of heaven is like treasure hidden in a field which someone has found; he hides it again, goes off happy, sells everything he owns and buys the field. 45Again, the kingdom of heaven is like a merchant looking for fine pearls; 46when he finds one of great value he goes and sells everything he owns and buys it. 47Again, the kingdom of heaven is like a dragnet cast into the sea that brings in a haul of all kinds. 48When it is full, the fishermen haul it ashore; then, sitting down, they collect the good ones in a basket and throw away those that are no use. 49This is how it will be at the end of time: the angels will appear and separate the wicked from the just 50to throw them into the blazing furnace where there will be weeping and grinding of teeth. 51Have you understood all this?' They said 'Yes.' 52And he said to them, 'Well then, every scribe who becomes a disciple of the kingdom of heaven is like a householder who brings out from his storeroom things both new and old.'

This Sunday's gospel is a collection of four parables, teaching us about the kingdom of heaven. Be content to choose one and remain with it.

To ensure that your meditation remains down to earth, you must clarify what for you is 'the kingdom of heaven'. This is a biblical expression which means 'what happens when God is really king,' and it includes his being king of an individual as well as of a community. You might translate it as 'growing spiritually' or 'getting closer to God.'

Follow the movement of the teaching: don't start by trying to understand what 'the kingdom' means; start with the parable and let it teach you about the kingdom. And let the details of the parable speak to you so that you can enter into it.

The first two parables – verse 44, and verses 45 and 46 – appear to be similar, but if you read them carefully you will find that they are actually quite different. The third parable – verses 47 to 50 – is different from the others in that an interpretation is added in verses 49 and 50. You need not, however, tie yourself down to this interpretation, as the parable can stand by itself.

The final parable, in verses 51 and 52, is different again in that it represents the moment when someone – in this case a wise person – becomes a disciple of the kingdom.

* * *

'He does not have a shred of bitterness, even after twenty-eight years of prison and abuse and injustice.'
Shridath Ramphal, speaking of Nelson Mandela
Lord, we thank you for people of faith:
    - ordinary people like our grandparents or elders in our parish community;
    - great people like Nelson Mandela.
They have developed an extraordinary serenity
in facing their problems.
They are like people who have chanced on a huge treasure
that was hidden in a field,
who have hidden it again and gone off perfectly happy
because they went and bought the field,
and now they know that they have nothing to worry about
for the rest of their lives.

Lord, we thank you for conversion experiences:
    - a Life-in-the-Spirit seminar,
    - a retreat, or a marriage encounter weekend,
    - meeting someone we knew we could trust.
Up till then we had been living scattered lives,
like a juggler trying to keep different pieces in the air all at once,
or a merchant forever looking for a pearl
more precious than the one he had just bought.
Now we knew that we had found a pearl of such great value
that we were willing to go off and sell everything we owned
and buy it.

'What has emerged with great clarity is the lack of a moral foundation for the formation of public policy in this most crucial area, that of human life and death.'
Cardinal Hume, after a parliamentary vote on abortion
Lord, our societies are floundering
because we equate means and ends.

Teach us that there are values that are like pearls,
so precious we would not dream of selling them;
on the contrary, we would sell everything we own
in order to buy them.

Lord, when we are doing good
we must not worry so much about ourselves,
wanting to make sure that we have the purest intentions.
Working for you is like the fishermen in Mayaro
letting out their nets:
good fish get caught in the net,
but all kinds of other things too
– old bottles, shoes, bits of galvanize –
that they will simply throw back into the sea.

'The family that prays together stays together.'
Lord, we thank you for prayer time in our families
– the family rosary, the Prayer of the Church,
our own family prayers.
Our lives together are like a great dragnet,
bringing in a haul of all kinds: good and bad experiences,
problems that need to be sorted out,
and others that seem important at the time
but eventually we realise that they are of no importance at all.
Our prayer time is when we put things into perspective,
like fishermen at the end of the day
sitting down and collecting the good fish in a basket
and throwing away those that are of no use.

'I see the Soviet Union as a country on the way to moral stability,
a country that has revived its old spiritual values and enriched them
with new ones.'
Mikhail Gorbachev, interview in Time magazine, June 1990
Lord, we pray for the leaders of nations.
Help them to be wise and to become disciples of your kingdom,
so that like good householders
they can bring from the storerooms of their cultures
new things as well as old.

Eighteenth Sunday in Ordinary Time

Gospel Reading: Matthew 14:13-21

13*When Jesus received the news of John the Baptist's death he withdrew by boat to a lonely place where they could be by themselves.* 14*But the people heard of this and, leaving the towns, went after him on foot. So as he stepped ashore he saw a large crowd, and he took pity on them and healed their sick.* 15*When evening came, the disciples went to him and said, 'This is a lonely place, and the time has slipped by; so send the people away, and they can go to the villages to buy themselves some food.'* 16*Jesus replied, 'There is no need for them to go: give them something to eat yourselves.'* 17*But they answered, 'All we have with us is five loaves and two fish.'* 18*'Bring them here to me' he said.* 19*He gave orders that the people were to sit down on the grass; then he took the five loaves and the two fish, raised his eyes to heaven and said the blessing. And breaking the loaves he handed them to his disciples who gave them to the crowds.* 20*They all ate as much as they wanted, and they collected the scraps remaining, twelve baskets full.* 21*Those who ate numbered about five thousand men, to say nothing of women and children.*

Verses 13 and 14 tell a story which typifies Jesus' ministry. We can read it from two perspectives:

a) Jesus as experienced by the people. He was the kind of leader people feel drawn to; they 'go after him' even if they have to go 'on foot' and even when he and his disciples are saddened by bad news and 'withdraw by boat to a lonely place where they can be by themselves'.

b) Jesus as he is in himself:
- sensitive so that when he hears that a great man has been martyred, he feels the need to withdraw to a lonely place;
- selfless so that even in a time of personal distress he finds the resources to reach out to those in need; he lets them bring out the best in himself.

The story invites us to celebrate leaders like Jesus. It also calls us to repentance so that we can be more like him, as individuals and as a church.

The story of Jesus' miraculous feeding (verses 15 to 21) is

unique in that it is told five times in the gospels – twice in St Matthew (here and in 15:32-38) and once in each of the other gospels. Clearly, the early Christians considered the incident crucial for understanding the person and ministry of Jesus. Each of the five accounts has details which are special to it and bring out its particular emphases. We take the account before us as the Word of God addressed to us here and now; we don't refer to the other accounts.

We can read the story as a teaching on the Eucharist (and this is how it is often read in the church) but it is better to read it in a wider sense, as a general teaching on Jesus' mission in the world. Reading the story in this way reminds us that the Eucharist is itself a living lesson ('sacrament') of Jesus' mission – and ours too. This is a point I developed in my booklet, *The Eucharist as Word* (published in 2001 by Veritas).

It is significant that the story does not lay emphasis on the miracle itself but on the gestures which precede and follow it – another indication that the miracle of the feeding is a 'sign', a lesson about life that we are called to celebrate and imitate. Being followers of Jesus does not mean having to 'work miracles' as he did. Though we may occasionally do extraordinary things, we must always see them as exceptional. What we are called to do always is to adopt his attitudes, expressed by his gestures in today's story.

We can identify three stages in the story.
- A preliminary stage in verses 15 to 17. These verses present a striking contrast between Jesus' approach and that of his disciples:
- the disciples want Jesus to 'send the people away'; he says, 'give them something to eat yourselves';
- they speak disparagingly of their situation, 'all we have is five loaves and two fish'; he welcomes what they have – 'bring them here to me'.

As always, we are invited to recognise that we have lived both stories. Jesus is our story of grace which we celebrate; the disciples are our story of sin for which we repent.

The miracle itself in verses 18 and 19. Here the focus is on Jesus alone:

- he orders the people to sit down on the grass; he is in control and does things in an orderly way;
- he takes the five loaves and two fish, raises his eyes to heaven and says the blessing; he is humble and reverent in the presence of the Giver of all gifts;
- he breaks the loaves and hands them to his disciples who give them to the crowd; he shares the food and shares his authority.

The fruit of the miracle in verse 20. Two points are made, applicable both to the Eucharist and to Jesus' entire mission:
- 'They ate as much as they wanted' reminds us that the Eucharist 'contains in itself all sweetness,' according to an ancient antiphon; it also reminds us that in 'Jesus communities' the needs of all are looked after.
- 'They collected the scraps remaining, twelve baskets full' brings out two points: the food is abundant, true of the Eucharist and of Jesus' ministry in general; the people receive it with reverence, also true of the Eucharist (the church has seen the veneration of the Real Presence as the fulfillment of this text) and of Jesus' ministry. In 'Jesus communities' people appreciate what they receive, and do not waste it (contrast with the fast food industry).

* * *

Lord, when we receive bad news
we want to withdraw to a lonely place by ourselves,
like Jesus when he heard the news
that John the Baptist had been beheaded.
We thank you for people who search us out, friends, family,
members of our parish community;
they leave their towns and go after us on foot,
and when they step ashore they take us out of our depression
so that we can once more exercise our healing power.

Lord, our church has been receiving news
of sexual scandals among clergy
and is tempted to withdraw to a lonely place.
Remind us of the large crowds who have left their towns
in need of spiritual sustenance

and have stepped on the shore before us.
Do not let us neglect them because of our pain.
Help us, like Jesus, to take pity on them and heal their sick.

*'The world has enough to satisfy everyone's need, but not enough to
satisfy everyone's greed.'* Gandhi
Lord, the reason why there is not sufficient food
in the world today
is that people are not concerned for one another.
When the prosperous see others in need
they respond like the disciples.
They want to send them away and tell them to go to the villages
to buy themselves some food,
although they know perfectly well that in fact
there is nothing in the villages for them to buy.
Send us leaders like Jesus
who will tell us that there is no need for the crowds to go away,
since we can give them something to eat ourselves.
Even if all we have with us is five loaves and two fish,
we can bring them to you
and raise our eyes to heaven in thanksgiving for what we have.
All will eat as much as they want,
and in fact there will be basketfuls of scraps remaining.

Lord, we thank you for our Caribbean housewives.
When visitors come to their homes and evening comes,
they don't send them away to buy themselves some food.
They tell their children,
'Let us give them something to eat ourselves.'
They take whatever five loaves and two fish they have,
raise their eyes to heaven and say the blessing,
and then share with their guests.
A strange thing happens – all eat as much as they want.
But these women don't waste anything;
they carefully collect whatever scraps remain.

Lord, we pastors tend to look on our ministry
as an eight-to-four job.
When we have ministered to people and healed their sick
we feel we have done enough.
Like the disciples of Jesus,
when evening comes we want to dismiss them.
Teach us rather to be like him, to let the people stay with us,
and to share what we have with them.

*'Development is the capacity of a society to tap the roots of popular
creativity, to free and empower people to exercise their intelligence and
collective wisdom.'* Kari Leavitt, Canadian economist
Lord, we pray for those who work in community development,
especially in Third World countries.
Often, when they find that a community lacks something,
their first thought is to send the people to get it elsewhere.
Teach them to be like Jesus, to say to local leaders,
'Bring what you have here to me,'
to thank you for what they bring,
and then hand it back to the leaders to give to the crowds,
trusting that all will have as much as they want.

Lord, we thank you for the Eucharist,
for the many times we were in a lonely place,
and your priest took bread, raised his eyes to heaven,
said the prayer of blessing,
then he broke the bread and gave it to us,
so that we ate as much as we wanted.

Nineteenth Sunday in Ordinary Time

Gospel Reading: Matthew 14:22-33

22*After having fed the crowds, Jesus made the disciples get into the boat and go on ahead to the other side while he would send the crowds away.* 23*After sending the crowds away, he went up into the hills by himself to pray. When evening came, he was there alone,* 24*while the boat, by now far out on the lake, was battling with a heavy sea, for there was a headwind.* 25*In the fourth watch of the night he went towards them, walking on the lake,* 26*and when the disciples saw him walking on the lake they were terrified. 'It is a ghost,' they said, and cried out in fear.* 27*But at once Jesus called out to them, saying, 'Courage! It is I! Do not be afraid.'* 28*It was Peter who answered. 'Lord,' he said 'if it is you, tell me to come to you across the water.'* 29*'Come,' said Jesus. Then Peter got out of the boat and started walking towards Jesus across the water,* 30*but as soon as he felt the force of the wind, he took fright and began to sink. 'Lord! Save me!' he cried.* 31*Jesus put out his hand at once and held him. 'Man of little faith,' he said 'why did you doubt?'* 32*And as they got into the boat the wind dropped.* 33*The men in the boat bowed down before him and said, 'Truly, you are the Son of God.'*

At first reading, today's passage looks like one story, but in fact several stories are woven into it, and we cannot meditate on them all at the same time. We therefore separate the various strands and focus on one at a time. We might eventually find a link between them (the early church did hand down the passage as a unity) but if we do find the link, it must happen spontaneously and in its own time.

In our meditation we choose our perspective. We can focus on Jesus, the ideal leader, parent, friend, spiritual guide; he is also the model of the church in the world, and indeed of any alternative community which brings hope to the rest of humanity. On the other hand we can focus on those to whom Jesus ministers – the disciples, the crowd, St Peter. They are ourselves when we have a deep experience of grace and salvation.

Verses 22 and 23. Jesus sends away both the disciples and the crowds so that he can go up on the hills by himself and pray. This is the moment when those of us who have authority over others feel the need to get in touch with our deepest selves. We are able to distance ourselves from those we have responsibility for.

By doing this we also give them the space to find themselves – an essential aspect of exercising authority. Even though, like Jesus, we end up having to go and rescue them, it is still a moment of growth for them and for us.

Verses 24 and 25. Jesus becomes aware (because he was at prayer?) that the disciples are in crisis; their boat is far out on the lake, they are battling against a high wind, he walks on the water to meet them. This is a deeply symbolical act in the Bible, since the Jews saw the sea as evil, the dwelling place of terrifying monsters. Jesus walking on the water then, especially in a storm, is a deeply moving picture of the good person walking boldly and confidently into an evil environment. Here again we can make the link with verses 22 and 23 – it was because he was faithful to his times of solitary prayer that he had the power to walk on the water.

Verse 26. The focus shifts to the disciples. When they see Jesus they are terrified, thinking 'it is a ghost', but he encourages them. We too when we panic, become suspicious and fearful even of goodness; only gradually do we recognise that it is a moment of grace.

Verses 28 to 32. The incident with St Peter is clearly a later addition to the main story. It has touched the imagination of Christians over the centuries, has been painted many times and has been the subject of countless sermons. Here again we can focus either on Jesus or on Peter:

- Jesus is the ideal leader and guide. The story reminds us that great leaders have the capacity to bring out the best in people – make them feel that they can step out and go beyond their usual limitations to do great things. A striking picture of the role of the church in society.
- Peter represents us when we take a bold step and then once we have stepped out become afraid. Jesus the true friend challenges but does not reject – he continues to offer Peter his support.

Verse 33. The climax of the story. Jesus finishes the task he set himself – he gets into the boat and the wind drops. We must

avoid an escapist interpretation. Jesus does not always calm
storms, what he always does is convey the message that he has
power over the forces of evil.

The disciples experience the victory of goodness over evil,
grace over sin, life over death. It is a moment of rest, of 'blessed
assurance' – 'the wind drops' – and of security – 'Jesus gets in
the boat'. They know they are in the presence of God, so they
'bow down before him'.

* * *

*'The more faithfully you listen to the voice within you, the better you
will be able to hear what is sounding outside.'* Dag Hammarskjold
Lord, teach us to be more like Jesus,
to know when the time has come for us to be alone;
to insist that even our closest companions leave
and to send away the crowds we have nourished,
so that we can go up to the hills by ourselves to pray.
In that place of inner silence
we become aware of our brothers and sisters
far out on the lake and battling with a heavy sea
and a head-wind.

*'Religion is often rejected as reactionary. Yet the Christian faith prop-
erly understood and wholeheartedly followed is a force for radical
change and renewal.'* Cardinal Hume
Lord, our civilisation is going through a great crisis.
We are like the apostles on a boat far from any shore,
battling with a heavy sea and facing a head-wind.
There are people who want to take risks,
to try new ways of doing things,
and to create alternative institutions.
They will know that the church is really the presence of Jesus
if they hear us calling them
to leave the safety of the boat and step out
even though it means walking on the water.

'I am disarmed of the will to overcome, to justify myself at the expense
of others, I am no longer on the alert, jealously guarding my riches.'
Patriarch Athenagoras
Lord, we pray that your church may be present to the world,
like Jesus walking on the water,
free of all desire to conquer or even to impress,
trusting only in your love and your truth.

'You know when you have met a saint; instead of feeling inferior, you
feel enormously affirmed.' Margaret Hebblethwaite, after interviewing
Cardinal Arns for *The Tablet*
Lord, we thank you for the great people
you send us on our life's journey.
They bring out the best in us so that, like Peter with Jesus,
we cry out, 'Tell me to come to you across the water!'

Lord, there are times when we feel so disillusioned
that even when you come to us with power
    - a friend whom we can trust,
    - an invitation to a retreat,
    - an opportunity for relaxation,
we think it is a ghost and cry out in fear.
But then we hear the comforting words,
'Courage, it is I, do not be afraid.'
Thank you Lord.

'The moment we cease to hold each other, the moment we break faith
with one another, the sea engulfs us and the light goes out.'
James Baldwin
Lord, we thank you for faithful friends,
the kind that when we feel the force of the wind and take fright,
we only have to say 'Save me!'
and at once they put out their hands and hold us.

Lord, prayer is experiencing that it is really you
who are there with us,
feeling the urge to go beyond our limitations
and to hear you say that we can do it;
then when we suddenly become aware of the risk
we have taken and feel afraid,
to experience that you have put out your hand and held us.
Thank you, Lord.

Lord, we pray that Jesus will be our model
in our work of spiritual guidance.
When we find that those we are guiding have little faith,
don't let us become impatient or reject them;
help us rather to put out our hands at once and hold them.

Twentieth Sunday in Ordinary Time

Gospel Reading: Matthew 15:21-28

21Jesus left Gennesaret and withdrew to the region of Tyre and Sidon. 22Then out came a Canaanite woman from the district and started shouting, 'Sir, Son of David, take pity on me. My daughter is tormented by a devil.' 23But he answered her not a word. And his disciples went and pleaded with him. 'Give her what she wants,' they said, 'because she is shouting after us.' 24He said in reply, 'I was sent only to the lost sheep of the House of Israel.' 25But the woman had come up and was kneeling at his feet. 'Lord,' she said 'help me.' 26He replied, 'It is not fair to take the children's food and throw it to the house dogs.' 27She retorted, 'Ah yes, sir; but even house dogs can eat the scraps that fall from their master's table.' 28Then Jesus answered her, 'Woman, you have great faith. Let your wish be granted.' And from that moment her daughter was well again.

This Sunday's gospel passage is in two sections,
- an introduction in verse 21,
- the main story in verses 22 to 28.

To get the significance of verse 21 we must look at the preceding passage which tells of the Pharisees' continued hostility to Jesus. It was because he was rejected by the religious leaders then that Jesus decided to 'leave that place' and 'withdraw' to a foreign environment, 'the region of Tyre and Sidon', and as a result experienced a radically new dimension to his mission. So often an experience of rejection leads to new possibilities being opened up. Our 'region of Tyre and Sidon' turns out to be a place of new beginnings.

Verses 22 to 28. This is another of the many stories of Jesus healing someone 'tormented by a devil'. We can be creative in interpreting what this means. We think of the demonic forces which 'torment' people and societies today – elitism in its many different forms, the desire to avenge old injustices, ruthless ambition. Many people are still 'shouting after us' looking to be healed.

Christians have always found the story difficult to interpret because of Jesus' seemingly harsh words to the Canaanite woman. Bible scholars have given various explanations to show that he was not as harsh as he seems to us today.

For some, it is a question of translation. In the original language the words were Jesus' symbolic way of explaining where he stood in his mission. He saw himself as 'sent to the lost sheep of Israel', meaning that he chose to start his life's work among the people he lived with – an admirable approach for all who embark on a programme of community renewal. Others see in Jesus' words a form of gentle teasing that was common among the rabbis of the time; it would have amused and not given offence. For others again, Jesus was giving the woman an opportunity to express her faith – like teachers who ask seemingly naïve questions as a way of drawing out the best in their students.

These explanations seem to me rather complicated, however. I feel it is better not to go into the question at all, but simply to join Jesus in celebrating the faith of this wonderful woman – letting her remind us of people who have made a deep impression on us, as she did for Jesus. We remember the times when we too could not help exclaiming, 'You have great faith!'

Two things are significant about her: she was a woman and a 'Canaanite' – a foreigner. She belonged to two groups therefore who were considered inferior by the religious leaders of the day and so is representative of all those who by their greatness challenge the false values of our culture.

As a woman she can be linked with Mary of Magdala – they were the first teachers of faith in the church. As a foreigner she opened a new era of evangelisation – the first gentile to receive the blessings of Jesus' ministry.

On both counts then, the 'Canaanite woman' represents the countless people in the course of history who started off as 'outsiders' and eventually brought a new richness to the church. We think of the so-called 'pagan nations' of the first centuries – Rome, Greece and Ireland – which brought out new dimensions to the message of Jesus. We think today of the church being renewed by the cultures of Africa, Asia, Latin America and the Caribbean.

Jesus celebrated the woman's faith and the first Christian communities recorded the story. They are models for the church of all times, including our own, telling us that we must celebrate the great men and women who by the example of their lives have shown up our petty prejudices.

The woman's concern is not for herself but entirely for her daughter. In her selflessness she reminds us of the great women of our time:

- Caribbean mothers moving heaven and earth to get their children into a good school;
- Latin American mothers campaigning to find out the truth of their husbands' 'disappearances';
- women gathering at the gates of prisons to bring clothes or food to their relatives who have been arrested – guilty or not.

The 'Canaanite woman' does not represent women only but all people who are passionately committed to a noble cause. All the various aspects of her faith are worth meditating on, starting from our experience of great people we have known.

For example, she was unconcerned about what others thought of her – she 'came out' and immediately 'started shouting'. Committed people don't mind making a nuisance of themselves.

Then there is the good humor which enabled her to turn Jesus' harsh words to her advantage, while keeping her dignity intact: 'I don't mind being considered one of the house dogs since that means that I have a right to scraps from the children's food.'

Turning our focus back to Jesus, we are touched by the extraordinary discretion of 'may your wish be granted'. He makes no mention of the problem she faced – a model for an age when benefactors (including church members) tend to proclaim on the housetops and in great detail what they have done for others.

* * *

Lord, you guide us in mysterious ways.
Sometimes we experience rejection and feel so deeply hurt
that we go away somewhere where no one knows us,
like Jesus withdrawing to the region of Tyre and Sidon.
But in your providence
some Canaanite woman is there waiting for us,
to ask for our help,
but also to give us a new understanding of faith.
Lord, we praise and bless you for our Caribbean mothers.

When their children are in need
there is nothing that will stop them.
They will continue shouting no matter who cares;
they will accept humiliation,
in fact they will see the humour in their situation,
but they will not rest until their wish is granted
and their children are well again.

'He who has never praised is not fully human.' St Alfonsus Liguori
Lord, we church leaders tend to think
that we must always be in the role of teachers,
we must always be models for others.
Teach us to be humble like Jesus,
to recognise publicly the great faith of others
and to let them evangelise us.

'Nature has produced a common right for all but greed has made it a
right for a few.' St Ambrose, 4th century
Lord, forgive us people of this twenty-first century,
that there are men and women who must be content to eat
scraps that fall from their masters' tables.

Lord, there are times
when we feel hurt by our church community.
We feel we don't belong at all,
that the community is not there to look after us.
Don't let us give in to discouragement or to bitterness.
Give us instead the faith of the Canaanite woman
so that we can recognise
that there are many scraps falling from the table
that can nourish us, and our wishes can in fact be granted.

Lord, your church has become narrow in its concerns:
    - almost exclusively focused on the Western world;
    - giving all its time and energy to the care of priests and reli-
    gious.
But now the church has heard the cry
of other Canaanite women:
    - people of third world cultures;

- oppressed minorities;
- lay people in need of spiritual guidance.
They have cried for liberation,
hoping even for scraps that fall from the master's table,
and their faith and perseverance have brought us
a new understanding of the church's mission.

Lord, theology had become a cold abstract exercise.
Today it has become a matter of ridding society of its demons,
racism, unemployment and unjust debt.
Some find that this kind of passion is unseemly,
like the disciples pleading with Jesus
to get rid of the Canaanite woman
because she was shouting after them.
But Jesus is with us and he knows
that people of faith must have their wishes granted.

Twenty-first Sunday in Ordinary Time

Gospel Reading: Matthew 16:13-20

13When Jesus came to the region of Caesarea Philippi he put this question to his disciples, 'Who do people say the Son of Man is?' 14And they said, 'Some people say he is John the Baptist, some Elijah, and others Jeremiah or one of the prophets.' 15'But you,' he said 'who do you say I am?' 16Then Simon Peter spoke up. 'You are the Christ,' he said, 'the Son of the living God.' 17Jesus replied, 'Simon son of Jonah, you are a happy man! Because it was not flesh and blood that revealed this to you but my Father in heaven. 18So I now say to you: You are Peter and on this rock I will build my church. And the gates of the underworld can never hold out against it. 19I will give you the keys of the kingdom of heaven: whatever you bind on earth shall be considered bound in heaven; whatever you loose on earth shall be considered loosed in heaven.' 20Then he gave the disciples strict orders not to tell anyone that he was the Christ.

This is a difficult passage for us Catholics to meditate on because in our church it is nearly always read with an apologetic purpose – to reinforce (or persuade others of) our faith in the primacy of the Pope and the infallibility of his teaching office. The apologetic purpose is important but in meditation we go further and discover in the text a message that will help us grow spiritually and experience the work of God in our lives.

The passage tells the story in three stages:
- verses 13 to 16, the dialogue between Jesus and his disciples leading to Peter's confession;
- verses 17 to 19, Jesus bequeaths his authority to Peter;
- verse 20, conclusion: Jesus gives them 'strict orders' not to tell anyone he is the Christ.

At all three stages we can focus either (a) on Jesus or (b) on those he relates with.

Verses 13 to 16: Jesus is proclaimed to be 'the Christ, the son of the living God', but as always in the gospels we should not isolate him from our experience. The passage invites us to recognise in this incident similar experiences in our lives and in the lives of great people we have known – 'anointed ones', the 'sons and daughters of the living God'.

So too we need not read the story of Jesus in a static way, as if he is settled in his identity. Once we choose to identify with his experience, we will naturally see him as making a journey to enter into his identity, and Peter as the one who affirms him on the way. This interpretation in no way takes away from Jesus' divinity. It merely reminds us of the sacredness of the journey to self; we make the journey precisely because we are in the image and likeness of God.

Interpreted in this perspective, the question 'who do people say the Son of Man is?' tells us where Jesus is in his life's journey. Caesarea Philippi is a watershed moment in his life; he feels the need to clarify where he is – has he established himself? communicated his message? been who he is called to be? As always happens to us if we are honest in our self questioning as Jesus is, he is blessed to have someone like Peter, a 'disciple', affirm him as 'the Christ, the son of the living God'.

Peter on the other hand is at the stage where he knows he must take a stand on the master he is following. He must answer from the truth of himself, not 'who do people say he is?' but 'who do I say he is?' We celebrate the person (it may be an event or God himself in a moment of prayer) who brings us to the point where we have to affirm the 'lordship' of Jesus or someone (a cause) in which he is incarnate.

Verses 17 to 20: Here is another watershed moment in Jesus' life, when he becomes conscious that he has found someone to whom he can hand over his mission. We experience similar moments when, as parents, teachers, friends, leaders of political parties or social movements, we realise with great joy that someone is going to carry on our work. Every aspect of Jesus' words is significant:

- He feels deep humility, an overwhelming sense of gratitude that this is the work not of flesh and blood but of God.
- He feels unbounded confidence in the future. This person is a sure foundation, a 'rock', and 'the gates of the underworld' will not 'hold out' against him or her.
- He is very happy to hand over his authority, to give this person 'the keys of the kingdom'. The authority is practical – it includes both 'binding and loosing.'
- He does this handing over with confidence too; whatever

decision the 'disciple' takes will be 'considered' ratified 'in heaven'.

Looking back on similar moments in our lives we may find that the 'Peter' we celebrated later disappointed us – lost the vision, betrayed us, turned out to be corrupt. The subsequent disappointment does not however take away from the sacredness of the original experience.

It is a wonderful moment for Peter too. He experiences himself as receiving a mandate to bind and to loose with the confidence that whichever decision he takes will be ratified in heaven.

Verse 20: Here again we can focus on Jesus. He represents us when we realise that the truth of what we are about is something we can share only with our close friends, not with everyone.

For the disciples it is the moment when they know with deep conviction ('gave them strict orders') that they cannot reveal the revolutionary character of their leader or cause.

* * *

'To have humility is to experience reality not in relation to ourselves but in its sacred independence.' Dag Hammarskjold
Lord, many people today are drifting through life,
unsure of their identity.
Remind them that your son Jesus too
had to make the journey to being himself.
Send them humble companions like Simon Peter
who will see them in their truth,
not replicas of anyone else, but your sons and daughters,
anointed by you for a particular mission in the world.

Lord, there was a time when we felt discouraged,
wondering if our work was in vain.
Then we came to a place, our own Caesarea Philippi,
and we found that there were people
who understood what we were about;
we knew at that moment
that the cause we had given our lives for
was now on a solid foundation,
the forces of evil would not hold out against it,
and we could hand it over with confidence to our successors.

Lord, every once in a while
you send us young people who are special to us
their teachers, parents or community leaders.
Whereas others have only a vague idea of the message
we are trying to convey,
they understand it perfectly.
We experience them as a gift,
we know that it was not our hard work
that revealed things to them;
it was you yourself who taught them.
Without being able to prove it,
we know for certain that they will never fail us.
Thank you, Lord, for these blessed ones.

*'Under the pontificate of John Paul II the church has discovered itself as
a companion in humanity's pilgrimage, no longer a fortress under
siege.'* Cardinal Koenig
Lord, we thank you that Jesus saw himself
as a companion of his disciples.
He entered into dialogue with them,
asking them to share with him how they saw his mission.
Naturally they were surprised;
they were not accustomed to teachers
who would relate to them like this,
and so they did not speak from their own conviction
but repeated what the learned people of the time were saying.
Jesus wanted them to share what was deep within them
because he knew that when people do that
it is not merely flesh and blood that is at work in them
but you yourself.
And so their little community grew together,
built on the rock of trust and sharing a foundation so solid
that the gates of the underworld could never hold out against it.

'Slaves wrested God from their captors.' Derek Walcott, Caribbean
poet reflecting on a Third World culture finding itself
Lord, we thank you for sending us great artists
who make us aware
that we have allowed others to keep us bound;
now we are set free and no power on earth can bind us again.

'Hope is the thing with feathers that perches in the soul
And sings the tune without the words and never stops at all.'
Emily Dickinson
Lord, we thank you for the wonderful gift
of the sacrament of reconciliation.
We remember the times when the priest told us
that we were free from the bondage of our sins
and we knew that what was loosed there in the confessional
was loosed in your presence in heaven.

Lord, forgive us church workers
for drawing attention to ourselves,
arrogating to ourselves sacred titles like 'prophet'
or 'anointed one'.
Help us to be humble like Jesus
when he gave his disciples strict orders
not to tell anyone that he was the Christ.

Twenty-second Sunday in Ordinary Time

Gospel Reading: Matthew 16:21-27

²¹*Jesus began to make it clear to his disciples that he was destined to go to Jerusalem and suffer grievously at the hands of the elders and chief priests and scribes, to be put to death and to be raised up on the third day. ²²Then, taking him aside, Peter started to remonstrate with him. 'Heaven preserve you, Lord,' he said, 'this must not happen to you.' ²³But he turned and said to Peter, 'Get behind me, Satan! You are an obstacle in my path, because the way you think is not God's way but man's.' ²⁴Then Jesus said to his disciples, 'If anyone wants to be a follower of mine, let him renounce himself and take up his cross and follow me. ²⁵For anyone who wants to save his life will lose it; but anyone who loses his life for my sake will find it. ²⁶What, then, will a man gain if he wins the whole world and ruins his life? Or what has a man to offer in exchange for his life? ²⁷For the Son of Man is going to come in the glory of his Father with his angels, and, when he does, he will reward each one according to his behaviour.'*

In meditating on this passage, we need to make some choices – guided, as always in lectio divina, by feelings, not reason. For example, we can focus on the disciples, and Peter in particular, so that the passage speaks to us about our relationship with Jesus or with someone who has been Jesus to us. We then celebrate the times when we have been brought to see how our way of thinking was 'human' and not according to God's plan.

I am proposing another approach however – to focus on Jesus, seeing him as our exemplar, the one in whose destiny we his followers are called to share. This is the approach of Hebrews 12:2: we 'keep our eyes fixed on Jesus' as the one who 'leads us in our faith and brings it to perfection.'

The passage is in two sections:
- verses 21 to 23, a narrative,
- verses 24 to 27, a collection of sayings.

I am proposing that we experience both sections as a unit, with the teachings flowing spontaneously from the narrative. This is always the teaching method of the Bible – truth flowing from experience.

We capture the power of the passage by situating it historically, remembering that the incident it relates came at a very significant moment in the life of Jesus. It is one all human beings
pass through – a moment of truth.

Up till then Jesus had been ministering in Galilee in the north
of Palestine, far from Jerusalem in the south. He had met with
great success at first: 'he went round the whole of Galilee ... his
fame spread throughout Syria ... large crowds followed him'
(Matthew 4:23-25; cf 7:18; 9:15).

Opposition to him had grown, however, mainly from scribes
(e.g. 9:11) and Pharisees (e.g. 12:1, 24). At this point in his life
then, Jesus decided that the time had come for him to confront
these opposing forces at the seat of their power, Jerusalem,
home of the scribes and Pharisees (15:1). It was a decision which
would have tragic consequences, but the passage shows that he
accepted them fully (verses 21-23), basing himself on his understanding of every person's life journey.

The passage then invites us to celebrate similar 'moments of
truth' we have lived through, when we chose a course of action
which we knew would cause hurt to people we loved and admired, and would bring us rejection and pain. We celebrate the
great men and women who have inspired us by the way they
entered courageously into their moments of truth – our saints,
'personal' or 'canonised'. We can also read it as the story of the
church (or of a group within it, like a religious order) taking a
decision to be more radical in its following of Jesus.

The passage is also a call to conversion in that it makes us
more aware that we – as individuals and as communities – do
not respond like Jesus. We pray that the spirit of Jesus will continue to live in our church, our families and the world.

Our meditation will enable us to recognise the different characters in the narrative. Who are 'the elders, chief priests and
scribes' – the 'experts' we must confront? Who is the 'Peter' – a
dear respected friend, and yet we must find the courage to say to
him, 'Get behind me'?

Through meditation on verses 21 to 23, the sayings in verses
24 to 27 will no longer be abstract theories, but lessons about life
which we have experienced concretely. We will be aware of the
things we would have 'lost' if we had tried to 'save' them, of

wonderful things we 'found' because we took the risk of losing them. We will feel convinced that there is nothing we would 'exchange' for the blessings which came to us as a result of our choices.

We will naturally pray for those who are facing moments of truth at present, with compassion since we know the pain involved, and also with confidence, since we are aware that Jesus is living his story in them.

* * *

Lord, we thank you for the times
when you allowed us to experience
the peace that Jesus bequeathed to us,
times when, like him, we had to make a difficult decision
we knew would not be pleasing to family and friends:
   - get married to someone from a different race or social class;
   - give up a well paid job and take one that offered little security but gave us satisfaction – teacher, artist, community leader;
   - enter the religious life;
   - join a radical movement;
   - bring up a child in a way others considered unconventional;
   - make a new beginning in a foreign country.
We made it clear to them that you had destined us
to go to this Jerusalem,
and that we knew we would have to suffer grievously
at the hands of the elders and chief priests and scribes,
and to be rejected, perhaps disowned and treated as dead,
but we were confident that in time we would be raised up.
Close friends, members of our family
and of our church community,
took us aside and started to remonstrate with us,
invoking your name,
saying, 'Heaven preserve you, this must not happen to you.'
But you gave us the grace to turn and say to them,
'Get behind me, Satan, you are an obstacle in my path;
the way you think is logical in your eyes,
but it is not what I know to be God's will for me.'
We understood then that to be followers of Jesus

we must walk in his footsteps
by renouncing ourselves and taking up our cross.
We are truly grateful now that we stuck by our decision.
What would we have gained if we had won the whole world
and lost the deep joy we have experienced?
Is there anything that life could have offered us
which we would exchange for the satisfaction we have had?
How true it is that the most precious things in life are those
which we end up losing if we try to save them:
  - friendships,
  - peace of mind,
  - a clear conscience,
  - a sense of achievement.
We discover them as life-giving
only if we take the risk of losing them.
We thank you for teaching us
that in life it is not important to please human beings,
no matter how experienced or how holy they are.
We are accountable only to our conscience,
knowing that the Son of Man is coming
in the glory of the Father with his angels
and will reward us according to our behaviour.

Lord, forgive us that in our church communities,
parishes and religious orders
we encourage submissiveness and conformity,
and even invoke your name in doing so.
Remind us that you want true followers of Jesus
to emerge among us,
men and women who are free,
who once they know that they are destined to go to Jerusalem,
will not be afraid of suffering grievously
at the hands of elders and chief priests and scribes,
and even to be put to death,
knowing they will rise again on the third day;
who are not afraid to take risks,
knowing that this is the only way to find their lives;
who will exchange nothing,
even all the possessions in the world,

for finding their true selves;
who will fear only the Son of Man
coming in the glory of his Father,
surrounded by his angels,
to reward all according to their behaviour.

Lord, we thank you that your church in many parts of the world
has chosen to identify more closely with Jesus
by adopting the cause of oppressed groups
  - ethnic minorities,
  - women,
  - homosexuals,
  - religious groups considered marginal.
Its leaders have often suffered grievously
at the hands of elders, chief priests and scribes,
some within the church itself,
others from the worlds of academia, business or the professions.
How true it is, Lord,
that if the church is preoccupied with saving itself,
it ends up losing its true identity;
it will live only if it remembers that the Son of Man is coming
in the glory of his Father,
and he will judge his church not on large numbers,
big buildings, or prestige in society,
but according to its behaviour.

Twenty-third Sunday in Ordinary Time

Gospel Reading: Matthew 18:15-20

¹⁵*Jesus said to his disciples: 'If your brother does something wrong, go and have it out with him alone, between your two selves. If he listens to you, you have won back your brother.* ¹⁶*If he does not listen, take one or two others along with you; the evidence of two or three witnesses is required to sustain any charge.* ¹⁷*But if he refuses to listen to these, report it to the community; and if he refuses to listen to the community, treat him like a pagan or a tax collector.* ¹⁸*I tell you solemnly, whatever you bind on earth shall be considered bound in heaven; whatever you loose on earth shall be considered loosed in heaven.* ¹⁹*I tell you solemnly once again, if two of you on earth agree to ask anything at all, it will be granted to you by my Father in heaven.* ²⁰*For where two or three meet in my name, I shall be there with them.'*

This passage is very different from the ones we read on the last two Sundays. Those were dramatic stories, marked by deep emotions and with deep implications for the characters involved. This is a little gem of a passage but with little drama; a very practical, common-sense teaching on that most common and most prosaic of community problems – conflict. It is deep wisdom teaching which continues to be valid for our time. Management has become a science today, and Jesus' teaching stands up well as a model of how to 'manage' conflict in any situation.

As usual with lectio divina, we do not moralise. The conclusion of our meditation is not 'Jesus tells us to do this,' but, 'Let us celebrate Jesus at work in the world.' We recognise moments of grace when we ourselves lived this teaching, and celebrate the great people who by word and example taught us to live it.

The teaching gives norms for dealing with local community conflicts – in families, neighbourhoods, church groups and workplaces – but also for the great conflicts of our time between races and ethnic groups, religions, nations, different social classes.

The passage is in two sections and we should try to see the link between them:
- verses 15 to 17 are the teaching;
- verses 18 to 20 give a spiritual foundation to the teaching.

It is therefore a good example of biblical teaching – practical moral teaching based on spirituality. Note that both aspects are valid for all people, believers or not.

The Jesus way of dealing with conflict is to go through a series of procedures, starting with those which will cause least hurt, and gradually moving to more severe ones, always making sure that the others have been tried and have failed.

Verse 15 is the first step, a one-to-one meeting marked by discretion and privacy – done 'by yourselves alone'. The conclusion has a touching simplicity – 'you have won back your brother.'

Verse 16 is the next stage, used only if the first has not worked. Those in authority must be humble enough to recognise when they lack the necessary qualities to influence the wrong-doer, and must seek help.

The text continues to stress the importance of discretion – just 'one or two others' are invited to help.

The quotation from Deutoronomy must be interpreted correctly. The setting of the teaching is not a court of law, but a human community. Jesus is merely drawing an analogy – just as in a court the prosecution needs help, we too need help in settling community conflicts.

Verse 17a is the third stage – recourse to the community. This can be interpreted as a plenary session or a meeting of the official leaders of the community. In either case the time for confidentiality is passed, the matter must be brought into the open.

Verse 17b brings in a new dimension. Jesus reminds us that a community must have its rules and a time comes when they must be insisted on. This verse complements what went before in a wonderful way. Without the previous verses, it would come across as harsh; without this verse, they would come across as naïve. By taking them together we enter into Jesus' holistic, extraordinarily balanced teaching.

The reference to 'pagans and tax collectors' is strange when we remember Jesus' special care for these two groups. We can however take the expression as it stands, referring it to those whom the community has a right to exclude. In the light of Jesus' other teaching, some would add, 'remember you have to reach out to them also.'

Verses 18 and 19 can be, and have often been, misinterpreted.

Perhaps under the influence of this teaching, church leaders have assumed the right to pronounce judgment in the name of God – even deciding who will be consigned to hell. Our meditation must not lead us there, fostering arrogance in the exercise of authority. This is specially important when we are dealing with social conflicts, religious ones in particular.

In the prayer below, I propose an interpretation which sees Jesus as the model authority figure. He is not the kind of person (parent, community leader, spiritual guide) who delegates responsibility and then takes it back. He doesn't want us to be always looking over our shoulders; he promises to back us in whatever we decide. The mention of 'the Father in heaven' could be a hint that God's way of delegating authority is the model for all fathers – physical and spiritual.

Jesus knows that there is always the possibility of our making mistakes. Verse 19 then means that God knows what we are really trying to do when we decide to exclude a member of our community. He will not necessarily accept our verdict, but he will look with approval at the ideal we wanted to affirm.

* * *

Lord, we thank you for sending us teachers
who show us how to handle quarrels
    - in our families, work places or church communities;
    - when we work together for social justice;
    - between different religions.
Like Jesus and all good teachers, they don't teach in the abstract,
but walk with us when we have to deal with a problem.
Someone does something wrong in our community:
    - treats another member unjustly;
    - is dishonest with money;
    - is unfaithful to marriage or religious vows;
    - compromises the ideals of the group.
We tend to talk about it among ourselves
and outside the community,
but you correct us through people like Jesus:
    - one of our parents, a brother or sister, an aunt or uncle;
    - someone in our workplace;
    - a leader in our church community;
    - a friend.

They make us go and have it out with the wrongdoer,
alone between our two selves,
so that if they listen to us,
without any fuss we have won back the brother or sister.
Things often don't work out as simply as that, however.
It sometimes happens
that those we try to correct don't listen to us.
This is the moment when we need Jesus again,
someone who will not allow us to give up,
who will show us that perhaps we were the wrong person
to make the approach,
  - we lacked the expertise,
  - didn't listen enough,
  - our race, nationality, age group or religion was too great an
    obstacle.
As in a court case where a prosecutor looks
for two or three witnesses to sustain a charge,
we must humble ourselves
and look around for one or two others,
people more trusted or competent than we are,
take them along with us and have a meeting
where we can talk things out honestly.
Sometimes this too fails,
and we thank you that once more you do not abandon us;
you send us a friend or mentor
who does not let us give up in discouragement,
makes us bring the problem to the community
and have it discussed at a general meeting.
Quite frequently it happens
that someone we would not have expected
comes up with a solution that is acceptable to all sides.
We thank you for those who help us accept the possibility
that even this may not succeed,
who stir up within us the honesty and courage
to lay down some laws
which will make it clear that those who do not observe them
can no longer be members of the community,
just as happened with pagans and tax collectors
in the time of Jesus.

To be able to take that kind of painful decision
we need to have confidence in ourselves.
Don't allow us to see you as the kind of father
who gives his children responsibility
and then blames them for exercising it.
Help us rather to recognise you
as the model Father, the heavenly one,
who has really entrusted the world to us
so that we don't have to be all the time
looking over our shoulders;
we know that whatever we bind on earth
you shall consider bound in heaven,
and whatever we loose on earth
you shall consider loosed in heaven.

Lord, we know that when we have to exercise authority
some members in our community will disagree with us.
Remind us that we are all looking for the same goals:
    - respect for the rights of all,
    - freedom for ourselves,
    - a sense of responsibility,
and that when we agree on anything you will grant it to us,
for where two or three of us meet in your name
you are there with us.

Lord, forgive us that when conflicts arise in our church
we make them public too quickly,
we do not take time to have things out
between ourselves alone first.
Forgive us further that when this doesn't work we give up;
we do not try to take one or two others along
and see if the matter can be settled at that level.
Forgive us again that at other times
we sweep wrongdoing under the carpet
instead of reporting it to the community
and if necessary excluding those at fault.
Our problem is that we do not trust that
wherever two or three of us are gathered in your name,
you are there with us.

We are afraid that you will hold our mistakes against us,
forgetting the promise of Jesus
that what we bind on earth will be bound in heaven
and what we loose on earth will be loosed in heaven.

Lord, we pray that our church will always work for harmony
between ourselves and other churches and religions;
that when there are conflicts
we will be the first to have things out between us
by ourselves alone,
if necessary bringing along members
from one or two other religious groups.
We pray that when we cannot resolve a conflict
we will be humble enough to report it
to a national ecumenical or inter religious organisation,
even an international group like the World Council of Churches.
Remind us that where we human beings meet in your name
whatever our faith, you are there with us.

Twenty-fourth Sunday in Ordinary Time

Gospel Reading: Matthew 18:21-35

21Peter went up to Jesus and said: 'Lord, how often must I forgive my brother if he wrongs me? As often as seven times?' 22Jesus answered, 'Not seven, I tell you, but seventy-seven times. 23And so the kingdom of heaven may be compared to a king who decided to settle his accounts with his servants. 24When the reckoning began, they brought him a man who owed ten thousand talents; 25but he had no means of paying, so his master gave orders that he should be sold, together with his wife and children and all his possessions, to meet the debt. 26At this, the servant threw himself down at his master's feet. "Give me time," he said, "and I will pay the whole sum." 27And the servant's master felt so sorry for him that he let him go and canceled the debt. 28Now as this servant went out, he happened to meet a fellow servant who owed him one hundred denarii; and he seized him by the throat and began to throttle him. "Pay what you owe me," he said. 29His fellow servant fell at his feet and implored him, saying, "Give me time and I will pay you." 30But the other would not agree; on the contrary, he had him thrown into prison till he should pay the debt. 31His fellow servants were deeply distressed when they saw what had happened, and they went to their master and reported the whole affair to him. 32Then the master sent for him. "You wicked servant," he said. "I cancelled all that debt of yours when you appealed to me. 33Were you not bound, then, to have pity on your fellow servant just as I had pity on you?" 34And in his anger the master handed him over to the torturers till he should pay all his debt. 35And that is how my heavenly Father will deal with you unless you each forgive your brother from your heart.'

Today's passage deals with the crucial issue of forgiveness, surely the most pressing of all our human problems, as individuals, as communities and as a human family. The future of humanity is in the hands of those who can forgive.

It is important to understand Peter's question correctly: it is not about being wronged many times (a situation which Jesus speaks about in Luke 17:4). Here, Peter is asking about one wrong. We are dealing then with a very deep hurt, the kind that remains with us for years and that we find ourselves having to forgive many times over. We think we have forgiven, but when we meet the person who hurt us we realise that we have to start forgiving all over again. This is the question then – how long do we continue with this struggle to forgive the one wrong?

We must think not merely of personal wrongs but of deep ethnic and racial wrongs, the kind that have nations torn by civil strife for generations – the human family knows so many of these at present.

As always, Jesus does not give us prescriptions; he invites us to enter into the God-like way of seeing things and leaves it to us to decide how we will act out of that consciousness.

Jesus' response is in the form of a parable, and the key to interpreting his message correctly is to understand how a parable is meant to be read. We are accustomed to learning (and teaching) through 'edifying stories.' In this kind of story the characters are either 'good' or 'bad'; we are meant to imitate the good ones and avoid being like the bad. It is always wrong to read a parable like that. We find that we identify one of the characters with God and end up with a strange God, one who tortures those who don't forgive their enemies, burns the cities of those who do not accept his wedding invitation, closes the door on the bridesmaids who come late for the wedding feast, and so forth. Many Christians have developed warped ideas of God as a result of reading Jesus' parables in this way.

A parable is an imaginative story which we enter with our feelings. We identify with the various characters as the story unfolds, until at a certain point it strikes us: 'I know that feeling!' This is a moment of truth, when we say, 'I now understand grace and celebrate the times when I or others have lived it,' or 'I now understand sin and experience a call to conversion.'

In this parable we see a man who is in a position of total helplessness; he is made to feel worthless, he has neither dignity nor freedom. His life, and that of his entire family, is in the hands of this king who makes him grovel before he will condescendingly set him free of his debts. He is not a bad man: he has been generous enough to lend money to someone who is in even greater need than he is, knowing full well that sooner or later he will have to return his own loan to the king.

The problem with him is that his spirit has been broken by

oppression. Hardship has extinguished the spark of generosity. Experience tells us how frequently this happens. He has been made to feel so helpless and impotent that when he finds someone with even less power than himself he oppresses him in turn.

The king also is a victim of oppression. He breaks out of the oppressive world when he forgives his servant (even though we can detect some condescension), but it doesn't last. The servant's meanness defeats him, he takes back his generous spirit and becomes as mean as the servant. Very different from our God!

The parable then makes us reflect on oppression, understood quite correctly as being indebted. What a terrible thing oppression is! It keeps everyone in bondage – the oppressed and the oppressors alike. It isn't God who keeps us in bondage, but we ourselves, and the parable tells us that we will continue in this bondage, 'handed over to torturers', unless someone makes a breakthrough and replaces meanness with generosity of spirit, the spirit of forgiveness, permanent and unconditional, 'from our hearts'.

We can reflect on the movement of oppression/forgiveness at different levels – on the world stage, in our countries, within our families and neighbourhoods, in our own hearts. In each case, we celebrate the people who have made the breakthrough.

In our own hearts: what unforgiven hurts still 'torture' us? We recognise the bitterness which keeps us in bondage, consuming our energies, preventing us from enjoying life and being at peace with those around us. We remember the times when we were able to free ourselves, even if only temporarily, like the king.

Within families and communities: so often we are concerned mainly about punishing the offender. We celebrate today the peacemakers among us, those who work through mediation to re-establish harmony within the community.

Within nations, especially between ethnic groups, social classes, religions. We think of Northern Ireland, former Yugoslavia, the Republic of Congo, Sri Lanka, India and Pakistan, the black community in the United States – the list can go on and on!

We think of the debt of the third world countries, causing anger, resentment and civil strife. Indifference to the plight of those who are in debt keeps the whole human family in bondage.

As we begin our prayer, let us listen to some of the prophetic voices of our time speaking of forgiveness to our modern world which is so much in need of it:

'The philosophy of retributive justice has brought nothing but chaos and widespread distress to families caught up in it. It has guaranteed a growing level of crime and has wasted millions of taxpayers' money. We need to discover a philosophy that moves from punishment to reconciliation, from vengeance against offenders to healing for victims, from alienation to integration, from negativity and destructiveness to healing and forgiveness. Retributive justice always asks first: how do we punish the offender? Restorative justice asks: how do we restore the well-being of the victim, the community and the offender?'
Vincent Travers OP in *Religious Life Review*, Sept/Oct 1995

'The experience of forgiveness leads us to a radical understanding of the doctrine of Grace. We are saved, not by getting it right, but by the love that redeems us while we are getting it wrong.'
Richard Holloway, *Dancing on the Edge*

'There will come a day when the martyr will be made to stand before the throne of God in defence of his persecutors and say, "Lord, I have forgiven in thy name and by thy example. Thou hast no claim against them any more".' A Russian Orthodox bishop wrote these words as he went to his death in one of Stalin's purges

'O Lord, remember not only the men and women of good-will, but also those of ill-will. But do not remember all the suffering they have inflicted on us; remember the fruits we have bought thanks to this suffering – our comradeship, our loyalty, our humility, our courage, our generosity, the greatness of heart which has grown out of all this. And when they come to the judgement, let all the fruits that we have borne be their forgiveness.' Prayer found in the clothing on the body of a dead child at Ravensbruck camp where 92,000 women and children died; in Mary Craig, 'Take up your Cross,' *The Way*, Jan 1973

'While waiting for the kingdom, make the kingdom.
While waiting for righteousness and peace, practice righteousness and
peace.
You want a paradise of love? Forgive.'
Carlo Carretto, *Summoned by Love*

Lord, we ask you to look with compassion
on the many people in our world who are in bondage
because they cannot forgive from their hearts.
What they have suffered may seem trivial to us,
a mere one hundred denarii,
but they are handed over to torture
until they have paid their debt of forgiveness.

We thank you for the great people of our time who, like Jesus,
work for the forgiveness of debts:
    - John Dear and the Fellowship of Reconciliation in
    Washington, DC;
    - the Sant Egidio Community in Rome;
    - the Tallaght Community Mediation Scheme in Dublin;
    - Archbishop Tutu and the Truth Tribunal in South Africa.
We thank you that these servants, following the way of Jesus,
are showing our contemporaries
that unless they forgive from their hearts
you have no choice but to leave them
and their communities in bondage.

We thank you for those who have taught our world forgiveness:
    - spouses who welcomed back those who had been unfaith-
    ful;
    - members of minority groups who work for racial harmony
    in their neighbourhoods;
    - devotees of traditional African religions in dialogue with
    the mainline churches;
    - Nelson Mandela;
    - Pope John Paul.
We thank you that, unlike the king in Jesus' parable,
they did not let themselves be turned aside
from the path of forgiveness,
 but forgave seventy-seven times.

Lord, have pity on the many countries
that are being torn apart by traditional hatreds;
send them men and women who will show their compatriots
that unless they forgive from their hearts
they will be forever tortured by hatred
and the desire for revenge.

Twenty-fifth Sunday in Ordinary Time

Gospel Reading: Matthew 20:1-16

[1] *Jesus told this parable to his disciples: 'The kingdom of heaven is like a landowner going out at daybreak to hire workers for his vineyard.* [2]*He made an agreement with the workers for one denarius a day, and sent them to his vineyard.* [3]*Going out at about the third hour he saw others standing idle in the market place* [4]*and he said to them, "You go to my vineyard too, and I will give you a fair wage."* [5]*So they went. At the sixth hour and again at about the ninth hour, he went out and did the same.* [6]*Then at about the eleventh hour he went out and found more men standing round, and he said to them, "Why have you been standing here idle all day?"* [7]*"Because no one has hired us," they answered. He said to them, "You go into my vineyard too."* [8]*In the evening, the owner of the vineyard said to his bailiff, "Call the workers and pay them their wages, starting with the last arrivals and ending with the first."* [9]*So those who were hired at about the eleventh hour came forward and received one denarius each.* [10]*When the first came, they expected to get more, but they too received one denarius each.* [11]*They took it, but grumbled to the landowner.* [12]*"The men who came last," they said, "have done only one hour, and you have treated them the same as us, though we have done a heavy day's work in the heat."* [13]*He answered one of them and said, "My friend, I am not being unjust to you; did we not agree on one denarius?* [14]*Take your earnings and go. I choose to pay the last-comer as much as I pay you.* [15]*Have I no right to do what I like with my own? Why be envious because I am generous?"* [16]*Thus the last will be first, and the first, last.'*

We have another parable this Sunday, one that many people find particularly difficult to interpret.

As I said in last week's meditation guidelines, method is always the root problem with interpreting parables, and to adopt the right method we must have a right understanding of what a parable is. It is not the kind of story where we identify 'good guys' and 'bad guys' and then draw the conclusion that we must imitate the good and avoid being like the bad.

A parable is like what we call today a 'short story'. We enter trustingly into the movement of it, identifying with the characters at the different stages, until we come to a point where we find ourselves saying, 'Yes! I recognise this experience' – an experience of sin to which we respond, 'Lord, have mercy', or a moment of grace for which we say, 'Thank you, Lord'.

The parable will then lead us to a new insight, a conversion, so that we have a better understanding of grace, of life and eventually of the nature of God. Of course, it will be an insight 'of the heart', one that touches us deeply, not abstract but based on experience, one that leads to deeper prayer.

In today's parable, therefore, we must resolutely refuse to enter into a discussion about whether the landowner was right or wrong, and especially to ask how he is like God. Once we follow that route we are into our heads, our imaginations are blocked, we are distracted from the task of interpreting the parable and letting it lead us where it will. The sign that we have interpreted the passage correctly is that we experience the inner freedom to move forward and be more creative in our God-given vocation.

Having got these principles of interpretation clear, we can divide the passage into six movements:
- verse 1: the hiring of the servants;
- verses 2-5: the fixing of the agreement and the later hirings;
- verses 6-7: the last hiring;
- verses 8-12: the complaint of those hired first;
- verses 13-15: the response of the landowner;
- verse 16: the final saying.

At each stage, we can identify with either one of the two protagonists – the landowner or the hired servants.

The climax of the story is in verses 8 to 15. The lessons Jesus wanted to teach are to be discovered here. Our meditation must be a slow journey through these verses, taking our time over each one.

We start with verses 8 to 12; they invite us to recall moments when we feel aggrieved at our lot in life: we have been hard done by, did not get what we deserved. On these occasions we always find ourselves making comparisons between ourselves and others, that vague but all-encompassing 'they'. 'They' did not have to work as hard as we did; 'their' families had fewer problems; 'their' age is more exciting; life was easier to cope with in 'their' time.

We then move to the landowner's response, which is in several steps. He shows compassion first; he is not condemning, and neither should we be, of ourselves or of others. He calls the man 'my friend', a simple but very touching gesture – the landowner understands how the man feels. We celebrate people who have shown us this kind of compassion, or times when we have been similarly compassionate to others.

The landowner then explains his position, logically and rationally. We think of ourselves having to deal with a friend's jealousy, a mother reassuring the child who feels left out, a manager reassuring workers who think that their work is not appreciated.

The landowner puts forward three arguments. The first is simply to reassure the worker that he has been justly treated, 'I am not being unjust to you, did we not agree on one denarius?' We must be careful to interpret this in the context of the parable, which is that of deep human relationships, even of our relationship with God. It is not therefore an employer negotiating with a trade union delegation, but a mother saying to her child, 'I have given you all my love'; it is a moment of prayer when God gives us the grace to be freed of jealousy and resentment and to relax in the 'blessed assurance' that he loves us unconditionally.

The landowner's second argument is also very touching: 'Have I no right to do what I like with my own?' We grasp here that envy is closely linked to possessiveness. We want to possess people (or things) because we are afraid that if we have to share them with others there will not be enough for us. Who are the people who taught us that this is not true, that someone can love us deeply and yet can be close to others in ways they are not close with us? This can happen even between spouses, as we know, and of course between us and God.

The third argument is in the form of a question. 'Why be envious because I am generous?' It is a further teaching on envy, through experience as always, the experience of a confrontation between an envious person and a generous one. Envious people calculate, look at what others have and they don't, what they could have got and didn't. Generous people are spontaneous, respond to situations as they present themselves, don't worry about pleasing everyone – but careful to be just. We have been and have met both kinds of people.

That then is the climax of the parable; but it would be good to retrace our steps to verse 1 and the image of the 'hiring'. The parable is a living lesson on both the value and the limitations of learning deep truths through images. It starts by inviting us to look on ourselves as workers hired to work in a vineyard. The image is valid. It is a touching way of understanding our vocation as parent, teacher, friend, spiritual guide or member of a community. They are all forms of service, and toilsome ones at that, '... a heavy day's work in all the heat'. Similarly, the staggered hirings in verses 2 to 5 are a powerful symbol of how the same vocation turns out differently for different people.

With verses 8 to 15 the story takes a radically new turn. It tells us, no! we are not the landowner's hired servants but his friends, free people, not 'hired' by anyone, not even by God. Look on God as a 'hirer of servants' and we misunderstand him completely. So too the rewards we receive for our service are not 'earnings' but gifts we receive with humble gratitude.

Making the journey from the image in verse 1 to having it corrected in verses 8 to 15 brings new life to the parable. By making the journey from 'God as hirer' to 'God as friend' or 'God as lover' we discover the wonder of love, human and divine.

The Pharisees did not make the journey, and we have all been like them at one time or another. How often have we Christians (and the church) made him into a cold calculator of rewards – a computer even! The parable throws out a challenge: do people experience in our words and actions the generosity and magnanimity of God?

The parable is a lesson in economics too. The world's economic system is based on the notion that everyone must receive only what they have worked for. The result is the ever-widening gap between rich and poor. The parable tells us that the wealthy are afraid to share God's gifts, they might not have enough for themselves! If humanity could enter into God's generosity, there would be plenty for all.

We can also focus on the concluding statement in verse 16 which is found many times in the gospels and in varied contexts. A deep wisdom saying, it can express our feelings when, in our meditation, we have moved from 'God as hirer' to 'God as friend'.

We celebrate moments when we have experienced the un-predictability of life as a grace; humble gratitude that we who were 'last' found ourselves 'first'; the conversion of recognising that someone we had rated 'last' was really 'first'; accepting to be 'last' and leaving it to God to make us 'first' whenever his time for doing so comes.

* * *

Lord, we thank you for the people in our lives
who taught us that true love is always generous
and helped us move beyond possessiveness and envy:
- one of our parents when we complained that they were paying more attention to a truant brother or sister than to us;
- a very dear friend of whom we began to be possessive;
- a spouse whose care for an in-law made us jealous;
- a leader trying to keep peace in the parish community.
They did not reject us, but were understanding,
like the landowner in the parable:
- they took time to reason with us;
- showed us that in fact their love for us had not been com-promised in any way;
- gradually brought us to the point where we could accept their love and go our way.
They were Jesus for us, teaching us the kind of person you are
and leading us to enter into your unconditional love,
and to be generous ourselves
in welcoming every member of our human family.

Lord, our modern culture is ruled by envy, not generosity,
and is tearing our human family apart.
Our contemporaries often think
that life's rewards should be calculated
on the basis of work done,
and as a result they are obsessed with rights:
- forever comparing their lot with that of others;
- grumbling that they have done a heavy day's work in all the heat;
- on the lookout to see if others who only work for an hour are treated the same as they are.

Lord, we thank you for the times
when you give us a glimpse of your kingdom,
invite us to enter into your generosity
and set us free from the bondage of envy.
Forgive us for when we grumble at you
for the way you share out your blessings,
comparing ourselves with others
who we think had things easier:
> - they were born in wealthier circumstances than we were
> and ended up being more successful in their careers;
> - they didn't need to study hard to succeed in examinations;
> - they got a lucky break when we didn't;
> - they led a dissolute life and then became fervent members
> of the church.

We thank you for sending us spiritual guides
who walk with us and help us move beyond these feelings:
> - a priest or other community leader,
> - one of our children,
> - a stranger with whom we found ourselves in conversation,
> - a member of another church.

They do not condemn us, but call us 'friend';
gently they show us
that the root of our problem is being calculating
instead of welcoming life as your gift;
they remind us of the many ways
in which life has been fair to us too:
> - we have had our successes,
> - got our own lucky breaks,
> - enjoyed many beautiful moments.

Now we find that we can face the challenges of life
with inner peace,
> - allowing you to do what you like with your own,
> - entering into your generosity,
> - knowing that at the end of the day you will be faithful to
> your covenant of everlasting love.

Like contented labourers who at the end of the day
take their earnings and go,
we accept what life brings us
and move forward to do the work
you want us to do in the world.

Lord, we pray that your church
will be the presence of Jesus in the world,
showing the wealthy nations of the world
and the wealthy people within individual nations
how false is the argument that they hold their position
because they have done a heavy day's work in all the heat,
and proposing to them the vision of your kingdom,
marked by generosity, not envy,
where those whose circumstances have allowed them
to work only one hour
receive a full reward.

Twenty-sixth Sunday in Ordinary Time

Gospel Reading: Matthew 21:28-32

28*Jesus said to the chief priests and the elders of the people: 'What is your opinion? A man had two sons. He went and said to the first, "My boy, you go and work in the vineyard today." 29He answered, "I will not go," but afterwards thought better of it and went. 30The man then went and said the same thing to the second who answered "Certainly, sir," but did not go. 31Which of the two did the father's will?' "The first," they said. Jesus said to them, 'I tell you solemnly, tax collectors and prostitutes are making their way into the kingdom of God before you. 32For John came to you, a pattern of true righteousness, but you did not believe him, and yet the tax collectors and prostitutes did. Even after seeing that, you refused to think better of it and believe in him.'*

On this 26th Sunday of Ordinary time we enter the final stage of Jesus' public ministry. Through our meditations on the Sunday gospel readings we accompany him on the different stages of his ministry. We began the journey with him in January, when he launched his career as an itinerant preacher in Galilee. We were with him on the 22nd Sunday when 'he began to make it clear to his disciples' that he must leave Galilee and go to Jerusalem. We stayed with him over the last three Sundays as he continued his teachings on the way there. We will be with him over the next eight Sundays while he ministers in Jerusalem.

The gospel readings of these last Sundays of Ordinary time reflect the tense atmosphere of Jesus' ministry in Jerusalem. He has come to the final confrontation between the 'chief priests and elders' and himself and all he stands for. It is literally 'a mortal combat' (sequence of Easter Sunday) since it will lead to his death, but he himself remains non-violent.

It would be good to let our meditation be influenced by this context. We celebrate similar moments of truth in our lives, or in the lives of great people we have known, important conversion experiences, painful but necessary, of being confronted by Jesus persons or having to confront 'chief priests and elders.'

Today's passage is in two sections:

- a parable in verses 28 to 31a;
- Jesus speaking in verses 31b to 32.

The parable is short and with few concrete details, so that we must make an effort to read it imaginatively. If we do this, we will get a feel for the different temperaments of the two sons.

'I will not go!' – the first son comes across as rough, impetuous, rebellious; but like many with that temperament, he simmers down once he 'thinks better of it'. From the second son's 'Certainly, sir' we get the picture of one who fawns, speaks with honeyed speech, but is superficial; he does not deliver. We can identify with both – as children or as parents!

Verses 31b and 32 are a call to conversion. We can feel the passion of Jesus, his frustration, and at the same time his deep admiration for those who have listened to the call.

The passage then is a meditation on conversions:
- important ones which change lives radically, e.g. giving up a life-long addiction, returning to the practice of faith after many years, accepting to be reconciled with a long-standing enemy;
- lesser ones that mark daily living, e.g. forgiving someone who has hurt us, shaking off discouragement, starting to pray regularly.

We can also celebrate group conversions – of a church community to a more humble presence in the world; of a nation to reconciliation; of humanity to a sustainable lifestyle.

We are free to focus either on the chief priests and elders, or on Jesus. As always we recognise them from our experience.

Jesus reminds the chief priests and elders that they have been refusing to listen to similar calls over a long period:
- John the Baptist preached and they did not listen;
- the tax collectors and prostitutes believed, they still did not listen;
- Jesus preached, they did not listen;
- the tax collectors and prostitutes listened and were now making their way into the kingdom, they still did not listen.
Now they are getting a chance again.

We have all lived through the experience of receiving repeated messages that we should change things in our lives. The messages come from different quarters – a member of our family, a friend, our bodies, the failure of someone close to us. We celebrate the final call when we eventually listen.

The passage reminds us that true conversion does not leave our egos intact. It is always a humbling experience, like the one Jesus calls the chief priests and elders to accept – seeing those we had looked down upon make their way into the kingdom before us. Conversion is always a turning of the tables, 'holy ones' exchange places with 'sinners.'

We can focus on Jesus, patient, courageous, forthright. We celebrate those who have been like him for us and for the world. The passage calls us to imitate him in carrying out our vocations as parents, teachers, friends, spiritual guides. The church must imitate him in its relationship with the wider community.

* * *

Lord, we thank you that in recent years
you have been leading your church
along the road to conversion.
Like the Pharisees in the time of Jesus
looking down on all those who did not keep the law,
we tend to condemn the modern world,
defining it in various negative ways:
    - a culture of death,
    - having lost the sense of sin,
    - atheistic,
    - immoral.
But the modern world has taught the church values of Jesus
that we had neglected:
    - respect for the human rights of all,
    - care for the environment,
    - the democratic spirit,
    - equality between men and women,
    - protection for minority religions.
You sent us prophetic figures, great men and women
 who were not members of our church,
but were, like John the Baptist, patterns of true righteousness:
    - Gandhi with his commitment to non-violence,
    - Martin Luther King and his struggle for civil rights,
    - Green Peace and other defenders of the environment,

- the World Council of Churches,
- leaders who fought to free their countries from colonialism,
- feminists.

Often the church was slow to believe in them,
and yet many of our contemporaries
whom we considered lacking faith, did.
We thank you for Pope John XXIII –
he challenged the church to read the signs of the times,
to recognise that we were saying 'Certainly, sir,' to you
but were not going to work in your vineyard.
He taught us to think better of it and humbly take our place
alongside those we considered tax collectors and prostitutes
but who were making their way into the kingdom before us.
Lord, send us church leaders like Jesus,
who will challenge us again.

Lord, we thank you for the great conversion moments of life,
when you send us Jesus to point out
tax collectors and prostitutes
making their way into the kingdom before us.
He speaks to us under various guises:
- one of our own children
- a fellow worker
- a preacher from another church.
He shows us how those
whom we consider to be spiritually inferior:
- unbelievers or atheists,
- the uneducated or illiterate,
- members of the gay community,
- adherents of religions called superstitious and primitive,
are keeping the commandments of Jesus better than we do:
- welcoming strangers into their homes,
- refusing to give in to discouragement,
- forgiving past wrongs.
Our first response is to be indignant
and refuse to accept the truth.
Like the first son in Jesus' parable, we say 'I won't go.'
We thank you for giving us the grace to think better of it
and accept the challenge to work in your vineyard today,

the world where we can no longer hide
behind feelings that we Christians are superior to others,
but must relate with all men and women as equals.

Lord, humanity today has its chief priests and elders:
- academics in universities and seminaries,
- consultants of the IMF and the World Bank,
- presidents and prime ministers of the wealthy countries.
We pray that our church may be the presence of Jesus
in our modern world,
calling on them to listen to your prophetic words:
- the ecological crisis
- the angry protests of the poor in every part of the world
- unending civil strife,
challenging them to recognise the little groups of people
who are building a better future for themselves and for us all:
- developing local communities,
- living in harmony with nature,
- relying on traditional medicine.
They are looked down upon as naïve idealists;
help us to proclaim to our contemporaries
that they are making their way into the kingdom
before the chief priests and elders.

Lord, we have all gone through our rebellious stage.
When anyone in authority told us to go and work in a vineyard
we always said, 'I will not go.'
We thank you for those who walked with us,
- parents or grandparents,
- school teachers,
- our first boss.
They did not get angry
or point to others who were saying 'Certainly, sir.'
Like Jesus, they waited for us to think better of it afterwards
and then go.

Twenty-seventh Sunday in Ordinary Time

Gospel Reading: Matthew 21:33-43

³³*Jesus said to the chief priests and the elders of the people: 'Listen to another parable. There was a man, a landowner, who planted a vineyard; he fenced it round, dug a winepress in it and built a tower; then he leased it to tenants and went abroad.* ³⁴*When vintage time drew near he sent his servants to the tenants to collect his produce.* ³⁵*But the tenants seized his servants, thrashed one, killed another and stoned a third.* ³⁶*Next he sent some more servants, this time a larger number, and they dealt with them in the same way.* ³⁷*Finally, he sent his own son to them. "They will respect my son," he said.* ³⁸*But when the tenants saw the son, they said to each other, "This is the heir. Come on, let us kill him and take over his inheritance."* ³⁹*So they seized him and threw him out of the vineyard and killed him.* ⁴⁰*Now when the owner of the vineyard comes, what will he do to these tenants?'* ⁴¹*They answered, 'He will bring those wretches to a wretched end and lease the vineyard to other tenants who will deliver the produce to him when the season arrives.'* ⁴²*Jesus said to them, 'Have you never read the scriptures: "It was the stone rejected by the builders that became the keystone. This was the Lord's doing and it is wonderful to see"?* ⁴³*I tell you, then, that the kingdom of God will be taken from you and given to a people who will produce its fruit.'*

Today's passage is complex. Several different strands have been woven into it, all with their own main characters, their own movement and their own atmosphere. In our meditation we need to look at each strand individually and then, if we are so inclined, to see a link between them.

It is first of all the story of the 'landowner', deeply grieved at the conduct of his tenants. His story is in four stages:

- he cares lovingly for the vineyard (verse 33a);
- he 'leases' it (verse 33b);
- the tenants reject his messengers (verses 34 to 38);
- his angry response (verses 40 to 41).

The landowner represents us when we give our all as parents, teachers, church or other community leaders. He also represents the founders of religious orders, social movements or political

240

parties. A time comes when we must all let go of our authority ('go abroad') and entrust to others the people or causes we have served. The parable reminds us of the shock we experience when we learn that our trust has been betrayed.

The landowner's final response is told in a very significant way. Jesus invites his audience to finish the story for him, agrees with their verdict (implicitly) and so (also implicitly) invites us to agree with them both. The landowner's response therefore is the model of what our spiritual tradition has called 'righteous anger'.

The landowner also represents God so that the parable invites us to enter into God's feelings when he sees how we human beings treat his precious sons and daughters and his beautiful nature. As always the God of the Bible (Old and New Testaments) is not calm and 'detached' as a false spirituality has depicted him – and encouraged us to imitate. 'Righteous anger' is a virtue we often fail to practice, especially in the light of the great crimes of our time: world poverty, racism and sexism, the sexual abuse of minors. Jesus is the person in our lives who invites us to repent of our false 'detachment' and enter into the anger of God.

The parable is also the story of the 'tenants' and here again we are invited to feel with them. We must however understand their frame of mind correctly. In many cultures today 'tenants' are poor people who are harshly treated by their landowners – the historical Jesus would have been on their side. The tenants in the parable are quite different. In the original context (as verse 43 shows) the tenants represent 'the chief priests and elders of the people'. Today they represent us to the extent that we belong to an oppressor group – individuals and civilisations – and lose the sense of being stewards of all we possess.

In the parable the 'tenants' become angry when they are reminded that the vineyard has been leased to them and they must be accountable for what they have done with it. Their anger grows ever more violent (verses 35 to 39). As the story develops, the root of their anger is revealed – they want to own the vineyard (verse 38b).

The parable then gives us the key to understanding abuse of authority in its many forms. Its root is always that we feel our

higher status being threatened in some way and lash out against the people or events we perceive as threats:
- one of our children rebels or befriends someone we don't approve of;
- sickness or old age forces us to change our lifestyle;
- a dear friend betrays our trust;
- a project fails which we had put a lot into.

The violence of the tenants in the parable may seem exaggerated on a first reading, but they are a dramatic reminder of the violence which is so much a part of our modern Western culture – against nature, minorities, men against women, adults against children. In each case it is a matter of 'tenants' being angry at being reminded that they are accountable.

The parable reminds us too that the sense of stewardship should be fostered by our religious faith. The fact is however that we religious people, 'chief priests and elders of our people,' can forget our dependence on God and no longer thank him for his gifts.

The parable is the story of the new tenants – ourselves when we become members of a church or religious community, a social movement, or political party. We too can become arrogant and complacent. Jesus is the person (or event) reminding us of two humbling realities:

a) We did not earn the right to be where we find ourselves; it was a free gift of God. The lesson is taught imaginatively as always in the Bible. We must be as humble as tenants who were hired only because others proved unworthy and the landowner was looking for someone to take their place.

b) We too must produce fruit. A warning must be sounded here: we must be careful not to interpret this as pandering to our culture's insistence that we human beings prove our worth by being 'producers'. That would be a gross misinterpretation of the image. The parable is inviting us to see the potential in all those entrusted to our care and approach them with corresponding reverence. This is of course applicable to our relationship with nature.

Finally the parable is the story of the landowner' son, ill-treated and killed but eventually become the cornerstone of a new era. We 'landowners' have been deeply hurt but we do not allow ourselves to despair – we know that if God's providence triumphs goodness will prevail.

* * *

Lord, we praise and we bless you for your gifts to us:
- our country with its mountains and valleys, its rivers and beaches, its trees and animals;
- our homes and all our possessions;
- our families, children, spouses and parents;
- our friends and spiritual guides;
- the communities in which we work and pray;
- our talents and the education we have received.
Truly you have planted a beautiful vineyard, fenced it round,
dug a winepress in it and built a tower,
and then you leased it to us.
We thank you for the privilege
of being tenants of your vineyard.
Forgive us, Lord, if we are resentful or angry
when we experience our frailty:
- ill health or the signs of old age,
- failure or ingratitude,
- criticism, especially when it is undeserved.
Yet these are your servants that you send
to remind us that we are only your tenants in this world,
and the season will soon arrive
when we will have to hand over the produce to you.

Lord, we thank you that not all tenants
are like those in the parable.
We remember with great gratitude those who have loved us
without being possessive
– parents, teachers, community leaders.
When the time came they were able to let go,
as calmly as any tenant-farmer delivering his produce
when the season arrives.

Lord, we thank you for the great prophets of our time:
- church leaders like Archbishop Romero and Dom Helder
  Camara;
- national leaders like Gandhi and Martin Luther King;
- many others in our countries and villages.
You sent them as your servants to the great ones of the world,
calling them to account for their tenancy.
They were seized and thrashed,
some were thrown out of the vineyard and killed.
But you have made them the keystones of a new age,
truly a wonderful thing to see.

Lord, you have called us to be members of your church;
forgive us that we so easily become arrogant,
as if we have earned the right to membership by our own efforts.

Forgive us for looking on our wealth
or the wealth of our country
as our own – to do with what we like.
Help us to be humble about our spiritual
as well as temporal gifts,
to be like people to whom land has been leased
only because others proved unfaithful,
and who know that at any moment
it can be taken from them just as easily,
to be given to others who will produce better fruit.

Twenty-eighth Sunday in Ordinary Time

Gospel Reading: Matthew 22:1-14

¹At that time Jesus began to speak in parables once again to the chief priests and elders of the people: ²'The kingdom of heaven may be compared to a king who gave a feast for his son's wedding. ³He sent his servants to call those who had been invited, but they would not come. ⁴Next he sent some more servants, "Tell those who have been invited," he said, *"that I have my banquet all prepared, my oxen and fattened cattle have been slaughtered, everything is ready. Come to the wedding." ⁵But they were not interested: one went off to his farm, another to his business, ⁶and the rest seized his servants, maltreated them and killed them. ⁷The king was furious. He dispatched his troops, destroyed those murderers and burnt their town. ⁸Then he said to his servants, "The wedding is ready; but as those who were invited proved to be unworthy, ⁹go to the crossroads in the town and invite everyone you can find to the wedding." ¹⁰So these servants went out on the roads and collected together everyone they could find, bad and good alike; and the wedding hall was filled with guests. ¹¹When the king came in to look at the guests he noticed one man who was not wearing a wedding garment. ¹²and he said to him, "How did you get in here, my friend, without a wedding garment?" And the man was silent. ¹³Then the king said to his attendants, "Bind him hand and foot and throw him out into the dark, where there will be weeping and grinding of teeth." ¹⁴For many are called, but few are chosen.'*

This passage and last Sunday's have much in common. They are both parables, each with its own dominant image – the vineyard last Sunday, the wedding feast today. Both belong to the last stage of Jesus' public ministry and remembering this could be helpful for our meditation. Jesus is in Jerusalem and the atmosphere is tense. The 'chief priests and elders of the people' continue refusing to accept Jesus' call to conversion; they will soon decide to hand him over to the Romans – a decision which leads to their own destruction. Jesus for his part does not give up. He continues to call them to repentance, although his teaching reflects his frustration at their blindness and hardness of heart. We can identify similar crisis moments in our lives,

246 LECTIO DIVINA WITH THE SUNDAY GOSPELS

- times when, like the chief priests and elders, we refused to read the danger signs – looking back now, we recognise that we were on the road to ruin, in our spiritual lives, in family or community life, in personal relationships;

- times when, like Jesus, we had to continue calling people to repentance even though we were deeply frustrated at their blindness.

The passage is in three sections:

- verses 1 to 10: First part of the parable: the invitation to the wedding feast

- verses 11 to 13: Second part of the parable: the wedding garment

- verse 14: The concluding statement.

As always we are free to take the sections separately or see them as a journey which we make.

Section 1: The image of the parable is of 'a king who gave a feast for his son's wedding', in other words a special kind of feast, one which celebrates the establishment of harmony. The parable therefore evokes a moment when a community (or an individual) is 'invited' to make an end of 'separateness' and a beginning of 'oneness' – within ourselves, in the world and in individual communities.

We think of groups being summoned to live together in harmony:

- within families,

- in individual countries, e.g. Northern Ireland, the Basque country, Sri Lanka,

- between neighbouring countries, e.g. India and Pakistan, Palestine and Israel,

- the different Christian churches,

- religions invited to collaborate with each other.

Within ourselves too, a time comes when we must resolve some inner conflict:

- between soul and body,

- an ideal and the reality we have to live,

- choosing between conflicting relationships.

Very often, as we know from experience, people prefer to remain divided. They are caught up in their own affairs (some to a 'farm' and others to a 'business') and reject those who 'invite them to the wedding'.

Their rejection takes different forms:

- at first they merely react angrily;
- then they maltreat the messengers, e.g. imprison them as the apartheid regime did to Nelson Mandela;
- they go further and put them to death, e.g. Gandhi and Martin Luther King.

We recognise that it is a moment of truth – as it was in the life of Jesus (see above). If the invited guests continue to reject God's invitation, they will themselves be 'destroyed' and their 'towns will be burnt'. This is what happened with nationalism in Europe between the World Wars, with British rule in India and with the apartheid regime.

Our meditation can focus on the 'guests' who eventually come in. They are ourselves when we experience a moment of grace in the form of a 'wedding':

- a family is reunited after long years of squabbling;
- an addict is finally converted;
- a church community finds new life through ecumenism or inter-religious collaboration;
- warring groups finally make peace.

Surprise is essential to these as to all experiences of grace (cf C. S. Lewis, *Surprised by Joy*). Spontaneously we exclaim, 'Imagine me being invited to this wedding feast!'

Section 2: This second part of the parable has two characters.

The king represents us when we insist that community (or personal) renewal must bear appropriate fruit. He is indignant at the guest's attitude and rightly so. As with last week's passage, what we see is an example of 'righteous anger'. We think of national leaders deeply frustrated as they see their newly liberated countries fall into corruption, communal violence, or class warfare.

The guest is insensitive and uncouth; he has no respect for the occasion or his fellow guests. His basic problem is that he does not feel awe at the privilege conferred on him. Identify with the terrible moment when his arrogance finally catches up with him and he, who was to be part of a royal occasion, is un-

ceremoniously 'thrown out into the dark', where there is 'weeping and grinding of teeth'.

Section 3 is a fitting conclusion to the parable. It is a typically
enigmatic saying of Jesus which can remain abstract but comes
alive if read imaginatively.

The saying reminds us of two stages in renewal. There is a
moment of 'being called'. We are happy to find ourselves members of a renewed group:

- the post-Vatican II church with its renewed liturgy, its involvement in the modern world, its active laity;

- a religious community which took the path of true poverty
and identifying with the poor;

- a racially integrated society.

A further stage arises when members become complacent
and take their blessings for granted. They suddenly realise that
they are 'not chosen' – they prove unworthy of their 'calling'.

* * *

'The more universal a work is the more it is divine.' St Ignatius
Lord, the modern world has become complacent
in its individualism.
Every nation looks after its own interests,
one making sure that its farms
are giving the highest possible yields,
another that its investments gain more and more profits.
Even the Christian churches have become individualistic,
each interested in getting more members than the others.
Today you remind us that this is not your plan at all.
You want humanity to be a family,
like guests at a wedding party, happy to be together,
swapping stories and laughing at one another"s jokes.
Help us followers of Jesus to be your servants
bringing this good news to our contemporaries.
We know that many, especially the prosperous,
will not be interested.
Sometimes we will be maltreated,
and some of us will be killed,
and this will result in further violence.

But we know too that many at the crossroads
are anxiously waiting to be invited,
and your wedding hall will be filled.

'Without a revolution of the Spirit, the forces which produced the in-iquities of the old order will continue to be operative, posing a constant threat to the process of reform and regeneration'. Aung San Suu Kyi, Nobel Peace Prize winner 1991

Lord, the people in many countries of your world
are deeply divided
    - Tamils and Sinhalese in Sri Lanka,
    - Hindus and Muslims in the Punjab,
    - Catholics and Protestants in Northern Ireland,
    - Israelis and Palestinians in the Holy Land.
Send them courageous men and women
who will summon them to unity,
like the king in the parable sending the servants
to invite guests to the wedding feast of his son.
The people they are sent to will often not be interested.
They will prefer to go off to their farms or to their businesses;
they will maltreat your messengers and sometimes kill them.
Lord, remind your prophets that they must not give up.
Your invitation stands, the banquet is all prepared,
oxen and fattened cattle have been slaughtered.
Though many have proved unworthy
there are men and women at the crossroads of the nation
who want unity and reconciliation;
the wedding hall can yet be filled with guests.

'Only those are truly great who are lifted above themselves by a faith which gives itself entirely.' Yves Congar

'If today's flourishing civilisations remain selfishly wrapped up in themselves, they could easily place their highest values in jeopardy; their continued greed will certainly call down upon them the judge-ment of God and the wrath of the poor, with consequences no one can foretell.' Pope Paul VI, *Populorum Progressio*

Lord, we thank you that recent popes
have been the voice of Jesus,
warning the nations of the world
that if they refuse your invitation to unity

they themselves will be destroyed and their towns burnt.
Lord, how quickly we become settled in our ways
in our families, communities, including the national community.
We choose not to be involved with others
and we do not let others become involved with us.
From time to time you invite us to come out of our isolation
and experience ourselves as part of a sharing community.
You send us messengers:
   - someone asks us to help in the church or in the village;
   - personal misfortunes make us dependent on our neighbours;
   - social problems like drugs or AIDS or unemployment begin
   to affect us as well.
Forgive us that we get angry with your messengers.
We are so insistent on maintaining our isolation
that we maltreat and even kill them.
We look back now and realise
that we were only postponing the need for change;
if we had continued that way
we would have been thrown out into the dark
where there would have been gnashing and grinding of teeth.

Lord, forgive us when we take your blessings for granted.
We move around unconcerned,
insensitive to the needs of others,
as if people who love us will always be there
to excuse and forgive.
We are like a guest going to a wedding reception in old clothes,
not bothering to excuse himself
or to thank the hosts for inviting him.
Lord, help us to see the error of our ways before it is too late
and we are bound hand and foot and thrown out into the dark.
Lord, help us always to be humble,
remembering that even if we were called
it doesn't mean we will always be chosen.

Twenty-ninth Sunday in Ordinary Time

Gospel Reading: Matthew 22:15-22

15*The Pharisees went away to work out between them how to trap Jesus in what he said.* 16*And they sent their disciples to him, together with the Herodians, to say 'Master, we know that you are an honest man and teach the way of God in an honest way, and that you are not afraid of anyone, because a man's rank means nothing to you.* 17*Tell us your opinion then. Is it permissible to pay taxes to Caesar or not?'* 18*But Jesus was aware of their malice and replied, 'You hypocrites! Why do you set this trap for me?* 19*Let me see the money you pay the tax with.' They handed him a denarius,* 20*and he said, 'Whose head is this? Whose name?'* 21*'Caesar's,' they replied. He then said to them, 'Very well, give back to Caesar what belongs to Caesar – and to God what belongs to God.'* 22*This reply took them by surprise, and they left him alone and went away.*

Today's passage is built around the saying in verse 21, 'Give back to Caesar what belongs to Caesar and to God what belongs to God.' It is a 'wisdom saying' and the passage invites us to enter into it with our feelings. Its truth should touch us so deeply that we are filled with gratitude, and also with humility as we realise that we do not live up to it – as individuals, as a church and as communities. The saying then becomes a call to repentance.

In order to bring the saying alive in this way, we need to read it in the context of a story, which is how it is presented to us, not as an abstract timeless truth but as a response to a situation. The question for us then is, when did we experience a similar situation? And then, who was the Jesus who spoke as he did?

We must be careful to interpret the saying correctly. In the course of the church's history, it has often been taken to mean that there are areas of life which are Caesar's domain and other areas which are God's. In fact the saying has been used to justify the claim that religious leaders should not 'interfere' in secular fields like politics, economics or culture.

This could not possibly be the meaning, however. The entire teaching of Jesus, indeed the entire Bible, insists that the whole

251

of creation 'belongs to God' – 'his is the earth and the fullness thereof'. There is no question of 'separate domains' therefore, since everything belongs to God.

The saying is rather about keeping priorities right. The Pharisees voice a concern which seems at first sight to be harmless but is in fact a 'trap'. They are not neutral. For them, paying taxes to Caesar is important, whereas for Jesus (as for all people whose priorities are right) it is only of relative importance: he says in effect, 'you can give back to Caesar whatever belongs to him (whatever has his head engraved on it); just make sure you don't give him what belongs to God'.

'What belongs to God' must be taken in a wide sense to mean what is so precious that we cannot make concessions where it is concerned – family, friendship, the sanctity of sex, self respect, compassion, humility, care for the poor, etc.

Jesus then is challenging the Pharisees to get their priorities right.

- His position can be expressed positively: treasure what is primary for you, and you will find that you will have no problem looking after ('paying your taxes' to) what is secondary.

- It can also be expressed negatively: don't take secondary things so seriously ('pay taxes to them') that you end up compromising what is primary.

We enter into the drama of 'whose head is this?' Feel Jesus' inner freedom (a hint of disdain) when he says, 'Well then, give it back to him.' On the other hand feel the terrible sadness of a priority gone wrong – allowing something that is sacred ('belongs to God'), to have 'Caesar's head' engraved on it.

The passage is intended to evoke memories of people or communities getting priorities wrong:
- parents who provide material benefits for their children but neglect to give them quality time;
- teachers who stress success in examinations and forget to praise those who are not successful but do their best;
- church leaders who are more concerned with what people think than with being faithful to the message of Jesus;
- public officials who work for popularity and compromise their integrity.
Jesus is the person (or community) pointing out that priori-

ties have gone wrong. As with all insightful statements, his answer is simple but surprising ('it took them by surprise') and deeply satisfying ('they left him alone and went away').

A sign that we have made a good meditation is that we identify with the Pharisees. If we find ourselves looking down on them, it means that we haven't really entered into the story. They represent us (sometimes an inner voice within us) when we voice concerns which are important but which are really 'a trap' in which more important values are lost. This situation occurs in:
  - our personal lives, e.g. concerns with job security, standing in the community;
  - the life of the church, e.g. concerns for large numbers, prestige, structures;
  - the development of a social movement, e.g. concern with taking political power, finances.

The details of how the Pharisees 'went about' asking their question are all significant and can help us recognise them from our experience:
  - they 'set traps': their concern hampers true growth;
  - they 'work it out': their arguments are very subtle; note in particular the unctuous language; we are never more 'pious' than when we are rationalising our fears and prejudices;
  - they do it 'between them': what they say represents the thinking of many, an entire class or even a culture.

The Pharisees' flattery in verse 16 is part of their 'trap', but we can take their words at face value. They were right to say that Jesus was 'an honest man' who 'taught the way of God in an honest way,' that he was 'not afraid of any one' and that people's rank 'meant nothing to him'. We celebrate people (or communities) like that; we read these words as a call to repentance.

* * *

'See the Divine self in all and all in the Divine self.' The Upanishads
Lord, there was a time when we had become
overly concerned for what was relatively unimportant:
  - what people thought about us,
  - being financially secure,
  - not making mistakes,
  - being hurt.

We recognise now that this concern
was undermining our priorities,
like the Pharisees working out between them
how to trap Jesus in what he said.
We thank you that you sent us Jesus,
    - close friends,
    - members of our community,
    - some of our children,
    - national leaders.
They made us aware of the malice in this concern,
told us that we were quite right
to give to Caesar what belonged to him
but that we had allowed ourselves
to give to Caesar what belonged to you alone.
We thank you, Lord, for the insight,
so simple and yet so surprising.
What had seemed an insoluble problem was now solved,
we left it alone and went our way. Thank you, Lord.

*'We ought not to consider our chance of living or dying, we ought only
to consider whether we are doing right or wrong.'* Socrates
Lord, from time to time you come into our lives
calling us to re-establish right priorities:
- through a bible passage or a homily;
- through some friend or a member of our family pointing out
our faults;
- when one of our dream projects collapses in failure.
Forgive us for refusing to hear what you are saying.
We know that if we did we would have to change our ways.
So like the Pharisees working out
how to trap Jesus in what he said,
we think up all kinds of arguments:
    - following this way will harm our health or hurt those dear
    to us;
    - it is against common sense and no one else is doing it;
    - it will offend powerful people and cause confusion in the
    community.
At such times we become very pious,
we say how much we long to be true and how open we are,

but really we are marshalling
a thousand reasons for staying as we are.
Lord, have mercy on us Pharisees.

Lord, our culture lays too much stress
on things that are important but secondary,
like wealth, prestige and popularity.
We are like the Pharisees in the time of Jesus
worrying about whether or not they should pay taxes to Caesar,
and so we end up setting traps for the idealists you have sent us
and are totally surprised at their answers.

Lord, we pray that we, the members of your church,
may be wise like Jesus
with the wisdom that comes from being honest,
from not being afraid of anyone
because people's rank means nothing to us,
and from giving you what belongs to you.
Once rooted in his wisdom we can escape from the traps
that are set for us by the false values of our time;
we will recognise the things that have Caesar's image on them
and have no problem giving them back to him.
On the other hand,
we will recognise the things that bear your image alone.

Thirtieth Sunday in Ordinary Time

Gospel Reading: Matthew 22:34-40

34When the Pharisees heard that Jesus had silenced the Sadducees, they got together 35and, to disconcert him, one of them put a question, 36'Master, which is the greatest commandment of the Law?' 37Jesus said, 'You must love the Lord your God with all your heart, with all your soul, and with all your mind. 38This is the greatest and the first commandment. 39The second resembles it: You must love your neighbour as yourself. 40On these two commandments hang the whole Law, and the Prophets also.'

Today's passage, like last Sunday's, is built around a saying of Jesus. I would say about it what I said about last Sunday's: it is a wisdom saying which the passage invites us to enter into with our feelings. Its truth should touch us so deeply that we are filled with gratitude, and also with humility as we realise that we do not live up to it – as individuals, as a church and as communities. The saying then becomes a call to repentance.

The two sayings are similar in that they are both teachings on wholeness:
- last Sunday's spoke of the wholeness which comes from recognising the sacredness of certain values – 'giving to God what belongs to him';
- this Sunday it is the wholeness which comes from recognising right priorities among our various obligations – 'which is the greatest of the commandments'.

Wholeness is presented in the form of a journey – we become whole by moving from fragmentation to wholeness. This is a crucial message for our times since fragmentation is one of the characteristics of our modern Western culture and the journey to wholeness one of its greatest challenges. Wholeness therefore defines our Christian mission today. Our special contribution to the modern world is to help ourselves and one another make the journey to wholeness – and this gospel passage shows us how this is achieved.

The passage is addressed to us as individuals in our various vocations – parents, community leaders, ministers of church communities, spiritual guides and counsellors; it is also addressed to us as the church of our time.

As always we read Jesus' saying, not merely as theory, but as testimony also. This was how he looked on life at this crucial stage of his journey, when he was in Jerusalem, facing the wrath of 'the chief priests and elders' (mentioned explicitly on two previous Sundays), arrest and crucifixion. A good approach to interpreting the passage is to start with Jesus – what was in his mind when he said this? So too a sign that we have made a good meditation is that we celebrate Jesus (and all the people like him) who have touched our lives.

The Pharisees and the Sadducees represent the fragmentation which Jesus rejected – and calls us to reject – in favour of wholeness. As we saw last week, a sign that we have made a good meditation is that we feel compassion for them – we know where they are coming from.

The passage traces the journey to wholeness as a movement from a solid foundation ('the greatest commandment') which leads to three consequences. The foundation is to put God in the first place, laying claim to our whole selves ('heart, soul and mind'). Once the foundation is set, three things fall into place:
- the neighbour;
- ourselves;
- the 'law and the prophets'.
Let us look at each stage of the movement.

The foundation – God
We often find ourselves stressed by our many obligations. One day we realise our root problem: we have allowed obligations to become important in themselves, whereas they are important only because they are linked to a basic obligation – our commitment to God, the centre of all our lives. We celebrate that moment of insight.

In our meditation we must make sure to interpret 'love' concretely. In our culture it has become vague – meaning many things and therefore nothing very precise. We need then to give it some 'body' – meaning such things as 'surrender ourselves to', 'put our trust in', 'choose to please'.

'All your heart, all your soul, all your mind': we do not have to give each of these a separate meaning. A cumulative effect is intended – 'your whole self'. The real stress is on 'all' which means in the concrete 'more than to any person, thing or cause'.

In fact, a good approach to the saying is to start by asking ourselves the question: 'Who (or what) do I love (surrender myself to, put my trust in, choose to please) more than any other?' That is God for me. The further question now is, 'Is this the true God, the Father of Jesus?'

First consequence – the neighbour
We then work our way 'downwards'. Once God is first for us we will find that love of our neighbour becomes our 'greatest commandment'. The two obligations 'resemble each other', meaning that we now choose to give our whole selves to our neighbour, spouse, children, community, the human family.

We celebrate the Jesus (person, community, event, Bible text, natural phenomenon) who led us to this wholeness.

Second consequence – neighbour and self become one
An important area of fragmentation in our modern Western culture is individualism. This concept, which is at the heart of most modern institutions, says that our first obligation as human beings is to look after ourselves. Individualism affects the whole gamut of human relationships – between individuals, nations, ethnic groups, religions etc. It has even affected the life of our church.

Jesus, however, (like all Jesus-like people) totally rejects individualism and upholds solidarity instead. His position is that we and our neighbour are one person – our destinies are inextricably intertwined. As the passage says, when we love our neighbour we are loving ourselves. This integration is another secret of wholeness and we celebrate the Jesus who teaches it by word and example.

Third consequence – 'the whole law and the prophets' fall into place
In Jesus' time 'the law and the prophets' referred to the Jewish ancestral tradition. We interpret it today of our own cultural traditions. The saying celebrates a time when we experience them as perfectly fulfilled ('hanging together') in Jesus. This say-

ing then rejects another source of fragmentation in our modern world (one which our church has contributed to) – the concept that Western culture is superior to others. A sign that Native Americans and people of Africa, Asia and Latin America have come to 'love' the Father of Jesus is that they reverence their 'whole law' and their 'prophets'.

Like last Sunday's saying, this one is presented in the context of a story and identifying with the different characters can help bring the story to life for us – always on condition that we don't look down on them but identify with them.

As we have seen, the Pharisees and Sadducees represent us at the beginning of our journey to wholeness. We can however focus on the fact that they 'got together' for the purpose of 'disconcerting' Jesus; this is significant because the Pharisees and Sadducees were usually at odds. They therefore represent us when we are afraid to make the journey to wholeness and ally ourselves with anyone who will collaborate with us in running away from it.

We can also consider each separately as representing us when, like the invitees to the wedding feast, we reject the call to wholeness:

- the Pharisees' learning had made them arrogant and complacent;
- the Sadducees were conscious of their standing in society and wanted to preserve it at all costs. Confronted with them, Jesus remains clear and focused because his priorities are right.

* * *

Lord, forgive us Christians for complicating
your very simple message.
Like the Pharisees, we have become very learned:
- we know canon law and all the laws of the church;
- we have listened to all the wise people, both ancient and modern;
- we have studied the background to the books of the Bible.
Like the Sadducees, we have influence in society
and know how to exercise power.
But the upshot of it all is
that we are never sure what we are to do

because one commandment is always in conflict with another,
and there is always some expert
who disagrees with what we decide to do.
Thank you, Lord, for sending us Jesus.
In one instant he cleared away all the undergrowth
we had allowed to cover up the truth
and we remembered that there is
really only one commandment:
    - that pleasing you is the only important thing in life;
    - that if we seek your will only, we end up loving others and
    doing what is best for ourselves.
Then suddenly all the many laws and prophets fall into place.

Lord, we thank you for the great teachers
who have touched our lives,
they were not learned like the Pharisees,
nor high class like the Sadducees,
but they taught us the basic lessons of life,
and ever since we have been able
to put laws and prophets into proper perspective.

Lord, according to the philosophy of individualism
the greatest commandment is to look after ourselves,
to seek prosperity for our immediate families
and for our countries.
To defend that commandment,
we quote scientists and doctors and lawyers,
allying ourselves with all sorts of people
with whom we do not normally associate.
Help us to be simple and uncompromising, like Jesus,
showing that loving others is the same as worshipping you
as well as the only sure way of loving ourselves,
and that all laws and prophets
must fall into line with this teaching.

The Feast of All Saints

Gospel Reading: Matthew 5:1-12
¹Seeing the crowds, Jesus went up the hill. There he sat down and was joined by his disciples. ²Then he began to speak. This is what he taught them:

³'Happy are the poor in spirit; theirs is the kingdom of heaven.

⁴Happy the gentle; they shall have the earth for their heritage.

⁵Happy those who mourn; they shall be comforted.

⁶Happy those who hunger and thirst for what is right; they shall be satisfied.

⁷Happy the merciful; they shall have mercy shown to them.

⁸Happy the pure in heart: they shall see God.

⁹Happy the peacemakers: they shall be called sons of God.

¹⁰Happy those who are persecuted in the cause of right: theirs is the kingdom of heaven.

¹¹Happy are you when people abuse you and persecute you and speak all kinds of calumny against you on my account.

¹²Rejoice and be glad, for your reward will be great in heaven; this is how they persecuted the prophets before you.'

The gospel reading for the feast of All Saints is the beatitudes according to St Matthew (which is also the reading for the Fourth Sunday in Ordinary Time). The church invites us to enter into this famous passage and discover the kind of holiness which we celebrate in this feast.

It would be a mistake to meditate on the whole passage together. Focus on the particular verse which you feel you would like to explore at this moment.

Each beatitude combines two things we do not usually associate – poverty and possessing the kingdom of God; gentleness and inheriting the land; mourning and being comforted. Let your meditation bring to mind a person in whom these opposites came together; that person is the saint, the 'blessed one' you celebrate.

In every case, you must discover the striking contrast between the two parts of the beatitude. If the combination does not surprise you, you have probably missed the meaning.

In addition to remembering others, you might want to celebrate moments when you experienced some of the blessedness in your own life.

The language of the beatitudes is biblical, and sometimes has to be interpreted. The confirmation of your experience is however the best guide to the correct meaning.

* * *

Lord, there are times in life when we know for certain
that what we are doing is right.
A sure sign is that we experience ourselves
as poor in spirit, carried along,
so that our own will and our opinions
do not matter in the slightest.
It does not matter either if people harass us,
or speak all kinds of calumny against us;
we feel blessed,
and we know that our reward is with you.
Thank you, Lord.

'We must live life less as an attempt to conquer new land and hold on to it, and more as a grateful response to the gifts of God.' Henry Nouwen
Forgive us, Lord, that even in a noble cause
we put so much effort into getting our way:
- as a church we are always trying to win converts;
- we are anxious to grow in virtue.
Teach us the gentle way by which
what we strive for comes naturally to us
like an inheritance.

'I have seen people put themselves through terrible torture – and die – because they were afraid of getting hurt.' James Baldwin
Lord, we thank you for those who taught us how to mourn:
- to look honestly at our envy, lust or racism;
- to accept that our youthful dreams have not been fulfilled,
- that friends have disappointed us.
We know now that by entering into the truth of our grief
we experience the blessedness of being comforted.

'To succeed in this country, an artist has to forget about what he can get out of his art and work for his own fulfilment.'
Ken Morris, Trinidadian artist, died in 1992
Lord, people are afraid to commit themselves.
They like to play at things,
try their hand here and there,
enter into relationships for a time only.
But as Jesus taught us,
only those who hunger and thirst for what they believe in
know what true satisfaction is.

'Closing your eyes won't help us, and either you help us or we will be on your doorstep.'
Lech Walesa to the British people, August 1992
Lord, unless the wealthy nations show mercy to the poor,
no mercy will be shown them.

'It is easy to show up the slime; it needs faith to see behind the dark forces a much more powerful force, the presence of the Holy Spirit.'
Karl Rahner
Lord, many things prevent us recognising you
in ourselves and in others
– lust, jealousy, ambition, a sense of failure.
We pray for purity of heart so that we may see you.

*'If you learn the art of being thoughtful,
you will be more like Christ.'*
Lord, we think that holiness means
accomplishing great things in your name;
but just to bring some harmony into the world is to be like you.

Thirty-first Sunday in Ordinary Time

Gospel Reading: Matthew 23:1-12

¹Addressing the people and his disciples, Jesus said, ²'The scribes and the Pharisees occupy the chair of Moses. ³You must therefore do what they tell you and listen to what they say; but do not be guided by what they do, since they do not practise what they preach. ⁴They tie up heavy burdens and lay them on men's shoulders, but will they lift a finger to move them? Not they! ⁵Everything they do is done to attract attention, like wearing broader phylacteries and longer tassels, ⁶like wanting to take the place of honour at banquets and the front seats in the synagogues, ⁷being greeted obsequiously in the market squares and having people call them Rabbi. ⁸You, however, must not allow yourselves to be called Rabbi, since you have only one Master, and you are all brothers. ⁹You must call no one on earth your father, since you have only one Father, and he is in heaven. ¹⁰Nor must you allow yourselves to be called teachers, for you have only one Teacher, the Christ. ¹¹The greatest among you must be your servant. ¹²Anyone who exalts himself will be humbled, and anyone who humbles himself will be exalted.'

Today's gospel passage contains several different teachings, each of them very deep and relevant to us today, and each expressed in its own imaginative language. Since they are all so special it might be better to focus on each one individually although we may come to see a common thread running through them all.

Another point to note is that the teachings are addressed to two different groups:
- the 'scribes and Pharisees' on the one hand,
- the 'people and his disciples' on the other.

In fact the focus shifts so that it is now one group that is being addressed and now the other. In our meditation we need to be conscious of the group being addressed and of how we identify with each.

The Pharisees are those in authority who adopt false values. A good meditation on them will avoid two errors – self-righteousness on the one hand, playing down the evil of what they do, on the other. We avoid self-righteousness by recognising something of ourselves in them (even if in a reduced way); we feel the evil of their ways by entering into Jesus' indignation.

The 'people' are us when we let ourselves be oppressed by others and some Jesus helps us to discover our freedom and dignity.

In either case we celebrate Jesus, the great teacher and leader:
- he is fearless in confronting the scribes and Pharisees, reminding us of times when we have been challenged by people, events or institutions - perhaps a biblical word;
- he believes in the common people and is deeply respectful of them – a wonderful model for community leaders, catechists and spiritual guides. A model too for the church community in our time.

Verses 1 to 3 are addressed to the common people. Jesus reassures them – they must not let themselves be awed by those in authority who do not practise the noble things they proclaim.

We remember times when we allowed ourselves to be overawed by others because:
- they were better educated,
- they belonged to a higher social class, to an ethnic group, culture or religion with a higher status,
- they were more 'respectable' in the eyes of our church community, neighbourhood, society.

Then some Jesus came into our lives (as individuals, church community or culture) and freed us from this dependency. We saw that those we had placed on a pedestal were flawed like all human beings and we felt liberated.

Verses 4 to 7 are addressed to those in authority.

Verse 4 speaks of their tendency to hand down laws without compassion. We think of
- church leaders unwilling to spend time counselling pregnant girls but condemning them when they have an abortion,
- education (including religious education) as handing down information rather than consciousness raising.

Verses 5 to 7 speak of the Pharisees' desire for external signs of honour. 'External signs' for us will include the different ways (including subconscious ones) in which we look for approval from our peers or from the wider community. This is a defect we can observe in the church as well.

We read these verses from two points of view:

- remembering moments of grace when we or our community became conscious of these faults in ourselves,
- celebrating Jesus people who brought us to this consciousness. We think of the great men and women, in our time and in history, who have challenged the structures of our organisation – including the church.

Verses 8 to 10 return to the common folk, reminding them of their right to be guided by conscience. This passage has been crucially important for the development of our church's wonderful teaching on the primacy of the individual conscience.

We celebrate the great theologians who have courageously upheld this teaching in the face of authoritarian tendencies in the church, e.g. Cardinal Newman, Bernard Häring, Hans Küng. They have been Jesus for our time.

Verses 11 and 12 (returning to those in authority) can stand on their own but we can also read them in the light of the previous teachings.

Verse 11 is a commandment, but we must avoid all moralising and read it as a story of grace – Jesus bringing good news. In Jesus we celebrate 'great people' – teachers, leaders, spiritual guides – who taught us by word and example to reject the arrogance of authority figures (the 'scribes and Pharisees' of our community) and who put themselves at the service of all.

Verse 12 is a factual observation which we are invited to recognise from our experience. It raises two possibilities:

- very gifted people 'exalted themselves' and ended up 'humbled' – looked down on by those who formerly admired them. Here again we must be careful to avoid self-righteousness. A sign that we have done so is that we feel very great sadness at the memory. What a pity!
- truly great people 'humbled themselves' and were 'exalted', they gave themselves in humble service and are now widely admired. Some have made the passage on the world stage, e.g. Gandhi, Martin Luther King, Dorothy Day; others in the context of our daily lives, e.g. parents, grandparents, teachers, neighbours.

We must not move too quickly to the second stage but spend time remembering (celebrating) the years of frustration. Our overall response must be from the heart – what a privilege to have known people like that!

The saying is a powerful reminder of how life brings surprises; it invites us to celebrate the Jesus who prepared us for this. It is also a call to the church to speak its prophetic word, warning our culture of how false its values are.

* * *

'A seemingly powerless person who dares to cry out the word of truth and to stand behind it with all his person and his life has surprisingly greater power, though formally disenfranchised, than do thousands of anonymous voters.' President Havel of Czechoslovakia, speaking when he was living under the communist regime
Lord, we thank you for those who live under tyrannical regimes
and keep up the spirits of fellow citizens, telling them, like Jesus,
that they have to obey those who occupy the chair of authority,
and do what they say,
but they must be guided by their own values,
and not the values of those who preach lofty principles
and do not practise them.

Lord, we who hold positions of authority in the church
wear garments that attract attention;
we are always given places of honour at banquets
and front seats in places of worship;
people often greet us obsequiously in market places
and give us titles of honour.
Preserve us, Lord, from setting store on all these things;
remind us that the greatest thing in our lives
is to be at the service of your people.

*'I shall not fear anyone on earth. I shall fear only God.
I shall bear ill will towards no one.
I shall not submit to injustice from anyone.'* Gandhi
Lord, there are times when people in authority
hold us in bondage.
We are terrified of displeasing them,
whatever they say is Bible truth to us.

Then you send a Jesus person into our lives who teaches us
about our own dignity:
>   - that we have only one Master and all men and women are
>   brothers and sisters to us;
>   - that we have only one Father, and he is in heaven; only one
>   teacher, the Christ.
Thank you, Lord.

*'The important thing for a woman soldier to remember is not to show
weakness. We wouldn't give men that satisfaction.'*
A woman officer in the Trinidad and Tobago Defence Force
Lord, in our culture no one wants to appear weak.
We pray that in our church communities
there may be no great honour
for those who pretend to be strong when they are not,
and that those who admit to being vulnerable may be respected.

Lord, we thank you for the various centres
that have been set up in our church
to care for unwed mothers.
They are a sign that we do not merely call for obedience
to your laws
but help people to bear their burdens.

*'Power comes from the people, but no sooner is that power acquired
than those who got the power begin to isolate themselves from people.'*
Cesar Chavez
Lord, have mercy on us who are in authority in the church,
in the state, in families.
How easy it is for us to hand down commandments,
tying up heavy burdens and laying them on the shoulders
of those in our charge,
but never lifting a finger to move those burdens.

'It is when I am weak that I am strong.' 2 Corinthians 12:10
Lord, we can always recognise a moment of grace.
It is one when we realise how we had been exalting ourselves
and now feel ennobled in our lowliness.

'Our fear is that a reinforced Europe may choose for its conscience the law of the strongest, the law of militarism, the old law of colonialism and of discrimination because of class, race and sex.'
Ecumenical Forum of European Christian Women, July 1990
Lord, we pray for the followers of Jesus
who are building the new Europe,
that they may consider it the highest honour in life
to be servants of the oppressed;
that among them self exaltation will be held in low esteem
while those who humble themselves will be exalted.

Thirty-second Sunday in Ordinary Time

Gospel Reading: Matthew 25:1-13

¹Jesus told this parable to his disciples: 'The kingdom of heaven will be like this: Ten bridesmaids took their lamps and went to meet the bridegroom. ²Five of them were foolish and five were sensible; ³the foolish ones did take their lamps, but they brought no oil, ⁴whereas the sensible ones took flasks of oil as well as their lamps. ⁵The bridegroom was late, and they all grew drowsy and fell asleep. ⁶But at midnight there was a cry, "The bridegroom is here! Go out and meet him." ⁷At this, all those bridesmaids woke up and trimmed their lamps, ⁸and the foolish ones said to the sensible ones, "Give us some of your oil: our lamps are going out." ⁹But they replied, "There may not be enough for us and for you; you had better go to those who sell it and buy some for yourselves." ¹⁰They had gone off to buy it when the bridegroom arrived. Those who were ready went in with him to the wedding hall and the door was closed. ¹¹The other bridesmaids arrived later. "Lord, Lord," they said "open the door for us." ¹²But he replied, "I tell you solemnly, I do not know you." ¹³So stay awake, because you do not know either the day or the hour.'

Today's passage is a teaching on 'what the kingdom of heaven will be like' (verse 1). This biblical expression means the coming of grace into the world. The passage therefore is a teaching on grace, inviting us to recognise and celebrate our experiences of grace, and to prepare ourselves for future comings.

'Will be' is a reminder that the final and definitive coming of grace lies in the future, but the teaching also refers to the many partial but real comings of grace that we and our communities (including the worldwide human family) have experienced.

The teaching is parabolic so it is important to remind ourselves of how we meditate on a parable:

- The parable comprises different characters; we choose the one(s) we want to identify with and read the parable from his or her (their) perspective.

- A 'crunch point' occurs at a certain stage of the story, a turning point which jolts us so that we know instinctively that this is the central moment in the parable. The 'crunch point' will be different for different people; indeed it will be different for us at different stages in our lives.

In this parable there are four possible 'crunch points':

- The moment of the cry, 'the bridegroom is here' (verse 6) – grace always takes us by surprise.
- The foolish bridesmaids find out that their lamps are going out and the wise ones will not give them oil (verses 7 to 9) – grace is always 'disturbing'.
- The wise bridesmaids go with the bridegroom into the wedding hall (verse 10) – grace is pure joy.
- The foolish bridesmaids come late and are told 'I don't know you' (verses 11 and 12) – grace brings feelings of remorse, despair even, but as a step to conversion.

In each case the bridesmaids represent two possibilities and we have been both at different times of our lives. The 'wise' (a better word than the Jerusalem Bible 'sensible') are ourselves at our best, the 'foolish' ourselves at our worst.

We can also focus on the bridegroom, remembering times when someone waited a long time for us to come to the best of ourselves (I took this approach in one of the prayers below).

Focusing on the person of Jesus can help bring the passage alive for us. At this point in his life, he is in Jerusalem, about to be arrested and crucified. The parable then becomes a testimony to his own attitude – he is a wise bridesmaid, ready for his moment of grace. It is also a heartfelt warning to his beloved disciples that they must not be like the foolish bridesmaids and miss their moment of grace when he is arrested. Who does he remind us of?

Verse 6: We can focus on either of two aspects of the moment of grace:

- It does not happen instantly, we have to wait a long time for it, so long that we 'grow drowsy (get a feel for that) and fall asleep'.
- When it comes, it is a surprise, like being wakened from sleep by a peremptory cry ('a rude awakening').

Verses 7 to 9: Grace always disturbs. It makes us fumble, look for solutions that are both impractical and unreasonable – like expecting the wise bridesmaids to give of their oil supply even though they risk not having enough, neither for themselves nor for others. We must make the effort to identity what Jesus meant by the 'extra flask' of oil. It is what makes the difference between 'good' and 'great', 'courageous' and 'heroic', 'run-of-the-mill' and 'special'.

Verse 10: The moment of grace is like entering into a great festive hall, accompanied by one we have long awaited. We think of:

- our marriage ceremony (or 25th or 50th anniversary);
- the first sexual experience;
- the return home of an addict;
- a moment of national reconciliation.

Verses 11 and 12: These verses are almost unbearably sad. We enter into the feelings of the rejected bridesmaids, the finality of the door being closed while the bridesmaids shout, 'open up,' the hopelessness of hearing the words 'I don't know you.' We can imagine the remorse – 'why wasn't I ready when he came?'

We think of similar experiences:

- parents wanting their children to open up to them after years of neglecting them;
- abusers faced with the break up of their families;
- national leaders trying in vain to get warring parties to be reconciled.

The teaching reminds us that we must live with the consequences of our choices. There is nothing airy fairy about Jesus – or about teachers like him.

Though this particular relationship can never be recovered, there will be other chances of healthy relationships – so the teaching is positive and a call to repentance.

The concluding verse 13 stands on its own. It is not strictly a comment on the parable since none of the bridesmaids actually 'stay awake'. The verse is rather a general teaching on 'staying awake' to the grace of the present moment – 'the day and the hour'. The deepest truth of every 'day and hour' is that the bridegroom has arrived. We give the word 'know' its full meaning of 'perceiving all the possibilities latent in ...'

* * *

Lord, you really like to keep us waiting:
    - for long years we struggled with an alcohol problem;
    - we thought that a difficult child would never settle down;
    - the parish youth group kept going from one crisis to the
    next.
Then, all of a sudden, out of the blue, the moment of grace came.
It was as if at midnight, when everybody had gone to sleep,
there was a cry, 'The bridegroom is here! Go out to meet him!'
We thank you that we did not give up hope;
somehow or other we had left ourselves open
to the possibility of better things:
we had kept an extra flask of oil alongside our regular supply,
so that we were able to trim our lamps
and welcome the bridegroom when he came.
Thank you, Lord.

'My mother don't have time to talk to me. I don't have her to tell me things. When she comes home from work, she only has time to clean the kitchen, go to sleep and back to work again.' A young boy in Trinidad
Lord, we pray for parents.
It is not easy for them.
They are frequently so tired at the end of the day
that when the children come to share their lives with them
they have grown drowsy and fallen asleep.
Give them that reserve of energy
so that they may never have to come knocking at the door
of their children's hearts
and hear the terrible words, 'I do not know you.'

Lord, we thank you for the experience
of the sacrament of reconciliation
celebrated after many years being away.
It was like arriving late at night, long after we were due,
and yet being welcomed with great joy
like a bridegroom being escorted into the wedding hall.

Lord, nowadays we are accustomed to doing things instantly,
turning a switch or putting in a plug.
So we tend to think that we can know people instantly too.
But having someone open up to us always takes a long time.
It is like being a bridesmaid
and having to wait late into the night
for the bridegroom to come, and then continue to wait,
and when we have almost given up hope that he will come,
to hear that he is there and we must go out to meet him.
It is only after that kind of waiting
that two persons can enter into deep intimacy.

*'I promise by thy grace that I will embrace whatever I last feel certain is
the truth, if I ever come to be certain.'* Cardinal Newman as he won-
dered whether he should join the Catholic Church
Lord, we pray for those who are searching:
  - those who, like Cardinal Newman, ask themselves if they
    should leave their church and join another;
  - young people not sure what their vocation in life is;
  - friends who cannot decide on marriage.
Give them the grace to continue waiting,
not pretending that the bridegroom has come if he hasn't,
confident that when at midnight there is the cry, 'He is here!'
they will go out to meet him.

Lord, we spend a lot of energy
fighting against the present moment:
  - blaming ourselves or others for mistakes of the past;
  - regretting that things are not as good as they could be;
  - anxious about how the future will be.
And so our eyes are closed to the possibilities
that are there in the present.
Teach us always to stay awake,
because we do not know the day or the hour of your grace.

*'Care for the dying is founded upon two unshakeable beliefs: that each
minute of life should be lived to the full, and that death is quite simply
part of life, to be faced openly and with hands outstretched.'*
Sheila Cassidy

Lord, we thank you for calling some of us
to minister to the dying.
Some are afraid, others angry or confused.
You want us to help them all to welcome you;
to teach people, as Jesus did,
that it is all right if we fall asleep when you are long in coming,
because we know that when the cry goes up,
'The bridegroom is here!'
we will merely trim our lamps
and go into the wedding hall with him.

Thirty-third Sunday in Ordinary Time

Gospel Reading: Matthew 25:14-30

[14]*Jesus spoke this parable to his disciples: 'The kingdom of heaven is like a man on his way abroad who summoned his servants and entrusted his property to them.* [15]*To one he gave five talents, to another two, to a third one, each in proportion to his ability. Then he set out.* [16]*The man who had received the five talents promptly went and traded with them and made five more.* [17]*The man who received two made two more in the same way.* [18]*But the man who had received one went off and dug a hole in the ground and hid his master's money.* [19]*Now a long time after, the master of those servants came back and went through his accounts with them.* [20]*The man who had received the five talents came forward bringing five more. "Sir," he said "you entrusted me with five talents; here are five more that I have made."* [21]*His master said to him, "Well done, good and faithful servant; you have shown you can be faithful in small things, I will trust you with greater; come and join in your master's happiness."* [22]*Next the man with the two talents came forward. "Sir," he said, "you entrusted me with two talents; here are two more that I have made."* [23]*His master said to him, "Well done, good and faithful servant; you have shown you can be faithful in small things, I will trust you with greater; come and join in your master's happiness."* [24]*Last came forward the man who had the one talent. "Sir," he said "I had heard you were a hard man, reaping where you have not sown and gathering where you have not scattered;* [25]*so I was afraid, and I went off and hid your talent in the ground. Here it is; it was yours, you have it back."* [26]*But his master answered him, "You wicked and lazy servant! So you knew that I reap where I have not sown and gather where I have not scattered?* [27]*Well then, you should have deposited my money with the bankers, and on my return I would have recovered my capital with interest.* [28]*So now, take the talent from him and give it to the man who has the five talents.* [29]*For to everyone who has will be given more, and he will have more than enough; but from the man who has not, even what he has will be taken away.* [30]*As for this good-for-nothing servant, throw him out into the dark, where there will be weeping and grinding of teeth".'*

This Sunday's passage continues last Sunday's. It too is a long parable telling us 'what the kingdom of heaven is like', i.e. 'what it is like' to experience grace coming into our world.

Most people find this parable difficult because of the master's seemingly exaggerated anger; also he is very hard on the third servant who was already less gifted than the others. If this is 'what the kingdom of heaven is like', then it is 'bad news' indeed. We must find an interpretation, therefore, which is both faithful to the text and also brings 'the good news of the kingdom' to all, but in particular to the 'little ones' (those with 'only one talent') of our communities.

The key to such an interpretation is to remember Jesus' situation when he gave this teaching. As with last week's passage, he was at the end of his public ministry, frustrated at the hardness of heart of the leaders of the people. The Mosaic tradition had taught generosity of spirit and compassion for the oppressed; the leaders had let this glorious tradition become their personal possession, an excuse for meanness and exclusiveness, a way of protecting their positions of privilege.

Jesus is highly indignant at what they have done with God's gift – rightly so. We need to enter into his feelings. The God of the Bible (Old and New Testament) is so passionately committed to the cause of the poor that when they are ill treated, 'his anger flares', as the first reading of the 31st Sunday reminded us. Nowadays we Christians tend to 'soothe' God's anger, whereas we should be asking for forgiveness that we are so passive (so lacking in anger) at the injustices of the world.

The 'property' in the parable then, is not personal wealth. To interpret it like that makes the parable a teaching on being good capitalists! The master then becomes a go-ahead CEO angry that his company has not made the profit it should have. The 'property' in the parable is God's precious gift intended to multiply and be life-giving for all. Its true purpose is distorted by the servant's meanness (this is why he is called 'good-for-nothing').

The parable then is giving two messages.

- To those who have been made to feel excluded from the kingdom ('tax collectors and prostitutes') Jesus brings the 'good news' that this is totally against God's will. In fact God is very angry that they are being excluded.

- To his disciples he issues a stern warning: do not fall prey to a similar narrow mindedness. The history of the church (like our individual stories) tells us how right he was to warn them. We all fall into the trap of seeing our talents as our personal possession that we can do what we like with. God's will is that we see them as gifts to be shared so that they can be multiplied.

We remember examples of something similar happening.

- The teaching of Jesus, so full of potential for transforming the world and yet so often 'hidden under a bushel'. Christians have 'dug a hole in the ground and buried it'.

- Nature, which God has made so bountiful, now become a matter for personal greed with the resultant scarcities.

- Family traditions of openness to all, allowed to degenerate into snobbishness and racism.

- Individual talents (physical, mental, spiritual) intended to be a blessing for families and societies, become things to be bought and sold.

We celebrate the 'Jesus person' who made us conscious of this betrayal.

The parable is not all negative. It shows another possibility – the first two servants, trusting and free spirited, and experiencing abundance. We celebrate people who have followed that path, communities too and social moments.

The master is also someone we can celebrate. He is the kind of leader who does not cling to power. He entrusts his 'property' (his cause) to those who work with him without counting the risk.

This parable is crucial teaching for our modern Western culture which glorifies mistrust as not merely necessary but actually beneficial. This aberration has affected the way we Christians now tend to see Jesus – our first concern becomes to 'protect' his message against our 'competitors', notably the adherents of other religions. Our faith then makes us mean spirited and elitist – we are no longer life-giving for the world.

Verse 29 is a teaching found in other contexts, e.g. Matthew 13:12 and Luke 8:18. We are free to meditate on it by itself therefore. Here again, the saying seems unfair but if read creatively turns out to be a little gem of wisdom. This 'thing' that when people 'have it' they are 'given more' whereas when people 'don't have it' even the little they have is 'taken away', is trust. People who have no trust in themselves, in others or in life, end up losing 'even what they have'. On the contrary, people who have that kind of trust end up being 'given more'.

The verse invites us to celebrate Jesus the teacher (and those who have played a similar role in our lives):

- he reassures those who trust that they are on the right track; there is not the slightest trace of cynicism in him; on the contrary his message is, 'go ahead and trust'. How we need teachers and leaders like that!

- he issues a stern warning to those who have no faith. 'Learn to believe in yourself'. Jesus doesn't molly coddle people, 'Get off your butt and stop pitying yourself! Otherwise you will lose everything you have.'

* * *

'If at times we are inclined to feel discouraged, let us not be dismayed. The human will remains the great force the Creator designed it to be.'
President Hassanali of Trinidad and Tobago, speaking to the nation after the attempted coup, July 1990
Lord, we thank you for the gift of free will.
It is this that enables us, even when we are discouraged,
to receive what life brings us,
like servants being entrusted with a certain amount of talents
by their master,
to go off promptly and make something of our opportunities,
and when the time for accounting comes,
to come forward cheerfully
and show what we have accomplished.

'If someone tells me that he doesn't believe in God, I ask him to describe the God he doesn't believe in, and I nearly always have to tell him that I do not believe in such a God either.' Lord Hailsham
Lord, forgive us church people
for giving others a wrong impression of you.
Many have heard that you are a hard man,
reaping where you have not sown
and gathering where you have not scattered.

As a result, they are afraid,
afraid to take risks, to trust themselves or to trust life.
And so the talents you have given them,
they dig a big hole in the ground and hide them.
Humanity suffers, and so do they.

Lord, when we get into positions of authority
we become afraid to trust people.
Teach us to be like Jesus.
He walked the earth for some years,
instructed his little community,
then, when he had lived his appointed time,
he entrusted his mission to his followers
giving each of us talents according to our ability;
then he set out on his journey back to you,
knowing that he would return after a very long time
and go through his accounts with us,
that even though some would hide their talents in the ground,
others would trade with them,
and his word would multiply indefinitely.

Lord, a mark of our civilisation is that everyone is afraid to fail.
That is because we demand too much of one another.
We expect to reap where nothing has been sown,
and to gather where nothing was scattered.
Then people do not take risks
and do not make of their talents what they could.

Lord, help us to face old age with trust in you and in ourselves,
knowing that you give us responsibilities
each one of us in proportion to our ability,
and once we are faithful in the small things you ask us to do,
you will trust us with greater things,
and we will join in your happiness.

'Our deeds do not simply disappear into the black hole of time.
They are recorded somewhere and judged.'
President Havel of Czechoslovakia
Lord, we thank you for those who keep alive in our society
the idea of judgement,
that you have entrusted your property to us,
and you will come back to go through your accounts with us.

'We are not on earth as museum keepers, but to cultivate a flourishing
garden of life and prepare a glorious future.' Pope John XXIII
Lord, we thank you for Pope John
and for all those who have made humanity more free,
urging us to see life in positive terms,
reminding us that the only thing
which seems to make you angry
is when we are afraid to use the talents you have entrusted to us
as if the world were ruled by a hard man
who reaps where he has not sown
and gathers where he has not scattered.

Lord, trust is the most precious of your gifts.
It is the kind of thing that when we have it we are given more
and end up having more than enough;
but if we do not have it,
then even the little we have is taken away.
We pray that we adults may hand on that gift to our children.

Thirty-fourth Sunday in Ordinary Time
The Feast of Christ the King

Gospel Reading: Matthew 25:31-46

31Jesus said to his disciples: 'When the Son of Man comes in his glory, escorted by all the angels, then he will take his seat on his throne of glory. 32All the nations will be assembled before him and he will separate men one from another as the shepherd separates sheep from goats. 33He will place the sheep on his right and the goats on his left. 34Then the King will say to those on his right hand, "Come, you whom my Father has blessed, take for your heritage the kingdom prepared for you since the foundation of the world. 35For I was hungry and you gave me food; I was thirsty and you gave me drink; I was a stranger and you made me welcome; 36naked and you clothed me, sick and you visited me, in prison and you came to see me." 37Then the virtuous will say to him in reply, "Lord, when did we see you hungry and feed you; or thirsty and give you drink? 38When did we see you a stranger and make you welcome; naked and clothe you; 39sick or in prison and go to see you?" 40And the King will answer, "I tell you solemnly, in so far as you did this to one of the least of these brothers of mine, you did it to me." 41Next he will say to those on his left hand, "Go away from me, with your curse upon you, to the eternal fire prepared for the devil and his angels. 42For I was hungry and you never gave me food; I was thirsty and you never gave me anything to drink; 43I was a stranger and you never made me welcome, naked and you never clothed me, sick and in prison and you never visited me." 44Then it will be their turn to ask, "Lord, when did we see you hungry or thirsty, a stranger or naked, sick or in prison, and did not come to your help?" 45Then he will answer, "I tell you solemnly, in so far as you neglected to do this to one of the least of these, you neglected to do it to me." 46And they will go away to eternal punishment, and the virtuous to eternal life.'

For the feast of Christ the King, in this Year A, the church chose a gospel passage which is the final teaching of Jesus' public life according to St Matthew; it therefore completes the lectionary's 'continuous reading' for the year.

Meditating on this passage in the light of the feast requires two clarifications.

Modern Western culture does not have kings – or queens. The few left do not exercise any real power; they play ceremonial roles and we associate them with pomp and pageantry. In the biblical culture, however, kings are leaders of their communities. They are 'judges' in the sense that they set moral standards for the community. Rightly then, today's gospel reading celebrates Christ's kingship as an act of 'judgement'.

The second clarification is that Jesus is a special kind of king – his way of 'judging' is very different from what prevails in the world. This is what the feast celebrates – the 'good news for the poor' of Christ's (God's) standards of judgement. It is also a call to repentance addressed to us as individuals and as a church, since our 'judgements' (in word or action) are often far removed from those of Jesus.

As always in the Bible, Christ's kingship is taught not in abstract language but through a dramatic story – an event we are invited to identify with.

The story is of a future, final judgement – like the parable of two weeks ago, 'the kingdom of heaven will be like this'. Our present judgements are never 'final', the final one will occur only 'when the Son of Man comes in his glory escorted by all his angels'. For now, all we can be certain of is that God's judgement will surprise us, and so we are humble in his presence. To the extent that we are complacent and self-satisfied we are not ready for God's judgement.

St Paul sums up our attitude: 'There must be no passing of premature judgement. Leave that until the Lord comes: he will light up all that is hidden in the dark and reveal the secret intentions of the human heart' (1 Cor 4:5).

This is not the whole picture, however. Today's passage invites us to remember the temporary and fleeting 'judgement moments' we have experienced:
- we became seriously ill;
- our marriage broke up;
- we fell into a fault we thought we would never succumb to;
- our country experienced national disaster, floods, famine, civil war.

These experiences are authentic encounters with God in that they reinforce the teaching of the entire Bible that when God comes into the world 'the lowly are lifted up and set in the company of princes', 'the barren wife bears countless children', 'the last come first'.

- We thought that certain people were the 'least'. Now we realise they were sacred, divine in fact, since what we did to them we did to Christ and what we refused them we refused to Christ.

- We thought that we met Christ by doing extraordinary things. Now we realise that it was in very mundane things, giving food to the hungry, drink to the thirsty, clothes to the naked, visiting the sick and those in prison.

- We thought we met Christ in moments of prayer or in holy places. Now we realise that we meet him when we feed and clothe those in need, when we visit hospitals and prisons.

- We realise that leadership in religious organisations counts for nothing before God. In his judgement, the only thing that counts is humble service.

As always in the Bible, the judgement causes two reactions and we have experienced them both at different times:

- wonderful relief at knowing we were right. Good actions which we (and others who had power over us – 'chief priests and elders') looked on as trivial were in fact truly great, recognised in the presence of God (and of all right thinking people) and never to be forgotten. It is a homecoming experience, we 'take for our heritage the kingdom prepared for us since the foundation of the world'.

- terrible sadness when we realise that we have missed the boat – like the foolish bridesmaids of two weeks ago. We are consumed by remorse, 'the eternal fire'. The contrast with the virtuous is striking; for them it was a homecoming, whereas these feel deep alienation – the fire was 'prepared for the devil and his angels', they 'go away' to their fate.

As on the past two Sundays, we remember the context of this teaching. Jesus' imminent crucifixion would be a 'judgement moment' in that it broke down all barriers:

- the humblest person there was the Son of God,
- the holy place was outside the city,
- the person of faith was a Roman soldier.

In those degrading circumstances, the 'son of man' was present 'in his glory escorted by all the angels, with all the nations assembled before him'. We remember experiences which seemed to be disasters but in fact were judgement moments showing us how wrong our values were.

We note once more how down-to-earth Jesus' judgement is. The sign that we have met him is that we discern between good and evil, 'goats and sheep are separated; one placed on the right, the other on the left'.

His teaching is not airy fairy – 'you must live with the consequences of your actions'. 'Good news' is implied however – 'other chances will arise so don't miss out next time'.

* * *

'It is we who lose when we allow the venom of hatred and revenge to circulate through our spiritual veins.'
Archbishop Pantin of Port of Spain, Trinidad
Lord, forgive us that in times of great crisis
– national or personal –
we become vengeful,
wanting to consign people to the eternal fire
prepared for the devil and his angels.
Help us to wait for the day
when the Son of Man comes to his glory,
escorted by all the angels, takes his seat on his throne of glory,
with all the nations assembled before him,
and separates good from evil,
as the shepherd separates the sheep from the goats.

Lord, we tend to think of you sitting passively on your throne,
indifferent to what is going on in the world.
But whenever we enter your presence,
it is always an experience of discernment,
of goodness being put on one side of you and evil on the other,
like sheep being separated from goats.

Lord, we thank you for those beautiful moments
when we relieved someone's pain:
    - someone was hungry and we gave them food, thirsty and
    we gave them drink;

    - we clothed someone naked, made a stranger welcome;
    - visited one who was sick, went to see a prisoner.
Quite suddenly it dawned on us
that we had experienced a blessed moment,
had a personal meeting with you
and had come to the best of ourselves;
we had taken possession of a kingdom
that had been prepared for us
since the foundation of the world.

Lord, part of each one of us has no compassion,
can see the hungry and never give them food,
see the thirsty and never give them anything to drink,
never want to make strangers welcome, clothe the naked,
or visit the sick and those in prison.
Sometimes this part of ourselves seems very influential,
but it is not the truth of ourselves;
it is evil, destined for the eternal fire
prepared for the devil and his angels.

Lord, a moment of grace is like coming home,
entering a kingdom prepared for us
since the foundation of the world.
Thank you, Lord.

'We can never really love others unless we feel a certain reverence towards them.' Cardinal Newman
Lord, help us to move from helping the poor with condescension
to experiencing that to do a favour
to one of the least of our brothers and sisters
is to be given the privilege of doing it to you.

Lord, we thank you for those who are grateful to us.
So often all we did was to help them in some basic way,
but they made us feel that we looked after you
and now deserve to be put on your right side.

Lord, we have to make a journey in our relationship with you.
At first, we think that we will draw close to you
by doing plenty of 'holy' duties.
Then we realise that you want us to be free and spontaneous,
just to be compassionate, and leave judgement to you.

*'The abdication by the Christian churches of one whole department of
life, that of social and political conduct, as the sphere of the powers of
this world and of them alone, is one of the capital revolutions through
which the human spirit has passed.'* R. H. Tawney
Lord, we pray that your church
will always proclaim Jesus' teaching
that when the Son of Man comes in his glory,
escorted by all the angels,
to take his seat on his throne of glory
with all the nations assembled before him,
his judgement will be based on
whether the hungry were given food
and the thirsty were given drink,
whether strangers were made welcome, the naked clothed,
and whether the sick and those in prison were visited,
because when these things are done
to the least of his brothers and sisters
they are done to him.

*'Christ himself wishes to be identified with and recognised in every
refugee.'* Pope John Paul II
Lord, we thank you for those
who make strangers to their country welcome.
In doing so, they are welcoming you.

*'Why can't Christians see the poor wounded part inside themselves?
Can they not see Jesus there? Why do they always have to see Jesus outside themselves?'* Carl Jung
Lord, we thank you for those people who have helped us to see
that this passage speaks of
what is naked within ourselves and needs to be clothed,
of the stranger in us needing to be made welcome,
the sick and the prisoner within us who must be visited.